Siegel's
PROPERTY

BRIAN N. SIEGEL
J.D., Columbia Law School
and
LAZAR EMANUEL
J.D., Harvard Law School

ASPEN

PUBLISHERS

111 Eighth Avenue, New York, NY 10011
www.aspenpublishers.com

© 2005 Aspen Publishers, Inc.
a Wolters Kluwer business
www.aspenpublishers.com

Aspen Publishers
Attn: Permissions Department
111 Eighth Avenue, 7th floor
New York, NY 10011

Printed in the United States of America.
1 2 3 4 5 6 7 8 9 0
ISBN 0-7355-5692-X

About Aspen Publishers

Aspen Publishers, headquartered in New York City, is a leading information provider for attorneys, business professionals, and law students. Written by preeminent authorities, our products consist of analytical and practical information covering both U.S. and international topics. We publish in the full range of formats, including updated manuals, books, periodicals, CDs, and online products.

Our proprietary content is complemented by 2,500 legal databases, containing over 11 million documents, available through our Loislaw division. Aspen Publishers also offers a wide range of topical legal and business databases linked to Loislaw's primary material. Our mission is to provide accurate, timely, and authoritative content in easily accessible formats, supported by unmatched customer care.

To order any Aspen Publishers title, go to *www.aspenpublishers.com* or call 1-800-638-8437.

To reinstate your manual update service, call 1-800-638-8437.

For more information on Loislaw products, go to *www.loislaw.com* or call 1-800-364-2512.

For Customer Care issues, e-mail *CustomerCare@aspenpublishers.com;* call 1-800-234-1660; or fax 1-800-901-9075.

Aspen Publishers
a Wolters Kluwer business

Acknowledgment

The authors gratefully acknowledge the assistance of the California Committee of Bar Examiners, which provided access to questions upon which many of the questions in this book are based.

Introduction

Although law school grades are a significant factor in obtaining a summer internship or entry position at a law firm, no formalized preparation for finals is offered at most law schools. For the most part, students are expected to fend for themselves in learning how to take a law school exam. Ironically, law school exams ordinarily bear little correspondence to the teaching methods used by professors during the school year. Professors require you to spend most of your time briefing cases. Although many claim this is "great preparation" for issue-spotting on exams, it really isn't. Because, in briefing cases, you are made to focus on one or two principles of law at a time, you don't get practice in relating one issue to another or in developing a picture of an entire problem or the entire course. When exams finally come, you're forced to make an abrupt 180-degree turn. Suddenly, you are asked to recognize, define, and discuss a variety of issues buried within a single multi-issue fact pattern. In most schools, you are then asked to select among a number of possible answers, all of which look inviting but only one of which is right.

The comprehensive course outline you've created so diligently, and with such pain, means little if you're unable to apply its contents on your final exams. There is a vast difference between reading opinions in which the legal principles are clearly stated, and applying those same principles to hypothetical essay exams and multiple-choice questions.

The purpose of this book is to help you bridge the gap between memorizing a rule of law and **understanding how to use it** in an exam. After an initial overview describing the exam writing process, you see a large number of hypotheticals which test your ability to write analytical essays and to pick the right answers to multiple-choice questions. **Read them—all of them!** Then review the suggested answers which follow. You'll find that the key to superior grades lies in applying your knowledge through questions and answers, not through rote memory.

GOOD LUCK !

Table of Contents

Preparing Effectively for Essay Examinations

The "ERC" Process.. 1

Issue-Spotting... 3

How to Discuss an Issue 4

Structuring Your Answer... 7

Discuss All Possible Issues... 8

Delineate the Transition from One Issue to the Next 10

Understanding the "Call" of a Question 10

The Importance of Analyzing the Question Carefully
    Before Writing... 11

When to Make an Assumption... 11

Case Names 12

How to Handle Time Pressures 13

Write Legibly.. 14

The Importance of Reviewing Prior Exams 15

As Always, a Caveat.. 16

Essay Exam Questions

Question 1 (Rule Against Perpetuities, Easements,
    Fee Simple Interests).. 19

Question 2 (Co-tenancies, Equitable Servitudes)........................... 20

Question 3 (Fee Simple Interests, Co-tenancies, Fixtures) 21

Question 4 (Co-Tenancy Rights and Disputes) 22

Question 5 (Easements, Trespass, Nuisance)................................ 23

Question 6 (Landlord-Tenant).. 24

Question 7 (Landlord-Tenant).. 25

Question 8 (Landlord-Tenant).. 26

Question 9 (Landlord-Tenant).. 27

Question 10 (Sales Contracts, Landlord-Tenant)............................ 28

Question 11 (Equitable Servitudes, Zoning) 29

Question 12 (Adverse Possession, Easements, Fee Simple Interests)......... 30

Question 13 (Equitable Servitudes, Reciprocal Covenants, Nuisance)....... 32

Question 14 (Statute of Frauds, Equitable Servitudes, Easements) 33

Question 15 (Equitable Servitudes, Reciprocal Covenants,
    Nuisance, Zoning, Easements) 34

Question 16 (Recording Statutes, Zoning) 36

Question 17 (Adverse Possession, Oil and Water Rights) 37

Question 18 (Recording Statutes) 38

Question 19 (Sales Contracts, Statute of Frauds, Adverse Possession,
Risk of Loss) 39

Question 20 (Estoppel by Deed, Recording Statutes,
Adverse Possession) 40

Question 21 (Conveyance by Deed, Co-tenancies, Adverse Possession) 41

Question 22 (Conveyance by Deed, Recording Statutes) 42

Question 23 (Recording Statutes, Mineral Rights, Co-tenancies) 43

Question 24 (Conveyance by Deed, Recording Statutes) 44

Question 25 (Conveyance by Deed, Escrow) 45

Essay Exam Answers

Answer to Question 1 49

Answer to Question 2 51

Answer to Question 3 54

Answer to Question 4 57

Answer to Question 5 61

Answer to Question 6 64

Answer to Question 7 67

Answer to Question 8 70

Answer to Question 9 73

Answer to Question 10 76

Answer to Question 11 79

Answer to Question 12 83

Answer to Question 13 87

Answer to Question 14 91

Answer to Question 15 94

Answer to Question 16 99

Answer to Question 17 102

Answer to Question 18 106

Answer to Question 19 109

Answer to Question 20 112

Answer to Question 21 115

Answer to Question 22 118

Answer to Question 23 121

Answer to Question 24 123

Answer to Question 25 126

Multiple-Choice Questions

Questions 1 through 104.. 131

Multiple-Choice Answers

Answers to Questions 1 through 104..................................... 177

Index

Alphabetical index, listing issues by the number of the question
    raising the issue.. 223

Preparing Effectively for Essay Examinations[1]

To achieve superior scores on essay exams, a law student must (1) learn and understand "blackletter" principles and rules of law for each subject; (2) analyze how those principles of law arise within a test fact pattern; and (3) write clearly and succinctly a short discussion of each principle and how it relates to the facts. One of the most common misconceptions about law school is that you must memorize each word on every page of your casebooks or outlines to do well on exams. The reality is that you can commit an entire casebook to memory and still do poorly on an exam. Our review of hundreds of student answers has shown us that most students can recite the rules. The students who do **best** on exams are able to analyze how the rules they have memorized relate to the facts in the questions, and how to communicate their analysis to the grader. The following pages cover what you need to know to achieve superior scores on your law school essay exams.

The "ERC" Process

To study effectively for law school exams you must be able to "*ERC*" (*E*lementize, *R*ecognize, and *C*onceptualize) each legal principle covered in your casebooks and course outlines. *Elementizing* means reducing each legal theory and rule you learn to a concise, straightforward statement of its essential elements. Without knowledge of these elements, it's difficult to see all the issues as they arise.

For example, if you are asked, "What is self-defense?", it is **not** enough to say, "self-defense is permitted when, if someone is about to hit you, you can prevent him from doing it." This layperson description would leave a grader wondering if you had actually attended law school. An accurate statement of the self-defense principle would go something like this: "When one reasonably believes she is in imminent danger of an offensive touching, she may assert whatever force she reasonably believes necessary under the circumstances to prevent the offensive touching from occurring." This formulation correctly shows that there are four separate, distinct elements which must be satisfied before the defense of self-defense can be successfully asserted: (1) the actor must have a **reasonable belief** that (2) the touching which she seeks to prevent is **offensive**, and that (3) the offensive touching is **imminent**, and

---

[1] To illustrate the principles of effective exam preparation, we have used examples from Torts and Constitutional Law. However, these principles apply to all subjects. One of the most difficult tasks faced by law students is learning how to apply principles from one area of the law to another. We leave it to you, the reader, to think of comparable examples for the subject-matter of this book.

(4) she must use no greater force than she ***reasonably believes necessary under the circumstances*** to prevent the offensive touching from occurring.

Recognizing means perceiving or anticipating which words or ideas within a legal principle are likely to be the source of issues, and how those issues are likely to arise within a given hypothetical fact pattern. With respect to the self-defense concept, there are four ***potential*** issues. Did the actor reasonably believe the other person was about to make an offensive contact with her? Was the contact imminent? Would the contact have been offensive? Did she use only such force as she reasonably believed necessary to prevent the imminent, offensive touching?

Conceptualizing means imagining situations in which each of the elements of a rule of law can give rise to factual issues. ***Unless you can imagine or construct an application of each element of a rule, you don't truly understand the legal principles behind the rule!*** In our opinion, the inability to conjure up hypothetical fact patterns or stories involving particular rules of law foretells a likelihood that you will miss issues involving those rules on an exam. It's ***crucial*** (1) to ***recognize*** that issues result from the interaction of facts with the words defining a rule of law; and (2) to develop the ability to ***conceptualize*** or ***imagine*** fact patterns using the words or concepts within the rule.

For example, a set of facts illustrating the "reasonable belief" element of the self-defense rule might be the following:

> One evening, A and B had an argument at a bar. A screamed at B, "I'm going to get a knife and stab you!" A then ran out of the bar. B, who was armed with a concealed pistol, left the bar about 15 minutes later. As B was walking home, he heard someone running toward him from behind. B drew his pistol, turned, and shot the person advancing toward him (who was only about ten feet away when the shooting occurred). When B walked over to his victim, he realized that the person he had shot was dead and was not A, but another individual who had simply decided to take an evening jog. There would certainly be an issue whether B had a reasonable belief that the person who was running behind him was A. In the subsequent wrongful-death action, the victim's estate would contend that the earlier threat by A was not enough to give B a reasonable belief that the person running behind him was A. B could contend in rebuttal that given the prior altercation at the bar, A's threat, the darkness, and the fact that the incident occurred soon after A's threat, his belief that A was about to attack him was "reasonable."

An illustration of how the word "imminent" might generate an issue is the following:

> X and Y had been feuding for some time. One afternoon, X suddenly attacked Y with a hunting knife. However, Y was able to wrest the knife

away from X. At that point, X retreated about four feet away from Y and screamed: "You were lucky this time, but next time I'll have a gun and you'll be finished." Y, having good reason to believe that X would subsequently carry out his threats (after all, X had just attempted to kill Y), immediately thrust the knife into X's chest, killing him. While Y certainly had a reasonable belief that X would attempt to kill him the *next time* the two met, Y would probably *not* be able to assert the self-defense privilege because the element of "imminency" was absent.

A fact pattern illustrating the actor's right to use only that force which is reasonably necessary under the circumstances might be the following:

D rolled up a newspaper and was about to strike E on the shoulder with it. As D pulled back his arm for the purpose of delivering the blow, E drew a knife and plunged it into D's chest. While E had every reason to believe that D was about to deliver an offensive impact on him, E probably could not successfully assert the self-defense privilege because the force he utilized in response was greater than reasonably necessary under the circumstances to prevent the impact. E could simply have deflected D's blow or punched D away. The use of a knife constituted a degree of force by E which was *not* reasonable, given the minor injury which he would have suffered from the newspaper's impact.

"Mental games" such as these must be played with every element of every rule you learn.

Issue-Spotting

One of the keys to doing well on an essay examination is issue-spotting. In fact, issue-spotting is *the* most important skill you will learn in law school. If you recognize a legal issue, you can always find the applicable rule of law (if there is any) by researching the issue. But if you fail to see the issues, you won't learn the steps that lead to success or failure on exams or, for that matter, in the practice of law. It is important to remember that (1) an issue is a question to be decided by the judge or jury; and (2) a question is "in issue" when it can be disputed or argued about at trial. The bottom line is that *if you don't spot an issue, you can't raise it or discuss it*.

The key to issue-spotting is to learn to approach a problem in the same way as an attorney does. Let's assume you've been admitted to practice and a client enters your office with a legal problem. He will recite his facts to you and give you any documents that may be pertinent. He will then want to know if he can sue (or be sued, if your client seeks to avoid liability). To answer your client's questions intelligently, you will have to decide the following: (1) what principles or rules can possibly be asserted by your client; (2) what defense or defenses can possibly be raised to these principles; (3) what issues may arise if these defenses are asserted; (4) what arguments can each side make to persuade the fact-finder to resolve the issue in his favor; and (5) finally, what will the *likely* outcome of each issue be. *All the issues which can possibly arise at trial will be relevant to your answers.*

How to Discuss an Issue

Keep in mind that *rules of law are the guides to issues* (i.e., an issue arises where there is a question whether the facts do, or do not, satisfy an element of a rule); a rule of law *cannot dispose of an issue* unless the rule can reasonably be *applied to the facts.*

A good way to learn how to discuss an issue is to study the following mini-hypothetical and the two student responses which follow it.

Mini-Hypothetical

A and B were involved in making a movie which was being filmed at a local bar. The script called for A to appear to throw a bottle (which was actually a rubber prop) at B. The fluorescent lighting at the bar had been altered for the movie—the usual subdued blue lights had been replaced with rather bright white lights. The cameraperson had stationed herself just to the left of the swinging doors which served as the main entrance to the bar. As the scene was unfolding, C, a regular patron of the bar, unwittingly walked into it. The guard who was usually stationed immediately outside the bar had momentarily left his post to visit the restroom. As C pushed the barroom doors inward, the left door panel knocked the camera to the ground with a resounding crash. The first (and only) thing C saw was A (about 5 feet from C), who was getting ready to throw the bottle at B, who was at the other end of the bar (about 15 feet from A). Without hesitation, C pushed A to the ground and punched him in the face. Plastic surgery was required to restore A's profile to its Hollywood-handsome pre-altercation look.

Discuss A's right against C.

Pertinent Principles of Law:

1. Under the rule defining the prevention-of-crime privilege, if one sees that someone is about to commit what she reasonably believes to be a felony or misdemeanor involving a breach of the peace, she may exercise whatever degree of force is reasonably necessary under the circumstances to prevent that person from committing the crime.

2. Under the defense-of-others privilege, where one reasonably believes that someone is about to cause an offensive contact upon a third party, she may use whatever force is reasonably necessary under the circumstances to prevent the contact. Some jurisdictions, however, limit this privilege to situations in which the actor and the third party are related.

First Student Answer

Did C commit an assault and battery upon A?

An assault occurs when the defendant intentionally causes the plaintiff to be reasonably in apprehension of an imminent, offensive touching. The facts state that C punched A to the ground. Thus, a battery would have occurred at this point. We are also told that C punched A in the face. It is reasonable to assume that A saw the punch being thrown at him, and therefore A felt in imminent danger of an offensive touching. Based upon the facts, C has committed an assault and battery upon A.

Were C's actions justifiable under the defense-of-others privilege?

C could successfully assert the defense-of-others and prevention-of-crime privileges. When C opened the bar doors, A appeared to be throwing the bottle at B. Although the "bottle" was actually a prop, C had no way of knowing this fact. Also, it was necessary for C to punch A in the face to assure that A could not get back up, retrieve the bottle, and again throw it at B. While the plastic surgery required by A is unfortunate, C could not be successfully charged with assault and battery.

Second Student Answer

Assault and Battery:

C committed an assault (causing A to be reasonably in apprehension of an imminent, offensive contact) when A saw that C's punch was about to hit him, and battery (causing an offensive contact upon A) when (1) C knocked A to the ground, and (2) C punched A.

Defense-of-Others/Prevention-of-Crime Defenses:

C would undoubtedly assert the privileges of defense-of-others (when defendant reasonably believed the plaintiff was about to make an offensive contact upon a third party, he was entitled to use whatever force was reasonably necessary to prevent the contact); and prevention-of-crime defense (when one reasonably believes another is about to commit a felony or misdemeanor involving a breach of the peace, he may exercise whatever force is reasonably necessary to prevent that person from committing a crime).

A could contend that C was not reasonable in believing that A was about to cause harm to B because the enhanced lighting at the bar and camera crash should have indicated to C, a regular customer, that a movie was being filmed. However, C could probably success-fully contend in rebuttal that his belief was reasonable in light of the facts that (1) he had not seen the camera when he attacked A, and (2) instantaneous action was required (he did not have time to notice the enhanced lighting around the bar).

A might also contend that the justification was forfeited because the degree of force used by C was not reasonable, since C did not have to punch A in the face after A had already been pushed to the ground (i.e., the danger to B was no longer present). However, C could argue in rebuttal that it was necessary to knockout A (an individual with apparently violent propensities) while the opportu-nity existed, rather than risk a drawn-out scuffle in which A might prevail. The facts do not indicate how big A and C were; but assum-ing C was not significantly larger than A, C's contention will probably be successful. If, however, C was significantly larger than A, the punch may have been excessive (since C could presumably have simply held A down).

Critique

Let's examine the First Student Answer first. It mistakenly treats as an "issue" the assault and battery committed by C upon A. While the actions creating these torts must be mentioned in the facts to provide a foundation for a discussion of the applicable privileges, there was no need to discuss them further because they were not the issue the examiners were testing for.

The structure of the initial paragraph of First Student Answer is also in-correct. After an assault is defined in the first sentence, the second sentence abruptly describes the facts necessary to constitute the commission of a battery. The third sentence then sets forth the elements of a battery. The fourth sentence completes the discussion of assault by describing the facts pertaining to that tort. The two-sentence break between the original men-tion of assault and the facts which constitute assault is confusing; the facts which call for the application of a rule should be mentioned *immediately* after the rule is stated.

A more serious error, however, occurs in the second paragraph of the First Student Answer. While there is an allusion to the correct principle of law (prevention of crime), the *rule is not stated*. As a consequence, the grader can only guess why the student thinks the facts set forth in the subsequent sentences are significant. A grader reading this answer could not be certain whether the student recognized that the issues revolved around the *reasonable belief* and *necessary force* elements of the prevention-of-crime privilege. Superior exam-writing requires that the pertinent facts be *tied* directly and clearly to the operative rule.

The Second Student Answer is very much better than the First Answer. It disposes of C's assault and battery upon A in a few words (yet tells the grader that the writer knows these torts are present). More importantly, the grader can easily see the issues which would arise if the prevention-of crime privilege were asserted (i.e., "whether C's belief that A was about to commit a crime against B was reasonable" and "whether C used unnecessary force in punching A after A had been knocked to the ground"). Finally, it also utilizes all the facts by indicating how an attorney would assert those facts which are most advantageous to her client.

Structuring Your Answer

Graders will give high marks to a clearly written, well-structured answer. Each issue you discuss should follow a specific and consistent structure which a grader can easily follow.

The Second Student Answer basically utilizes the *I-R-A-A-O format* with respect to each issue. In this format, the *I* stands for the word *Issue*; the *R* for *Rule of law*; the initial *A* for the words *one side's Argument*; the second *A* for *the other party's rebuttal Argument*; and the *O* for your *Opinion as to how the issue would be resolved*. The *I-R-A-A-O* format emphasizes the importance of (1) discussing *both* sides of an issue, and (2) communicating to the grader that where an issue arises, an attorney can only advise her client as to the *probable* decision on that issue.

A somewhat different format for analyzing each issue is the *I-R-A-C format*. Here, the *I* stands for *Issue;* the *R* for *Rule of law;* the *A* for *Application of the facts to the rule of law;* and the *C* for *Conclusion. I-R-A-C* is a legitimate approach to the discussion of a particular issue, within the time constraints imposed by the question. The *I-R-A-C format* must be applied to each issue in the question; it is not the solution to the entire answer. If there are six issues in a question, for example, you should offer six separate, independent *I-R-A-C* analyses.

We believe that the *I-R-A-C* approach is preferable to the *I-R-A-A-O* formula. However, either can be used to analyze and organize essay exam answers. Whatever format you choose, however, you should be consistent throughout the exam and remember the following rules:

First, *analyze all of the relevant facts.* Facts have significance in a particular case *only as they come under the applicable rules of law*. The facts presented must be analyzed and examined to see if they do or do not satisfy one element or another of the applicable rules, and the essential facts and rules must be stated and argued in your analysis.

Second, you must communicate to the grader the *precise rule of law* controlling the facts. In their eagerness to commence their arguments, students sometimes fail to state the applicable rule of law first. Remember, the *R* in either format stands for *Rule of Law*. Defining the rule of law *before* an analysis of the facts is essential in order to allow the grader to follow your reasoning.

Third, it is important to treat *each side of an issue with equal detail.* If a hypothetical describes how an elderly man was killed when he ventured upon the land of a huge power company to obtain a better view of a nuclear reactor, your sympathies might understandably fall on the side of the old man. The grader will nevertheless expect you to see and make every possible argument for the other side. Don't permit your personal viewpoint to affect your answer! A good lawyer never does! When discussing an issue, always state the arguments for each side.

Finally, don't forget to *state your opinion or conclusion* on each issue. Keep in mind, however, that your opinion or conclusion is probably the *least* important part of an exam answer. Why? Because your professor knows that no attorney can tell her client exactly how a judge or jury will decide a particular issue. By definition, an issue is a legal dispute which can go either way. An attorney, therefore, can offer her client only her best opinion about the likelihood of victory or defeat on an issue. Since the decision on any issue lies with the judge or jury, no attorney can ever be absolutely certain of the resolution.

Discuss All Possible Issues

As we've noted, a student should draw *some* type of conclusion or opinion for each issue raised. Whatever your conclusion on a particular issue, it is essential to anticipate and discuss *all of the issues* which would arise if the question were actually tried in court.

Let's assume that a negligence hypothetical involves issues pertaining to duty, breach of duty, proximate causation, and contributory negligence. If the defendant prevails on any one of these issues, he will avoid liability. Nevertheless, even if you feel strongly that the defendant owed no duty to the plaintiff, you **must** go on to discuss all of the other potential issues as well (breach of duty, proximate causation, and contributory negligence). If you were to terminate your answer after a discussion of the duty element only, you'd receive an inferior grade.

Why should you have to discuss every possible issue if you are relatively certain that the outcome of a particular issue would be dispositive of the entire case? Because at the commencement of litigation, neither party can be **absolutely positive** about which issues he will prevail upon at trial. We can state with confidence that every attorney with some degree of experience has won issues he thought he would lose, and has lost issues on which victory was assured. Since one can never be absolutely certain how a factual issue will be resolved by the fact-finder, a good attorney (and exam-writer) will consider **all** possible issues.

To understand the importance of discussing all of the potential issues, you should reflect on what you will do in the actual practice of law. If you represent the defendant, for example, it is your job to raise every possible defense. If there are five potential defenses, and your pleadings only rely on three of them (because you're sure you will win on all three), and the plaintiff is somehow successful on all three issues, your client may well sue you for malpractice. Your client's contention would be that you should be liable because if you had only raised the two additional issues, you might have prevailed on at least one of them, and therefore liability would have been avoided. It is an attorney's duty to raise **all** legitimate issues. A similar philosophy should be followed when taking essay exams.

What exactly do you say when you've resolved the initial issue in favor of the defendant, and discussion of any additional issues would seem to be moot? The answer is simple. You begin the discussion of the next issue with something like, "Assuming, however, the plaintiff prevailed on the foregoing issue, the next issue would be . . ." The grader will understand and appreciate what you have done.

The corollary to the importance of raising all potential issues is that you should avoid discussion of obvious non-issues. Raising non-issues is detrimental in three ways: first, you waste a lot of precious time; second, you usually receive absolutely no points for discussing a point which the grader deems extraneous; and third, it suggests to the grader that you lack the ability to distinguish the significant from the irrelevant. The best guideline for avoiding the discussion of a non-issue is to ask yourself, "Would I, as an attorney, feel comfortable about raising that particular issue or objection in front of a judge"?

Delineate the Transition from One Issue to the Next

It's a good idea to make it easy for the grader to see the issues you've found. One way to accomplish this is to cover no more than one issue per paragraph. Another way is to underline each issue statement. Provided time permits, we recommend that you use both techniques. The essay answers in this book contain numerous illustrations of these suggestions.

One frequent student error is to write two separate paragraphs in which all of the arguments for one side are made in the initial paragraph, and all of the rebuttal arguments by the other side are made in the next paragraph. This is *a bad idea*. It obliges the grader to reconstruct the exam answer in his mind several times to determine whether all possible issues have been discussed by both sides. It will also cause you to state the same rule of law more than once. A better-organized answer presents a given argument by one side and follows that immediately in the same paragraph with the other side's rebuttal to that argument.

Understanding the "Call" of a Question

The statement *at the end of* an essay question or of the fact pattern in a multiple-choice question is sometimes referred to as the "call" of the question. It usually asks you to do something specific like "discuss," "discuss the rights of the parties," "what are X's rights?" "advise X," "the best grounds on which to find the statute unconstitutional are:," "D can be convicted of:," "how should the estate be distributed?," etc. The call of the question should be read carefully because it tells you exactly what you're expected to do. If a question asks, "what are X's rights against Y?" or "X is liable to Y for: . . ." you don't have to spend a lot of time on Y's rights against Z. You will usually receive absolutely no credit for discussing issues or facts that are not required by the call. On the other hand, if the call of an essay question is simply "discuss" or "discuss the rights of the parties," then *all* foreseeable issues must be covered by your answer.

Students are often led astray by an essay question's call. For example, if you are asked for "X's rights against Y" or to "advise X," you may think you may limit yourself to X's viewpoint with respect to the issues. This is *not correct*! You cannot resolve one party's rights against another party without considering the issues which would arise (and the arguments which the other side would assert) if litigation occurred. In short, although the call of the question may appear to focus on the rights of one of the parties to the litigation, a superior answer will cover all the issues and arguments which that person might *encounter* (not just the arguments she would *make*) in attempting to pursue her rights against the other side.

The Importance of Analyzing the Question Carefully Before Writing

The overriding *time pressure* of an essay exam is probably a major reason why many students fail to analyze a question carefully before writing. Five minutes into the allocated time for a particular question, you may notice that the person next to you is writing furiously. This thought then flashes through your mind, "Oh, my goodness, he's putting down more words on the paper than I am, and therefore he's bound to get a better grade." It can be stated *unequivocally* that there is no necessary correlation between the number of words on your exam paper and the grade you'll receive. Students who begin their answer after only five minutes of analysis have probably seen only the most obvious issues, and missed many, if not most, of the subtle ones. They are also likely to be less well-organized.

Opinions differ as to how much time you should spend analyzing and outlining a question before you actually write the answer. We believe that you should spend at least 12 to 18 minutes analyzing, organizing, and outlining a one-hour question before writing your answer. This will usually provide sufficient time to analyze and organize the question thoroughly *and* enough time to write a relatively complete answer. Remember that each word of the question must be scrutinized to determine if it (1) suggests an issue under the operative rules of law, or (2) can be used in making an argument for the resolution of an issue. Since you can't receive points for an issue you don't spot, it is usually wise to read a question *twice* before starting your outline.

When to Make an Assumption

The instructions for a question may tell you to *assume* facts which are necessary to the answer. Even when these instructions are *not* given, you may be obliged to make certain assumptions about missing facts in order to write a thorough answer. Assumptions should be made only when you are told or when you, as the attorney for one of the parties described in the question, would be obliged to solicit additional information from your client. On the other hand, assumptions should *never be used to change or alter the question*. Don't ever write something like "if the facts in the question were . . . , instead of . . . , then . . . would result." If you do this, you are wasting time on facts which are extraneous to the problem before you. Professors want you to deal with *their* fact patterns, not your own.

Students sometimes try to "write around" information they think is missing. They assume that their professor has failed to include every piece of data necessary for a thorough answer. This is generally *wrong*. The professor may have omitted some facts deliberately to see if the student *can figure out what to do* under the circumstances. In some instances, the professor may have omitted them inadvertently (even law professors are sometimes human).

The way to deal with the omission of essential information is to describe (1) what fact (or facts) appear to be missing, and (2) why that information is important. As an example, go back to the "movie shoot" hypothetical we discussed above. In that fact pattern, there was no mention of the relative strength of A and C. This fact could be extremely important. If C weighed 240 pounds and was built like a professional football linebacker, while A tipped the scales at a mere 160 pounds, punching A in the face after he had been pushed to the ground would probably constitute unnecessary force (thereby causing C to forfeit the prevention-of-crime privilege). If the physiques of the parties were reversed, however, C's punch to A's face would probably constitute reasonable behavior. Under the facts, C had to deal the "knockout" blow while the opportunity presented itself. The last sentences of the Second Student Answer above show that the student understood these subtleties and correctly supplied the essential missing facts and assumptions.

Assumptions should be made in a manner which keeps the other issues open (i.e., they lead to a discussion of all other possible issues). Don't assume facts which would virtually dispose of the entire hypothetical in a few sentences. For example, suppose that A called B a "convicted felon" (a statement which is inherently defamatory, i.e., a defamatory statement is one which tends to subject the plaintiff to hatred, contempt, or ridicule). If A's statement is true, he has a complete defense to B's action for defamation. If the facts don't tell whether A's statement was true or not, it would *not* be wise to write something like, "We'll assume that A's statement about B is accurate, and therefore B cannot successfully sue A for defamation." So facile an approach would rarely be appreciated by the grader. The proper way to handle this situation would be to state, "If we assume that A's statement about B is not correct, A cannot raise the defense of truth." You've communicated to the grader that you recognize the need to assume an essential fact and that you've assumed it in a way that enables you to proceed to discuss all other issues.

Case Names

A law student is ordinarily *not* expected to recall case names on an exam. The professor knows that you have read several hundred cases for each course, and that you would have to be a memory expert to have all of the names at your fingertips. If you confront a fact pattern which seems similar to a case which you have reviewed (but you cannot recall its name), just write something like, "One case we've read held that . . ." or "It has been held that. . . . " In this manner, you have informed the grader that you are relying on a case which contained a fact pattern similar to the question at issue.

The only exception to this rule is in the case of a landmark decision (e.g., *Roe v. Wade*). Landmark opinions are usually those which change or alter established law.[2] These cases are usually easy to identify, because you will probably have spent an entire class period discussing each of them. *Palsgraf v. Long Island Rail Road* is a prime example of a landmark case in Torts. In these special cases, you may be expected to remember the case by name, as well as the proposition of law which it stands for. However, this represents a very limited exception to the general rule which counsels against wasting precious time trying to memorize and reproduce case names.

How to Handle Time Pressures

What do you do when there are five minutes left in the exam and you have only written down two-thirds of your answer? One thing **not** to do is write something like, "No time left!" or "Not enough time!" This gets you nothing but the satisfaction of knowing you have communicated your personal frustrations to the grader. Another thing **not** to do is insert in the exam booklet the outline you may have made on a piece of scrap paper. Professors will rarely look at these.

First of all, it is not necessarily a bad thing to be pressed for time. The person who finishes five minutes early has very possibly missed some important issues. The more proficient you become in knowing what is expected of you on an exam, the greater the difficulty you may experience in staying within the time limits. Second, remember that (at least to some extent) you're graded against your classmates' answers and they're under exactly the same time pressure as you. In short, don't panic if you can't write the "perfect" answer in the allotted time. Nobody does!

The best hedge against misuse of time is to *review as many old exams as possible*. These exercises will give you a familiarity with the process of organizing and writing an exam answer, which, in turn, should result in an enhanced ability to stay within the time boundaries. If you nevertheless find that you have about 15 minutes of writing to do and five minutes to do

2 In Constitutional Law and Criminal Procedure, many cases will qualify as "landmark" cases. Students studying these subjects should try to associate case names with the corresponding holdings and reproduce both in their exam answers.

it in, write a paragraph which summarizes the remaining issues or arguments you would discuss if time permitted. As long as you've indicated that you're aware of the remaining legal issues, you'll probably receive some credit for them. Your analytical and argumentative skills will already be apparent to the grader by virtue of the issues that you have previously discussed.

Write Legibly

Make sure your answer is legible. Students should *not* assume that their professors will be willing to take their papers to the local pharmacist to have them deciphered. Remember, your professor may have 75 to 150 separate exams to grade. If your answer is difficult to read, you will rarely be given the benefit of the doubt. On the other hand, a legible, well-organized paper creates a very positive mental impact upon the grader.

Many schools allow students to type their exams. If you type your exam, you'll probably be in a room with a lot of other people who are typing theirs. Some schools may have programs that allow you to type on your laptop or on a school laptop. If it's your own laptop, the school will provide software that blocks you from accessing any other programs or information on your hard drive while you type the exam. Computer-typing is not widely available, however, so if you type you will more than likely be typing on a typewriter. If the constant clack-clack-clack of typewriters keeps you from concentrating, you shouldn't type. If you do write your exam on a typewriter, be sure to leave at least one blank line between typewritten lines, so that handwritten changes and insertions in your answers can be made easily.

If you decide against typing, your answer will probably be written in a "bluebook." It is usually a good idea to write only on the odd numbered pages (i.e., 1, 3, 5, etc.). You may also want to leave a blank line between each written line. These things will usually make the answer easier to read. If you discover that you have left out a word or phrase, you can insert it into the proper place by means of a caret sign ($\wedge$). If you feel that you've omitted an entire issue, you can write it on the facing blank page. A symbol can be used to indicate where the additional portion of the answer should be inserted. While it's not ideal to have your answer take on the appearance of a road map, reference to an adjoining page by means of a symbol is much better than trying to squeeze six lines into one, and the symbol will help to indicate to the grader where the same symbol appears in another part of your answer.

The Importance of Reviewing Prior Exams

As we've mentioned, it is *extremely important to review old exams*. The transition from blackletter law to essay exam can be a difficult experience if the process has not been practiced. Although this book provides a large number of essay and multiple-choice questions, *don't stop here*! Most law schools have recent tests on file in the library, by course. We strongly suggest that you make a copy of every old exam you can obtain (especially those given by your professors) at the beginning of each semester. The demand for these documents usually increases dramatically as "finals time" draws closer.

The exams for each course should be scrutinized *throughout the semester*. They should be reviewed as you complete each chapter in your casebook. Generally, the order of exam questions follows the sequence of the materials in your casebook. Thus, the first question on a law school test may involve the initial three chapters of the casebook; the second question may pertain to the fourth and fifth chapters; etc. In any event, *don't wait* until the semester is nearly over to begin reviewing old exams.

Keep in mind that no one is born with the ability to analyze questions and write superior answers to law school exams. Like any other skill, it is developed and perfected only through application. If you don't take the time to analyze numerous examinations from prior years, this evolutionary process just won't occur. Don't just *think about* the answers to past exam questions; take the time to *write the answers down*. It's also wise to look back at an answer a day or two after you've written it. You will invariably see (1) ways in which the organization could have been improved, and (2) arguments you missed.

As you practice spotting issues on past exams, you will see how rules of law become the sources of issues on finals. As we've already noted, if you don't *understand* how rules of law translate into issues, you won't be able to achieve superior grades on your exams. Reviewing exams from prior years should also reveal that certain issues tend to be lumped together in the same question. For instance, where a fact pattern involves a false statement made by one person about another, three potential theories of liability are often present—defamation, invasion of privacy (false, public light), and intentional infliction of severe emotional distress. You will need to see if any or all of these legal remedies apply to the facts.

Finally, one of the best means of evaluating if you understand a subject (or a particular area within a subject) is to attempt to create a hypothetical exam for that subject. Your exam should contain as many issues as possible.

If you can write an issue-packed exam, you probably know that subject well. If you can't, then you probably haven't yet acquired an adequate understanding of how the principles of law in that subject can spawn issues.

As Always, a Caveat

The suggestions and advice offered in this book represent the product of many years of experience in the field of legal education. We are confident that the techniques and concepts described in these pages will help you prepare for, and succeed, at your exams. Nevertheless, particular professors sometimes have a preference for exam-writing techniques which are not stressed in this book. Some instructors expect at least a nominal reference to the *prima facie* elements of all pertinent legal theories (even though one or more of those principles is *not* placed into issue). Other professors want their students to emphasize public policy considerations in the arguments they make on a particular issue. Because this book is intended for nation-wide consumption, these individualized preferences have *not* been stressed. The best way to find out whether your professor has a penchant for a particular writing approach is to ask her to provide you with a model answer to a previous exam. If a model answer is not available, speak to upper-class students who received a superior grade in that professor's class.

One final point. While the principles cited in the answers to the questions in this book have been drawn from commonly used sources (i.e., case-books, hornbooks, etc.), it is conceivable that they may be inconsistent with those taught by your professor. In instances where a conflict exists between our formulation of a legal principle and the one which is taught by your professor, *follow the latter!* Since your grades are determined by your professors, their views should always supplant the views expressed in this book.

Essay Exam Questions

Question 1

Oscar was the owner of Sandyacres, a seafront property that lies between a highway and a public beach. Thirty-three years ago, he sold Alan an option to purchase the southeast quarter of Sandyacres for $2,500. The option agreement provides that the option can be exercised "by Alan or by his widow at any time while either shall live." Alan promptly recorded the agreement. Alan and his wife are alive.

Thirty years ago, Oscar constructed a tunnel through a sand dune on Sandyacres to provide convenient access to the beach. He also conveyed to Nabor, an adjoining owner, a right-of-way easement across Sandyacres and through the tunnel to the beach for Nabor and his motel guests to use. This deed of conveyance was acknowledged before a notary public whose commission had expired. Nabor promptly recorded the deed. Three years ago, the tunnel collapsed. It has not been reconstructed.

Twenty years ago, Oscar granted Sandyacres for value to Edward "in fee simple so long as he never marries." Edward, who had no actual knowledge of Oscar's transactions with Alan and Nabor, promptly recorded his deed. Edward is alive and has never married.

Client is now negotiating to buy Sandyacres from Edward. Client plans to build a resort hotel, a portion of which will sit directly above the collapsed tunnel.

A title insurance company has agreed to insure Client's title to Sandyacres subject to exceptions that might arise out of each of the following matters:

(1) Alan's option agreement;
(2) the conveyance to Nabor; and
(3) the conveyance to Edward.

Discuss how you would advise Client regarding the extent, if any, to which each of the matters referred to in the title insurance exceptions may affect her rights in Sandyacres if she purchases that property.

Question 2

Owen owned Blackacre, which consisted of a house on a lot. He conveyed Blackacre to his two children, Sam and Doris, by a deed that reads as follows: "Owen hereby grants Blackacre to Sam and Doris, to be held by them jointly." The deed was duly recorded.

Thereafter, Sam borrowed money from Bank and gave Bank a mortgage on Blackacre to secure repayment of the loan. In the mortgage document, Sam covenanted for himself, his successors and assigns, that Blackacre would not be used for any purpose other than as a single-family residence.

Sam died before the loan became due. His will left all his property to his friend Tom. As applicable law permits, Bank elected not to file a claim against Sam's estate or to call the loan, but rather to rely on whatever rights it had under the mortgage.

Shortly after Sam's death, the area in which Blackacre is located was rezoned to permit multiple-family dwellings. Tom decided to convert the house on Blackacre into a three-unit apartment building.

Bank, upon learning of Tom's plans, sought an injunction against Tom to prohibit the conversion.

Doris brought an action against Bank and Tom to quiet title to Blackacre in herself.

Discuss the result in each case.

Question 3

Ten years ago, O, the owner of Blackacre, executed a conveyance thereof "to A and B, exclusively, as joint tenants, with right of survivorship, to be used as a parking lot, but if said premises should ever be used for a different purpose, then this conveyance shall immediately become void." At the time of this transfer, A and B each had an independent retail establishment located across the street from Blackacre. A and B immediately began using Blackacre as a parking area for the convenience of their customers. Four years later, B sold her store and her interest in Blackacre to C.

One year after the sale to C, C decided to enlarge his store. He asked A if A would have any objection to C building a storage facility on Blackacre that would encompass approximately 20 percent of that parcel. C told A that without such increased storage area, it was not economically feasible for C to enlarge his retail establishment. A told C that he had no objections. To save time and money, C installed a prefabricated aluminum structure on Blackacre using metal bolts that were permanently attached to a suitable concrete foundation. C then expanded his retail store by adding a second floor to it. C and A continued to invite their customers to park on the rest of Blackacre. O made about five or six trips to A's store during the time that the storage facility was being erected, parking in the Blackacre lot in three instances.

One year after the storage facility had been erected, O executed a conveyance of all his "right, title and interest in and to Blackacre" to M. O died shortly thereafter, leaving all of his property to H (his only heir at law). It is now four months after O's death, and H has demanded possession of Blackacre from A and C. In addition, M has advised A and C that he owns Blackacre.

Discuss the respective rights of M, A, C, and H.

Question 4

Three years and four months ago, two brothers, Bill and Murray, bought 20 acres of land as joint tenants on the outskirts of the City of Myth. Originally, they each intended to build their family homes on the land and farm the remainder for extra income. However, Murray ran into some financial difficulties and was unable to build a house.

Bill constructed two single-family dwellings on the premises. He and his family occupied one of the dwellings and rented the other dwelling to Henrietta and her family for $500 per month. In addition, Bill paid the taxes on the land each year and also paid the fire insurance premiums on the two houses. Four months ago, Henrietta and Bill verbally entered into a one-year lease.

Bill cleared the remaining acreage of its timber. He sold the timber and kept the money for himself. He then cultivated the land and planted half of it as a fruit orchard and the other half as seasonal crops. Each year, he harvested the fruit and the seasonal crops and sold them. He kept all of the income for himself.

Six months ago, Murray had paid off all of his debts and was ready to build his house. Bill told him, "Listen, buddy boy, I'm the one who has taken care of this land all these years. You're not going to just come in here now and take out fruit trees or growing crops in order to build your stupid house." Murray, greatly upset, has sued Bill for possession of the premises, half the rentals paid by Henrietta over the years, half the value of the timber sold by Bill when he cleared the land, half the value of the crops harvested by Bill, and half the reasonable rental value of the property occupied by Bill. When Bill was served with the summons, he became so angry that he countersued for partition of the land in kind.

(1) Discuss fully the merits of Murray's suit against Bill. Include in your discussion any counterclaims that Bill might have against Murray.

(2) Can Henrietta be obliged to vacate the land?

(3) If Bill dies before the suit is tried and is survived by his wife Mary, to whom he leaves all his property, how does this affect Murray's claim?

Question 5

Alex owns Redacre. Bert owns an adjacent property, Greenacre. Alex delivered to Bert a signed deed reciting that Alex "conveys to Bert a four-foot wide strip across the middle of Redacre for an underground sewer line in order to connect a sewer line from Bert's apartment house on Greenacre with the city sewer line under the street adjacent to Redacre."

Bert installed an underground sewer line that extended from his apartment house through the strip across Redacre to the adjoining street.

Thereafter, Bert conveyed to Clyde a portion of Greenacre and an easement for a sewer line across another portion of Greenacre to connect with Bert's sewer line. Clyde planned to build an apartment house on his portion of Greenacre.

A year after Bert's conveyance to Clyde, and without Bert's knowledge, Alex connected a sewer line from his factory on Redacre to Bert's sewer line on Redacre. This overloaded Bert's line, causing it occasionally to back waste up into Bert's apartment house.

After Bert discovered the connection made by Alex, Bert disconnected Alex's Redacre sewer line from his own. He did not notify Alex of his action and, by the time Alex learned of it, Redacre had been damaged by waste discharging from Alex's open sewer line.

Alex then learned of the conveyance to Clyde and of Clyde's plans to construct an apartment house.

Bert commenced a lawsuit against Alex seeking an injunction and damages. Alex's defense asserted that Bert had a nonexclusive easement.

In a properly pleaded cross-action, Alex sought relief (a) against Bert for damages to Redacre caused by the discharge of waste onto Redacre, and (b) against Clyde to enjoin Clyde's proposed use of Bert's sewer line across Redacre.

(1) Discuss whether Bert should succeed in his action against Alex.

(2) Discuss whether Alex should succeed in her action against Bert.

(3) Discuss whether Alex should succeed in her action against Clyde.

Question 6

L and T entered into a written lease of a completely furnished dwelling for a period of one year at a rental of $250 per month, commencing on September 1, 2002. The lease contained a clause allowing T "to give up possession and terminate his liability for rent if the premises, through no fault on T's part, are destroyed or damaged so as to be uninhabitable."

X, the previous tenant of L under a lease that expired August 31, 2002, wrongfully held over and remained on the premises until December 1, 2002, when T took possession. During this period, L refused to take any action to oust X, although repeatedly requested to do so by T.

Shortly after going into possession, T was injured when a bedroom chair collapsed under his weight. Several of the screws pulled loose and came out of the softwood frame. There is no evidence that L knew of the chair's defective construction or that L was negligent.

On March 1, 2003, T paid his rent up to date, surrendered possession, and moved out because the roof had deteriorated and had begun to leak badly. L informed T that he refused to accept the surrender, but he would attempt to relet the dwelling for T's account. On May 1, 2003, T relet the premises to Y for the remainder of the term at a rental of $200 per month.

There are no applicable statutes. Discuss any rights and duties of L and T.

Question 7

L rented (by a signed written lease) a furnished apartment in his building to T, a law student, for two years, beginning June 1. When T arrived at the apartment on June 1, R (the prior tenant) was still there. T complained to L, and L evicted R on June 15. T came into possession of the apartment on June 16. In early July, some children playing baseball broke a windowpane in T's apartment. T demanded that L replace the windowpane, but L refused. Rain coming through the broken pane caused damage to the living room floor, which began to warp.

The apartment above T's was occupied by C, a member of the famous rock group, the Pebbles. The Pebbles rehearsed daily (typically 2:00–6:00 p.m.), which interfered with T's law studies so much that she complained repeatedly to L. On July 15, three of C's friends (the other members of the Pebbles) were arrested at C's apartment and charged with possession of narcotics. The noise stopped immediately thereafter.

On August 30, T discovered that the stove in her apartment was no longer functioning. On August 31, T, disgusted with all these events, knocked on L's door, tendered the key to L, and said, "This place is a zoo; I wouldn't live here if you paid me!" L took the key without saying a word. L now comes to you wanting to sue T for both the accrued and prospective rent (T has yet to pay any rent). Discuss what you would advise L.

Question 8

On February 1, 2002, O leased space in an office building to T, effective as of that date "for an aggregate rent of $48,000, payable at $2,000 on the first day of each month." The properly executed written agreement also provided, *inter alia*:

(1) Lessee shall not assign or sublet the leased premises without the written consent of Lessor, which shall not be unreasonably withheld;

(2) Lessee shall install all fixtures required for operation of a retail clothing store at the premises, which fixtures shall belong to Lessor at the conclusion of the lease term;

(3) Lessee shall keep such fixtures fully insured for Lessor's benefit; and

(4) Lessee shall not hold Lessor liable for the negligent acts of Lessor's employees or agents.

T installed the necessary fixtures and commenced operation of the store. In early April 2003, T decided to retire and introduced S to O as a possible successor. O, shortly thereafter, delivered the following written statement to T: "Without prejudice to my rights, I consent to adding S to the lease." That same day, T assigned the lease to S, but reserved the right to reenter the premises if S failed to pay rent due to O.

In May 2003, S installed dry cleaning and pressing equipment valued at $4,500.

S made all his rent payments on time and removed his inventory prior to February 1, 2004. However, because the new premises that S was to occupy had been damaged by a fire, S was unable to remove the dry cleaning and pressing equipment by that date. On February 10, 2004, S received a note from O that stated: "Rent will be due for one more year since you're still occupying my property." A copy of this note was mailed to T at his old address, but T had moved in the interim and the letter was not forwarded to T's new address. On February 15, 2004, S introduced Z to O as a possible successor, but O refused to accept Z because of Z's ethnic origin.

On April 1, 2004, O's night security guard accidentally dropped a lighted cigarette into a can of dry cleaning fluid that S had left at the premises. The ensuing explosion and fire gutted the premises and destroyed the fixtures and equipment, valued at $2,500 and $4,500, respectively, at the time of the accident. S had allowed the insurance to lapse on February 1, 2004. On April 10, 2004, S notified O that he no longer considered himself to be liable for rent.

Discuss O's rights against T and S.

Question 9

Lisa owns a five-story commercial building. On January 1, 2003, she leased the top floor to Tom for a five-year term at a rent of $500 a month. A written lease was signed by both parties. It contained a restriction that the premises could be used only "as a dance studio and for no other purpose." It also provided that "Landlord shall not lease space in the building to any competitor of Tenant." The lease did not contain any express warranties or disclaimers.

Tom moved in immediately and began to operate a dance studio. In June 2003, he sold his dance studio business to Alice, one of his instructors, and assigned the lease to her. The assignment did not contain any express assumption or assignment of contract rights clauses.

In January 2004, a dance student fell through a floor board. When the board was replaced, it was discovered that, even though the building met building code requirements, the floor was not strong enough to support a dance studio.

In February, Lisa rented the basement to Charles, who used it for aerobic exercise classes.

Alice wrote to Lisa demanding that Lisa have the floor reinforced and that she cancel the lease with Charles because his aerobic exercise classes competed with her dance studio. Lisa refused both requests. On July 1, 2004, with the rent up-to-date through June 30, Alice mailed the studio key back to Lisa and moved out of the building. She has paid no rent since moving. Lisa has made all reasonable attempts to mitigate the loss.

Lisa has now sued both Tom and Alice for the rent due.

Discuss how the court should rule.

Question 10

Omar owns a gasoline station. Tom is the lessee and operator of the gas station under a three-year written lease running from January 1, 2002, through December 31, 2004. The monthly rental is $1,000 payable on the first business day of each month. Tom remained in possession beyond the expiration date and continued to pay the rent as before.

On January 31, 2005, Tom offered to purchase the premises from Omar for $80,000, with title to pass in 90 days. Omar verbally accepted the offer, and the parties agreed that no additional lease payments would be required of Tom. With Omar's knowledge, Tom then installed new gas pumps, lube racks, and wheel alignment equipment at an aggregate cost to him of $18,000.

On March 5, a portion of the building was damaged by a mudslide caused by a severe rainstorm. Tom asked Omar either to repair the damage caused by the mudslide (cost approximately $1,600) or to reduce the purchase price by a corresponding amount. Omar refused. On March 15, Tom informed Omar that, under the circumstances, he was moving out and had no more interest in purchasing the property. On March 17, Tom vacated the premises.

Two weeks later, Tom received a letter from Omar telling him that the property had been relet to Jill for $800 a month, effective April 1, 2005. Omar also stated that he held Tom responsible for both the rent for the months of February and March and the $200 per month difference in the rent that would accrue through the end of the year. Omar further informed Tom that he had signed a contract to sell the premises to Samuel, with title to pass on January 1, 2006. It is now April 5, 2005. Tom has decided that he still wants to purchase the gasoline station on the original terms to which Omar had agreed.

Discuss the probable outcome of the following actions:

(1) an action brought by Tom against Omar to enforce specific performance of the agreement of sale, and

(2) an action by Omar against Tom for rent from February through December 2005.

Question 11

Owen owned a city block consisting of eight lots, each of which he had purchased from a different owner. In 2000, he conveyed by deed Lots 1 and 2 to Xavier Corporation, which built a department store thereon. The deed, which had been recorded promptly, contained covenants by Owen for himself, his heirs, successors and assigns (1) to provide, maintain, repair, and keep available a parking area for at least 500 automobiles on the remainder of the block for the nonexclusive use of department store customers; and (2) to refrain from selling tires or petroleum products on any of the remaining lots.

Owen then developed a shopping center with a 550-car parking lot on Lots 3 through 8. In 2002, he sold the shopping center to Annie, who knew about the covenant restricting the sale of tires and petroleum products, but was unaware of the covenant about the parking lot.

A municipal zoning ordinance encompassing the area in which the shopping center is located prohibits freestanding signs more than 15 feet high.

Annie now proposes to build a service station on the shopping center parking lot, which will eliminate 100 parking spaces. A marketing survey reveals that unless the station has a 50-foot-high freestanding sign to attract customers from a nearby freeway, the service station will be unprofitable. A 15-foot sign will be barely visible from the adjoining streets.

(1) Discuss whether Xavier can prevent Annie from building the service station.

(2) Assuming that Xavier cannot prevent Annie from building the service station, discuss whether the municipality can prevent Annie from erecting a 50-foot sign in the parking area.

Question 12

Alicia has just shown you a deed that was recorded 40 years ago. This document reads as follows:

> In consideration of love and affection, I hereby grant Sweetholm to my friend Josiah and the heirs of his body, this conveyance to take effect 10 years from the date hereof, provided that if Josiah dies without issue the estate is to go to my brother Ludwig and his heirs, and further provided that if animals, birds or children are ever kept on the property, the estate is to cease and determine.
>
> Signed, Vladimir

You ascertain from Alicia that her house, with its surrounding grounds of about 10 acres, is known as Sweetholm. Alicia tells you that she bought Sweetholm from Josiah's niece, Jennifer, 11 years ago. The deed transferred to Alicia "all my right, title, and interest in Sweetholm." Alicia also tells you that, when she bought the property, the guest house near the southwest boundary of the estate was occupied by Danny, Jennifer's cousin. Danny had visited Jennifer 12 years ago and decided to stay to work on a novel. Jennifer had asked Alicia to let Danny stay there for a while, "since he was finding himself." Alicia said it probably would be "all right, if Danny did not get in her way." Alicia thought it might be a good idea to have a male on the property to frighten away prospective thieves. Soon after Jennifer vacated Sweetholm, Danny built a separate mailbox outside the guest house and placed a doormat in front of the entrance that read "Welcome to Danny's."

It appears that the estate bordering Sweetholm on the west, Laurel Hill, was purchased 14 years ago by Wilson, a scientist doing research on the territorial habits of wild dogs, coyotes, and wolves. Wilson had captured several wolves and brought them to Laurel Hill. When Alicia took over the property from Jennifer, Wilson talked to her about the wolves. Alicia promised him, in a valid writing, that she would allow the wolves to wander freely over Sweetholm. The wolves soon manifested their territorial behavior and took up residence on the southwest corner of Sweetholm.

Unfortunately, when Danny saw one of the animals wandering around near the guest house about two months ago, he suddenly took it into his head that it would make a nice pet. Danny enticed the wolf into his enclosed patio and kept it there, even after it resisted his first efforts to make friends and bit his hand when he tried to feed it.

About a week ago, Alicia received an unpleasant visit from Trivers, another scientist with whom Wilson is working, who had purchased Laurel Hill from Wilson last summer. Trivers threatened to sue Alicia because Danny had tampered with a subject involved in his experiment. Alicia became upset with the whole situation, evicted both Danny and the wolves from Sweetholm that very evening, and hastily constructed a chicken-wire fence on the western boundary of Sweetholm so that the wolves could not get back in. Last night, (1) Danny called and claimed that he owned the guest house, and (2) Trivers called and threatened to obtain an injunction requiring Alicia to remove the chicken-wire fence.

Alicia asks you whether Trivers and Danny really have any viable claims against her. She also wants to know whether there are any other people who might show up to claim an interest in Sweetholm.

In response to your initial questions, Alicia tells you that Vladimir is dead and Josef is his sole heir; that Ludwig is dead and Richard is his sole heir; and that Josiah is also dead, but Jennifer, his niece and only heir, is still alive. You have also learned that the statute of limitations for actions to recover real property is 10 years. Please evaluate the possible claims of Danny, Trivers, and any other person(s) you think might have a plausible claim to some interest in Sweetholm.

Question 13

Twenty years ago, Owen subdivided his family estate into several hundred building lots, which he sold during the following few years. Most, but not all, of the deeds contained restrictions that required setbacks of at least 50 feet from the street, single-story ranch-style houses, all garages to be located on the rear quarter of the lots, and white split-rail fences.

Alex purchased Lot 15 from Owen 10 years ago. There was no restrictive covenant in his deed, but she built a ranch-style house 65 feet from the street with a garage on the rear quarter of the lot.

The deeds to Lots 14 and 16, which adjoin Lot 15 on either side, did contain the above restrictions. Although Lots 14 and 16 had been sold and passed through several owners, they were among the few lots that were unimproved when Alex bought Lot 15.

Baker bought Lot 14 last year and later built an expensive home that complied with the restrictions in the original deed from Owen. She started building an elaborate swimming pool, but lost her job before the pool was completed. She then quitclaimed her interest in Lot 14 to Commercial Bank in lieu of foreclosure. Two months after the Bank took title, Alex's prize flower bed slid into the excavation Baker had dug for her pool.

Dave now owns Lot 16 and plans to build a two-story brick house, with an attached garage, set back 15 feet from the street. Alex asked Dave to comply with the deed restrictions. When Dave refused, Alex erected a brick wall 20 feet high on her lot, adjacent to and paralleling the entire boundary with Dave's Lot 16. Alex painted the side of the wall facing Dave's lot black and coated it with creosote, a foul-smelling preservative. This wall would darken Dave's planned house and make use of his patio unpleasant.

All deeds were recorded. Owen no longer owns any of the lots, but lives in an exclusive hotel that overlooks the subdivision.

(1) Discuss whether Alex can prevent Dave from building as planned.

(2) Discuss whether Owen can prevent Dave from building as planned.

(3) Discuss whether Dave has any rights against Alex.

(4) Discuss whether Alex can recover from Commercial Bank.

Question 14

Albright owned adjoining lots in a city, Lots 1 and 2, each improved with a single-family residence. The lots are located in a district where business buildings were rapidly replacing houses. Albright sold Lot 1 to Bayard, who planned to erect a large commercial structure that would require a deep foundation. The parties agreed orally that Bayard should be permitted to excavate without providing support for the house on Albright's remaining lot since Albright intended to replace it with a similar commercial structure.

A period of depression for business followed the sale, and Bayard postponed his plans to build while Albright abandoned his plans and sold Lot 2 to Cullom, who repaired and occupied it as her home.

Economic conditions improved, and Bayard razed the house on his lot. While this was being done, Bayard discovered that the pipe connecting Cullom's house with the public sewer ran across the Bayard lot. The pipe was beneath the surface of the land outside where the house had been, but it was above the surface in a "crawl space" beneath the floor of the razed house where the basement was not fully excavated. The right to maintain such a line was not reserved in Albright's deed to Bayard and was not disclosed in any recorded document.

Bayard demanded that Cullom remove the sewer line and also notified her to protect her house against possible subsidence during the excavation for the new building Bayard was about to build. Cullom consulted qualified engineers, who advised her that the cost of strengthening her foundation and the cost of securing a new outlet for the sewer would be prohibitive.

Discuss the respective rights of Bayard and Cullom.

Question 15

One acre parking lot and cemetery	Lot 12	Lot 11	Lot 10	Lot 9	Lot 8	Lot 7	Easement for Lots 2–6
	Lot 6	Lot 5	Lot 4	Lot 3	Lot 2	Lot 1	

Fifteen years ago, Vera inherited the tract of land described above, consisting of Lots 1–12. Ten years ago, she sold Lots 1–4 and 7–10. The deeds to these lots imposed an easement over the northerly 15 feet of Lots 1–5 for the use and benefit of Lots 2–6. This easement presently provides the only access to Lots 2–6. The deeds to Lots 1–5 and 7–10 also contained the following restriction: "To preserve high quality within this development, this lot is conveyed on condition it be used solely for residential purposes, and any other use may be enjoined and shall be cause for forfeiture." Immediately, residences were built on Lots 1–4 and 7–10. Lot 5 remained vacant. Vera sold Lot 6 five years ago to Barb, without including any restrictions in the deed.

Three years ago, Barb, a rock music promoter, began operating a nightclub on Lot 6. One year ago, Phil purchased Lot 5. The deed he received from Vera was identical to that received by Lot owners 1–4. Phil built a family home, but has frequently complained to Barb about the noise level emanating from Barb's club, especially on weekends.

All of the deeds were recorded.

Occasionally, inebriated patrons of Barb's club throw empty bottles on the lawns of Lots 1–5.

Fifteen months ago, a zoning ordinance was enacted and Lots 1–12 were zoned "Single Family Residential." Barb ignored this zoning change.

Barb's club has prospered. Three months ago, by quitclaim deed, Barb acquired a 1-acre parcel adjoining Lot 6 on the west from Farmer to use as a parking lot and cemetery. Farmer owns another 59 acres of rural land surrounding Vera's tract on the north, west, and south. Barb now plans to use a few rooms in the building on Lot 6 for a mortuary featuring recently deceased rock stars. The dead stars would then be buried in the cemetery.

Yesterday, despite Phil's appearance and objections, the County Commissioners rezoned Lot 6 and the parking lot to "Commercial," stating that Farmer's adjacent land was a likely site for a shopping center. This rezoning permits Lot 6 and the parking lot to be used for mortuaries and nightclubs. As Phil left the meeting, he told Barb that he intended to retain an attorney and use every means legally available to close or hinder Barb's nightclub and mortuary operations.

Barb consults you before investing any more money in Lot 6 or paving the parking lot. She wants to know what legal action Phil and the owners of the other lots might take, what defenses she might reasonably assert, and what the likelihood is that she will be successful. Discuss.

Question 16

For many years, Olga operated a tavern on property owned by her at 2 Harvard Place in the town of Waterbury. On June 13, 1998, she broke her leg and closed the tavern, but did not remove any of the merchandise or fixtures. She reopened the tavern on September 19, 1998.

On July 1, 1998, Waterbury adopted a zoning ordinance (effective immediately) restricting use of property on Harvard Place to single-family dwellings, but providing for continuation of any existing nonconforming uses by the owner or successors in title, subject to the following provision:

"No nonconforming use, once abandoned, shall be reinstated. For the purpose of this section, 'abandoned' is defined as cessation of the nonconforming use for six or more consecutive months."

On March 15, 2000, Olga executed and delivered a grant deed to 2 Harvard Place to Dr. Baker to pay a past-due bill for personal medical services. Baker allowed Olga to continue to operate the tavern and did not record her deed immediately.

On September 5, 2000, Olga, for valuable consideration, executed and delivered a conveyance of "all my right, title and interest in 2 Harvard Place" to Charles, who had no knowledge of Baker's deed. Dr. Baker recorded her deed on October 1, 2000, and Charles recorded his deed two days later.

Charles operated the tavern continuously from September 15, 2000, to January 19, 2002, when he closed the tavern because his liquor license was suspended for nine months by the State Board of Liquor Control.

(1) Discuss who should prevail in a quiet title action between Baker and Charles.

(2) If Charles prevails, discuss whether he will be legally entitled to reopen the premises as a tavern when the suspension of his liquor license terminates.

Question 17

Twelve years ago, Able purchased a 400-acre tract of land in the state of Myth. The north end of this tract is bounded by a flowing river. Two years later, Able died. He was survived by one daughter, who didn't know until two months ago that her father had bought the tract of land. Eleven years ago, Baker built a fence around the 400-acre tract and began growing crops on it. Baker has paid taxes for all but four of the years he has occupied the land.

Four years ago, Carla asked permission to drill some test wells on the tract occupied by Baker to determine whether there were oil deposits beneath the land. After determining that there appeared to be substantial oil deposits, Carla asked Baker to lease the land to her for oil and gas production. Baker told Carla that he was not the true owner, and so he could not give Carla permission to drill. Carla then bought an adjacent tract of land and drilled wells to produce oil from the reservoir underneath both Baker's and Carla's tract. Baker, realizing that Carla probably would deplete the oil supply, drilled wells on the tract he occupied and pumped oil into storage tanks, waiting for the price of oil to go up. Carla has been selling her oil as it is produced, rather than storing it.

Eight years ago, Baker had begun appropriating 100,000 cubic feet of water per day from the river to irrigate his crops. When there was a drought two years later, Baker built an earthen dam to create a pool from which to irrigate the tract. This dam reduced the flow of water to downstream owners, most of whom relied upon it for manufacturing purposes. Baker also entered into a contract with City, a small town two miles away. Baker agreed to drill several water wells and to sell the water produced to the City. The result was to reduce the general water table in the area.

Baker has just discovered that one of Carla's wells was not drilled properly and encroached upon the substrata of Baker's tract.

Assuming Myth requires possession for 10 years in order to gain title by adverse possession, discuss the following:

(1) What rights does Baker have in and to the 400-acre tract?

(2) What rights, if any, does Carla have against Baker involving the oil?

(3) What rights do the downstream owners have as to the water in the river?

(4) What rights does Baker have against Carla regarding the oil produced from the slant-hole well?

Question 18

A was the owner of Blackacre, a vacant tract of land. A conveyed Blackacre to B by warranty deed on July 1, 2001, and B recorded the deed on December 1 of that same year. A then conveyed Blackacre to C by warranty deed on September 1, 2001. C conveyed Blackacre to D by quit-claim deed on November 1, 2001, and D recorded the deed the next day. D later discovered that C's deed was unrecorded. She obtained C's deed from him and recorded it on February 1, 2002. The land was still vacant at the time of the conveyance to D, but D immediately went into possession. Neither C nor D had actual notice of the prior conveyance by A to B at the time each received their respective deeds. C paid a fair price for Blackacre in cash; D took the quitclaim deed from C in full satisfaction of an ante-cedent debt. When B learned that D was in possession of Blackacre, he brought an action to recover possession from D. B notified A of the lawsuit, but A was not a party and did not participate therein.

The applicable recording statute provides: "Every conveyance of real property is void as against any subsequent purchaser of the same property in good faith and for a valuable consideration, whose conveyance is first duly recorded." Discuss the following questions.

(1) What result in B's action?

(2) What result if the last six words were omitted from the recording statute?

(3) If judgment is for D, what is B's recourse against A?

Question 19

On Daughter's twenty-first birthday, her father, Vendor, gave her a house and lot to which Vendor had a good record title. The gift was made orally, and Vendor gave Daughter the keys to the house. Daughter promptly took possession and occupied the premises for the next six years. During this time, she made substantial improvements to the house at considerable expense. At the end of the six years, Daughter's business required her to move to another city, and she listed the property with a local real estate agent for sale or to rent.

After Daughter vacated the premises, Vendor, without Daughter's knowledge, entered into a written contract to sell the house and lot to Purchaser, with transfer of title and possession to take place in 60 days. Purchaser paid Vendor one-half of the purchase price when they signed the contract. When Vendor and Purchaser were negotiating the sale, Purchaser told Vendor that he intended to raze the building and erect a commercial structure on the land, and the intended improvement would not be in conflict with the local zoning ordinance. Purchaser inspected the premises at the time of the contract, but Daughter was not in possession; there were no "For Sale" signs nor were there any other indications of Daughter's interest. A preliminary title insurance report obtained by Purchaser disclosed no such interest.

Two days before the scheduled transfer, fire destroyed the house, but through no fault of Vendor. In the meantime, Purchaser learned that Daughter claimed title to the premises and he found another lot better suited to his purposes. He then notified Vendor that he considered the contract terminated and demanded the return of his payment.

Discuss the rights and obligations of Vendor, Daughter, and Purchaser, and to what relief, if any, each is entitled.

Question 20

Twenty-two years ago, Owens purported to sell Greenacre to Able for $1,000 cash. Greenacre is a parcel of unimproved mountain land that is inaccessible by road during six months of each year due to snow. Owens gave Able a deed that granted Greenacre to Able in fee simple and contained all warranties of title. Able did not have a title examination made. Able immediately recorded his deed and obtained an unsecured loan from Bank. He used the funds to build a vacation cabin on the land. Unknown to Able, Owens's grandmother was the true and sole owner of Greenacre.

Since the time of the purported transfer, Able has paid taxes on Greenacre and lived in the cabin for one month each summer. The cabin and land have otherwise been unoccupied. Bank placed a metallic sign on the land at the time the cabin was built that read: "Built by Able with financing from Bank." The sign has remained in place ever since.

Five years ago, Owens borrowed $5,000 from Charlie. Three years ago, Owens's grandmother died, leaving Greenacre to Owens by will. Recently, Charlie induced Owens to deed Greenacre to him in full satisfaction of the $5,000 debt, which was then three-and-a-half years past due. Charlie had no actual knowledge of Able's claim to Greenacre. Owens's grandmother had no knowledge of the purported transfer to Able or of Able's activities on Greenacre.

Title searches in the state are customarily made in the grantor/grantee indexes of the official records. The recording statute reads:

"Any unrecorded conveyance is deemed void as against a subsequent taker for value and without notice."

Discuss the rights of all the parties to Greenacre.

Question 21

Henry was the owner of Greenacre, a vacant parcel of land in the state of Utopia. Twelve years ago, Henry handed his friend JoAnn a warranty deed granting "all my land in the state of Utopia to my niece and nephew Paula and Mark as joint owners." Henry orally advised JoAnn that he wanted his niece and nephew to have Greenacre since they were the only ones who loved him, but that he wanted to live there until he died. The deed was not recorded.

Paula died eight years ago. Soon afterwards, Henry, who had become angry at Mark's lack of devotion toward him, conveyed Greenacre by a quitclaim deed for $5,000 to Ruth. Ruth was aware of the deed from Henry to Paula and Mark, but she thought that because the deed to Paula and Mark had not been recorded, she would have priority to Greenacre. Ruth promptly recorded her deed. Ruth then built a two-bedroom house upon Greenacre, immediately made it her home, and has lived there ever since.

Three months ago, Henry died. Mark thereafter learned for the first time of Henry's deed to him and Paula. Mark consults you about his rights and informs you that (1) he recorded his deed (which JoAnn delivered to him when Henry died), and (2) Henry owned no land in Utopia except Greenacre.

Advise Mark as to his rights in Greenacre and against Ruth.

Question 22

Ollie owned Goldacre, an oil-rich ranch in the state of Lotus. Five years ago, Ollie summoned her foreman, Art, into her office and handed Art a deed transferring Goldacre to Art, and said, "I want you to have Goldacre if I die before you."

Four years ago, Ollie's accountant, Cap, discovered that Art had been embezzling. Ollie immediately discharged Art. With Cap as a witness, Ollie called in her bookkeeper, Bill, showed Bill a deed conveying Goldacre to Bill and said: "I am now giving Goldacre to you. You have the combination to my safe. When I die, get this deed out of my safe and record it."

A month later, Ollie discharged Bill for incompetence. Before leaving, Bill, without Ollie's knowledge, took the deed to Goldacre from the safe.

One year later, Ollie told Cap she had revoked both of the deeds to Art and Bill and that she wanted to retire. Nine months ago, Ollie conveyed Goldacre to Cap for a valuable consideration. Cap recorded the deed immediately. Ollie died two months later. Art recorded his deed one day after Ollie died, and Bill recorded his deed one day later. At Ollie's funeral, Bill and Art informed Cap of their respective recordations.

Cap then mortgaged Goldacre to Elk Mortgage Co., which recorded it the same day.

Elk Mortgage Co. has now brought an action for declaratory relief to determine the rights of Art, Bill, Cap, and Elk Mortgage Co. in Goldacre. Discuss their respective rights.

Question 23

Oscar was the owner of Goldacre, a heavily wooded area. On July 1, 2000, Atwell and Oscar entered into a contract whereby Atwell purchased all minerals in and under Goldacre. Since neither of them wholly trusted the other, they decided to have the contract acknowledged and recorded. To this end, they enlisted the services of a clerk at a nearby bank. After Atwell and Oscar had duly signed and sworn to their identities, the clerk affixed a seal and stamped statement. However, the statement indicated that the clerk's notary commission had expired three days before the contract was executed. Neither Oscar nor Atwell noticed this lapse, nor did the register of deeds who copied it into the record books and indexed it.

On September 1, 2000, Atwell assigned her interest in the contract with Oscar to Baker by a valid and properly executed and acknowledged document. Baker properly recorded the assignment at once. As a part of the deal, Baker had agreed to convey one-half of the minerals in and under Goldacre to Atwell in fee simple. To effectuate this intent, Baker executed a properly drafted warranty deed purporting to convey one-half of the minerals in Goldacre to Atwell and her heirs. The deed was properly signed and acknowledged, and Baker delivered it to Atwell. Atwell was preparing to leave the country on vacation, so she put the deed in her safe deposit box without bothering to take it to the register of deeds.

On January 2, 2001, Baker paid Oscar the total sum due under the contract between Oscar and Atwell, and received from Oscar a properly signed and acknowledged grant deed, conveying to him in fee simple "all the minerals in and under Goldacre." Baker immediately recorded the grant deed. Atwell got her deed out of her safe deposit box and recorded it on July 5, 2002. In August 2002, Baker went to his uncle Peter and pointed out the possibilities in mining. In return for a properly executed and acknowledged deed in fee simple to "all minerals in and under Goldacre," Peter paid Baker $5,000 in cash. Peter did not bother to examine the title, but he did record his deed on the day it was tendered to him, August 15, 2002.

Peter recently learned that Baker has suddenly left the country and has disappeared. Peter subsequently ordered a title report and learned all of the facts described above. Peter plans to commence operations to build roads, move in heavy equipment, and open mines on Goldacre as soon as possible. Peter had the ore quality appraised and thinks the operation will be profitable. Advise Peter as to the status of his title. Assume a statutory structure with a race/notice recording statute and a grantor/grantee index.

Question 24

In July 1995, Bob gave a quitclaim deed to Blackacre to his favorite niece, Joanne. When he gave the deed to her, he told her that he'd like to live on Blackacre until he died, to which Joanne agreed. Subsequently, Bob became unhappy with Joanne because he heard she was running around with the "disco crowd." This information was erroneous, but Bob nevertheless notified Joanne in writing that he had revoked the deed to Blackacre. Joanne did not respond to Bob's letter.

In January 2002, Bob sold Blackacre for $30,000 to Frank by quitclaim deed; Frank had no knowledge of the transfer to Joanne. George, Bob's nephew, had recently rented Blackacre from Bob for a nominal amount, but he voluntarily vacated when Bob asked him to leave, immediately after Frank bought the land.

In July 2002, Frank gave Blackacre to C (his cousin) by means of a warranty deed, and C immediately recorded Frank's deed. However, in October 2002, Joanne recorded the deed Bob had given her, even though she had recently learned of the alleged transfer of Blackacre from Bob to Frank. In December 2002, C recorded the deed from Bob to Frank.

Joanne and C now both claim the land.

Discuss who would have priority to Blackacre as between Joanne and C, and whether Frank can recover the $30,000 he paid to Bob.

Question 25

Art was the record owner of Greenacre, a vacant tract of land. Art and Barb discussed the sale of this land to Barb, and they orally agreed on a purchase price of $5,000 in cash. Art then typed up a statement setting forth all the terms that had been agreed upon. This included the fact that Art would deliver to Carl, a real estate broker, a warranty deed conveying Greenacre to Barb and that Carl would hand deliver the deed to Barb if Barb paid Carl the purchase price within one month.

Art placed one copy of this statement — unsigned, unwitnessed, and undated — in an envelope and mailed it to Barb. When Barb received it, she telephoned Art and told him that the statement accurately reflected their understanding and that she would deliver $5,000 in cash to Carl within the month in accordance with their agreement.

Art then executed the warranty deed, complete in all respects, and gave it to Carl with a copy of his statement.

One week later, Art learned that a highway was to be built near Greenacre, greatly increasing its value. Art immediately wrote to Carl, telling Carl he had changed his mind and wanted the deed returned to him.

One day later and before Carl had received Art's last letter, Barb called Carl and said she had to show the deed to her bank to obtain a loan for the $5,000. Carl sent the deed to Barb, who promptly recorded it and immediately executed and delivered a warranty deed for Greenacre to Dale.

Barb disappeared and has not paid the $5,000 to Art or Carl.

(1) In an action to quiet title between Art and Dale, discuss who will prevail.

(2) Discuss what rights, if any, Art and Dale have against Carl.

Essay Exam Answers

Answer to Question 1

(1) Alan's ("A") option agreement:

Does the option to purchase Sandyacres ("S/A") violate the Rule Against Perpetuities ("RAP")?

Under the RAP, executory interests and contingent remainders are void unless they must vest, if at all, within 21 years after an ascertainable life in being at the time the interest was created. The option agreement probably would constitute an executory interest since it could cut off the grantor's interest at a subsequent point in time. The agreement might therefore violate the RAP because of the possibility that (1) A's present wife might die, (2) A might then remarry a woman who is younger than 33 years old (i.e., not a life in being at the time the interest was created), and (3) the second wife might then outlive A and attempt to exercise the option more than 21 years after A's death. It might be contended in rebuttal, however, that the words "by his widow" in the option agreement should be read as including only A's present wife since this was probably the only person A and Oscar ("O") had in mind when they made the agreement. It should also be noted that some states have passed statutes whereby the reference to a "spouse" of a living person is conclusively presumed to be that person's then extant husband or wife.

Thus, unless this jurisdiction has enacted a statute as described above or recognizes the presumption contained therein, Client ("C") should be advised that the validity of A's option is doubtful.

(2) The conveyance to Nabor ("N"):

Whether the easement granted in favor of N is valid against Edward ("E")(and thereby against C) turns upon the resolution of the following questions.

(a) Did E have notice of N's easement?

In some states, a defective recording (including one involving a faulty acknowledgment) does not provide constructive notice to a subsequent purchaser. Thus, E would not be subject to N's express easement because such an interest terminates automatically when land is subsequently purchased for valuable consideration by a party who had no notice of the earlier transfer. Constructive notice is not deemed to be given by a void document. However, N probably could contend in rebuttal that in most jurisdictions, where the defect is latent (i.e., does not appear upon the face of the document), a subsequent grantee is deemed to be on constructive notice of the earlier interest; further, many jurisdictions have curative statutes, whereby a defect in a document is deemed to be remedied when no dispute arises with respect to it for a specified period of years (usually 10 to 15 years). Here, 30 years passed without any dispute. Finally, a few states permit a defective document to afford at least inquiry notice to a subsequent grantee (and in such an instance, E would have learned of N's easement had he asked O or N about it). Thus, the validity of N's easement vis-à-vis C depends upon the applicable rule in this jurisdiction.

(b) Did the destruction of the tunnel terminate N's easement?

It is unclear as to whether the beach would be accessible without the tunnel. Assume that it would not be.

The majority view is that when an easement is destroyed through no fault of the servient tenement owner, the easement terminates and the servient tenement owner has no obligation to reconstruct it. Since the tunnel simply collapsed and is no longer in existence, it probably would be held that N's easement terminated. It seems that N has, in a manner, acquiesced in this result by (apparently) not making any demand upon O to reconstruct the tunnel.

Thus, N's easement probably has ceased to exist even if E had notice of it. C can be advised that this issue would not be a problem.

(3) The conveyance to E:

The interest conveyed to E by O appears to be a fee simple determinable (an estate that terminates upon the occurrence of a stated event, at which time the land is automatically returned to the grantor). In the event that E married, S/A would revert automatically back to O. While E is free to transfer his interest in S/A, the land nevertheless would revert back to O if E subsequently married. It may be argued, however, that the condition of E remaining unmarried is void on public policy grounds since most states seek to encourage, not discourage, the institution of marriage. In such event, the anti-marriage clause would be deemed deleted from O's grant of S/A to E, which would result in E having been granted a fee simple absolute (the most unrestricted estate and that of the longest duration). C should therefore be advised that if this jurisdiction has an obvious pro-marriage public policy, it is possible that S/A would **not** revert back to O even if E eventually married.

Thus, C should be advised that it appears the conveyance to E is good and that E would be able to pass good title to C.

Answer to Question 2

Bank ("Bk") v. Tom ("T"):

Whether Bk can obtain an injunction against T will depend upon the resolution of the following issues.

(a) Did Owen ("O") create a joint tenancy or tenancy in common when he transferred Blackacre ("B/A") to Sam ("S") and Doris ("D")?

This threshold issue must be resolved because if O did create a joint tenancy and these events occurred in a "lien" state (addressed below), Bk's interest in B/A might be completely extinguished by S's death.

Whether an estate is held in joint tenancy or as a tenancy in common depends on both the grantor's language and the surrounding circumstances. In a joint tenancy, each tenant owns an equal interest in the whole property. By contrast, in a tenancy in common, each tenant has a separate, undivided interest. The most important distinction between the two is that a joint tenancy carries with it a right of survivorship, whereas the tenancy in common does not. Bk will argue that joint tenancies are normally disfavored and that they should not be found to exist without specific granting language (i.e., "with right of survivorship"). In response, T would contend that since S and D were related, O probably intended to keep B/A in the family. T's argument is buttressed by the fact that there was only a single residence upon B/A. O probably would not have created a situation where either sibling could devise his or her interest, thereby forcing the other sibling to share B/A with a stranger. A court could find that despite O's awkward language, a joint tenancy was created by O's grant to S and D.

(b) What is the effect of S's mortgage?

If a tenant in common encumbers his interest and then fails to repay the obligor, the creditor will succeed to the tenant in common's interest. Thus, if this grant were determined to create a tenancy in common, Bk and D would share B/A as tenants in common. However, if B/A has been granted in joint tenancy, the effect of one joint tenant mortgaging his interest may depend upon whether the jurisdiction is a "title" or a "lien" state, that is, whether the state treats the mortgage as a transfer of title or as a lien to secure repayment. In "title" states, the mortgage of a joint tenant results in a severance of the joint tenancy (and it turns the estate into a tenancy in common), and so Bk would succeed to S's interest if its loan were not repaid. If this is a "lien" state, however, there is a split in authority. In some jurisdictions, Bk's interest would be extinguished by S's death. In other jurisdictions, the lien would simply attach to the survivor's interest in the mortgaged portion of the property, and Bk's interest would, in essence, be the same as in a "title" state.

(c) Assuming this is a "title" state and Bk retained an interest in B/A after S's death (or even assuming this is a "lien" state that treats Bk's interest in the same fashion as a "title" state), can Bk enforce the covenant in the mortgage document against T?

Since Bk is seeking an injunction (rather than monetary damages), the covenant would be analyzed as an equitable servitude ("ES"). For the burden of an ES to run with the land, (1) the original parties must have intended it to run; (2) the burden must touch and concern the allegedly burdened land (and in some states, the benefit must also touch and concern the land of the party seeking to enforce the ES, but assume that is not the case here); and (3) the party against whom enforcement is sought must have either actual, inquiry, or constructive notice of the ES (although some states eliminate this element where gratuitous donees are involved). The first element is satisfied since the mortgage document specifically states that it is to be binding upon S's successors and assigns. The second element also appears to be satisfied because the burden specified is that the land is to be used only for a certain purpose — single-family dwellings. Finally, if the mortgage was recorded (which Bk would have done in the normal course of business), T would be chargeable with notice of the restriction. Thus, the covenant should be good against T (or D) if B/A was held in joint tenancy and this is a "title" state.

(d) Assuming the ES runs with the land, should a court enforce it against T or D?

T would argue that since the area has been rezoned (albeit after S's death), a change in the entire neighborhood is likely to occur soon, thereby making enforcement of the restriction against him inequitable. T's argument likely would fail because a change in zoning alone is not sufficient evidence of changed conditions to warrant lifting a residential restriction. T probably would also argue that allowing him to convert the house to a three-unit apartment building would increase the value of Bk's interest in the land. Bk would argue, however, that its original reasons for wanting S to covenant not to use B/A for any purpose other than as a single-family dwelling have not changed, and that both its original intent and agreement should be respected and upheld. Bk would argue further that the question of whether a potential increase in the value of Bk's interest will change Bk's decision should remain within Bk's discretion. Given the fact that the ES runs with the land, a court should enforce it against T or D. Thus Bk would be able to prevent the conversion.

D v. T and Bk:

D could quiet title in herself if (1) B/A had been granted to S and D in joint tenancy, and (2) no severance occurred when S mortgaged his interest in B/A to Bk. If B/A had been conveyed as a tenancy in common, *or* if this jurisdiction is a "title" state (or a "lien" state that treats the Bk's interest in the same fashion as a "title" state), D's action would *not* be successful.

Answer to Question 3

Rights of H and M:

H would contend that the estate originally given to A and B was a fee simple
subject to a condition subsequent. The granting language contained the
phrase "but if," and these words are usually associated with a condition
subsequent that is subject to a grantor's right of reentry. In some jurisdictions, a right of reentry cannot be conveyed by an *inter vivos* transfer
to someone other than the party presently in rightful possession of the
premises. If this is such a jurisdiction, O's attempt to give M an interest
in Blackacre ("B/A") was ineffective. Thus, the right of reentry would
have passed to H at O's death. Since the condition subsequent occurred
when B/A was used for a purpose different than parking (i.e., as a storage
facility), H could assert that she is now entitled to possession of B/A. This
assumes that O's inaction during the year he was aware of the storage
facility would not constitute a waiver of his right of reentry, and this
also assumes that the statute of limitations for reentry in this jurisdiction
is longer than one year.

In a small minority of jurisdictions, an attempt to make an *inter vivos*
transfer of a right of reentry results in it being extinguished completely.
However, we'll assume that this jurisdiction does not adhere to that view.

M would argue in rebuttal that the language in the granting document was
that of a fee simple determinable since using the words "shall" and "void"
demonstrate that B/A will immediately cease being owned by A and B if it is
used for any purpose other than as a parking lot. Consequently, O would
have retained a possibility of reverter. Even though the states are in dispute
about whether a possibility of reverter can be transferred *inter vivos*, the
prevailing view is to allow it. Assuming this jurisdiction has adopted the
majority view, and assuming that it doesn't matter whether O's conveyance
to M was a sale or a gift (the facts are not clear on this point), a possibility of
reverter can be transferred by O *inter vivos* and thus it was transferable to
M. Therefore, M would argue, O retained no interest in B/A that could pass
by inheritance to H.

Since courts dislike forfeitures, when confronted with vague granting
language, there is a judicial tendency to construe it as a fee simple subject
to a condition subsequent rather than a fee simple determinable. However, here O's insertion of the words "shall" and "void," which seems to
intend an automatic forfeiture, probably would result in M prevailing on
this issue, so that as between H and M, M's claim to B/A would be stronger.

Rights of A and C:

A and C could assert several arguments in rebuttal.

First, they could claim that the triggering event has not occurred since the granting language should be read as allowing for the termination of their fee interest only if the land is used **exclusively** or **primarily** for another purpose. Because the majority of B/A still serves as a parking lot, they would argue that it is not being used "for a different purpose." H and M, of course, would contend that the word "different" should be interpreted literally (i.e., if B/A is used for **any** purpose other than exclusively as a parking lot). While this is a close question, given the judicial reluctance to disturb established property interests, it is likely that A and C would prevail on this issue.

Second, as noted earlier, in many states there is legislation requiring that a possibility of reverter or right of reentry be exercised within a specified period of time, or that right is deemed to be extinguished. To the extent that such legislation applied in this situation, it would be asserted by A and C.

If no such legislation exists or it doesn't apply (because the specific period within which such right must be exercised has not expired), A and C might still contend that O (and through him, H or M) waived or should be estopped from enforcing the provision in question. After all, O failed to object to the storage facility on B/A after knowing that it was being built. The facts indicate that O visited the store five or six times, parking in the lot on three of those occasions, while the storage facility was being erected, and thus he must have known about it. In addition, since O did not object and instead appeared to acquiesce, C incurred substantial expense in enlarging his store. While M or H could contend in rebuttal that it is unclear whether O was actually aware that C was building a permanent nonparking structure on B/A (rather than, for example, a multilevel parking facility), it is likely that A and C would prevail.

If H or M did prevail on the above, A might contend that B's transfer to C of B's joint tenancy interest severed the joint tenancy and resulted in B/A converting to a tenancy in common (i.e., each tenant has a separate, undivided interest rather than equal interest in the whole). A would argue that since C violated the conveyance from O, H or M should succeed only to C's interest in B/A. However, H or M probably could successfully contend in rebuttal that O's grant encompassed all of B/A and clearly designated A and B as joint tenants.

Can C remove the storage facility?

If the prefabricated storage facility constitutes a "fixture," C would not be entitled to remove it. In determining if personalty has become a fixture (and therefore a part of the land), the courts ordinarily focus upon the intention of the party who annexed the item to the realty. This intention is usually determined from an analysis of several factors: (1) the permanence with which the item has been affixed to the land, (2) the extent of damage that will occur to the land if the fixture is removed, and (3) the usefulness of the land without the personalty at issue. H and M might contend that C intended the prefabricated storage facility to be permanently affixed to B/A, as evidenced by the facts that (1) C presumably intended to operate the retail store indefinitely, and (2) metal bolts were attached to a concrete foundation. C could argue in rebuttal, however, that (1) a prefabricated structure by its very nature is usually detachable from its cement foundation with relatively minor damage to the land, and (2) where an item is used in the land occupier's business, there is ordinarily a presumption that he intended to take it with him if the commercial operation ceased to exist. C is likely to prevail, and therefore C could remove the storage facility.

Answer to Question 4

(1) Murray ("M") v. Bill ("B"):

Possession of the premises:

Each co-tenant has an equal right of possession and use of the concurrently owned property. An ouster occurs when the tenant who is not in possession attempts to physically occupy the premises and the occupying tenant refuses to allow access. If an ouster does occur, the ousted joint tenant is entitled to recover his pro rata share of the reasonable fair rental value of the premises from the other. M might pretend that an ouster had occurred three years and four months ago because B occupied the land, leased one-half of the real property to Henrietta, and paid taxes on it. However, it is unlikely that M's argument would prevail because the conduct described above is consistent with the rights of a co-tenant in joint tenancy property. Nevertheless, B's refusal to permit M to enter the land six months ago ("Listen, buddy boy . . .") probably would constitute an ouster, assuming M physically tried to occupy the land (the facts indicate only that M was "ready to build his house"). If there was an ouster, B would be liable to M for one-half the reasonable rental value of the land for the six-month period preceding the partition action, unless a partition of the land had occurred prior to that time, as discussed below.

Lease to Henrietta ("H"):

The majority view is that rents received by one co-tenant from leasing a portion of joint tenancy property must be shared with the other co-tenant(s). Thus, B probably would be liable to M for one-half of the rent payments received from H. In many states, however, B would be entitled to deduct monies he expended for improvements that enhanced the rental value of the property. Thus, if the second house B built enabled B to charge H $500 rent, but without the structure the land would have rented for only $100 per month, B would be entitled to offset $400 each month against the rentals received from H, up to the total amount he spent, before dividing the rental income with M.

Rental obligation of B:

While there is a minority view to the contrary, an occupying tenant ordinarily need not pay rent to a nonoccupying joint tenant. Each tenant has an equal right to occupy the land and equal responsibility to maintain the land (in this instance, paying taxes and insurance). Thus, in B's countersuit for partition (discussed below), he would be able to deduct the taxes and insurance payments from any rent he received from H.

Sale of timber:

A co-tenant who derives net income as a consequence of an activity that depletes the land is usually accountable to other co-tenants for their *pro rata* share of the profits. M could therefore contend that B is liable for one-half of the net income derived from B's sale of timber. B could conceivably argue that since trees can be replanted and regrown over time, the land has not been permanently depleted. However, M probably could successfully respond that because growing trees to the timber stage ordinarily takes a very long time, B's actions should be viewed as permanent in nature. Thus, B probably would be liable to M for one-half of the profits from the timber.

The concept of waste is most often applied to life tenants and tenants for years where the holder of a future interest claims damage. However, in a few jurisdictions, a co-tenant has been found liable for waste when she diminished the value of the joint tenancy land. Here, though, the overall value of the land may actually have been increased by clearing the standing timber. If so, B could argue that his acts ameliorated the situation and that therefore M should not recover any damages. B could also argue that his actions were motivated by a desire to make a more profitable use of the land (i.e., to cultivate fruit and crops) rather than by a desire to cause injury to it. It is therefore unlikely that an action for waste would be successful.

Profits from fruit and crops:

A co-tenant need not ordinarily account to other co-tenants for profits derived from the land that do not deplete the property. In some jurisdictions, however, B would be liable to M for one-half of the profits derived from the fruit and crops **after** M was refused entrance onto the land. The rationale is that B's ouster prevented M from helping B cultivate the orchard and crops.

Improvements:

Ordinarily, a co-tenant is not entitled to immediate reimbursement for improvements made upon the land. However, she usually receives a *pro rata* credit in the event of partition (to the extent that such improvements have enhanced the value of the land). Thus, to the extent not previously deducted from rental payments received from H, B would be entitled to recover one-half of the costs incurred in (1) creating the fruit orchard and crop field, and (2) building the two houses upon the land.

Partition:

A joint tenant ordinarily has an absolute right to bring an action for partition at any time. Where possible, the courts prefer to divide the land into equal shares. "Equal shares" in this context does not necessarily mean that each co-tenant receives exactly the same amount of land. Rather, it means that B and M will each receive land equal in value. The facts are silent about the value of the two houses, the fruit orchard, and the crop field. If the land cannot be divided equally, a court may require the co-tenant who would receive land of greater value to make up the difference through a cash payment to the other co-tenant (sometimes referred to as owelty).

(2) Rights of H:

A joint tenant may ordinarily lease all or a portion of the land to a third party, subject to the right of other co-tenants to use the entire property. Assuming that title to the land was recorded in the county records, H probably would be deemed to be on constructive notice of the fact that B or M might seek a partition of the land at any time. In a partition action, the sale of premises ordinarily is made free of an existing lease. In the event of a physical partition, the parcel set off to the lessor/co-tenant remains subject to the lease. Thus, while H may have a cause of action against B for damages resulting from her eviction as a consequence of the partition action, H probably would not be able to successfully resist the eviction itself. If, however, the land upon which H lives is distributed to B in the partition action, H probably could prevent B from dispossessing her until the conclusion of the lease term. Since the lease term did not exceed one year, there would be no necessity for a writing signed by B for the contract to be enforceable.

(3) B's death before trial:

When one joint tenant dies, his interest automatically passes to the surviving joint tenants. M would therefore contend that he became the sole owner of the property upon B's death. Mary could contend in rebuttal that a partition of the land actually occurred before B died due to (1) B's prior lease of a portion of the land to H or (2) B's commencement of the action for partition. While the traditional view was that a lease of her interest by a joint tenant severed the joint tenancy, the modern view is to the contrary. Thus Mary would not succeed on this point. Nor would Mary's second contention be convincing. While there is a minority view that supports it, the prevailing view is that the mere filing of a partition action does not automatically result in a severance of the joint tenancy; there is always the possibility that the parties may reconcile their differences or that the suit may be dismissed prior to a court decree dividing the property. Consequently, if B dies before the trial, it is likely that Mary's interest dies too.

Answer to Question 5

Bert's ("B") action against Alex ("A"):

Whether B can successfully obtain an injunction against A depends first upon whether B's substantive rights have been violated. B might initially contend that he was granted a fee interest across the middle of Redacre ("R/A") since the grant states only that A conveys to B "a four-foot wide strip" across R/A. However, A could probably successfully contend in rebuttal that the words quoted are qualified by the additional words "for an underground sewer line." While ambiguities are often construed against the grantor, courts are obligated to interpret a document in accordance with the parties' intent. Here, it is unlikely that A intended to gratuitously transfer a four-foot wide strip across the middle of her property to B, and the facts do not indicate that B has attempted to make any use of the strip other than for purposes of the sewer line. Consequently, the grant probably would be construed as an easement to run an underground sewer line to the adjacent public street.

An easement appurtenant is the right by one landowner (the dominant estate owner) to make a limited, nonexclusive use of another's land (the servient estate owner). The servient estate owner cannot unreasonably interfere with the dominant estate owner's use of the easement. B could probably successfully contend that causing his sewer line to overload and occasionally back waste up into his apartment constituted a tortious interference with the easement. Thus, A's reliance on the fact that B's easement was nonexclusive probably will **not** be considered dispositive by the court.

B might also be able to contend that A, by causing the waste to back up into B's apartment house, was responsible for a series of trespasses upon B's apartment house and land. A trespass occurs when the defendant has intentionally intruded upon, beneath, or above the surface of the plaintiff's land. Restatement (Second) of Torts §159. Plaintiff need not prove the defendant knowingly violated plaintiff's property rights; all plaintiff need show is that defendant intended to enter plaintiff's land. B should be able to show that A acted intentionally (i.e., should have realized that by attaching her sewer line to B's, it was substantially certain that, as a result, B's line would overflow).

A might claim that in order to sustain a trespass action, the plaintiff must ordinarily be entitled to immediate possession of the affected land. If all of the apartments on Greenacre ("G/A") were rented to third parties, A could contend that B was not a proper plaintiff to an action for trespass. However, even if all the apartments were rented to third parties, B would probably still be responsible for the common areas within and around the structure. Since B would arguably have a right to immediate possession of these areas (albeit nonexclusive), he could probably successfully maintain an action in trespass for the damages resulting from A's conduct with respect to the sewer pipe.

In the alternative, B might assert a cause of action for nuisance against A. A nuisance occurs when the defendant has, in a nontrespassory manner, caused an unreasonable and substantial interference with, or impairment of, the plaintiff's use of his land. Under this theory, it is not necessary for B to have an immediate right to possess the land. Here, the sewage discharges certainly would interfere substantially with B's use and enjoyment of his property as an apartment house. B probably could argue successfully that A acted negligently in attaching another sewer line to B's existing line.

Can B obtain an injunction against A?

Ordinarily, one can obtain an injunction only when monetary damages would be inadequate and/or when multiple lawsuits can be avoided. B can probably successfully argue that (1) money damages are **not** adequate since the possibility of contamination and resulting sickness always exists in unsanitary conditions, (2) B might have difficulty attracting tenants to his apartment house in the future if it became widely known that he often has serious plumbing problems, and (3) multiple lawsuits will be avoided since B would have a new right of action each time A's attachment to the sewer line caused a waste backup onto G/A. Thus, in addition to the damages B should recover from A (discussed above), B should also be able to obtain an injunction against A.

Can A succeed in her action against B?

A could assert a trespass action against B based on B going on A's property and disconnecting the sewer line. In rebuttal, B could argue that he was acting out of public necessity. The privilege of public necessity arises when the interest sought to be protected outweighs the interest invaded and the actor was motivated primarily by the public (as opposed to her private) good. B will contend that a public necessity existed, given the unsanitary conditions in the apartment house on G/A and the danger of illness resulting therefrom. (There would be no point for B to argue private necessity since, in such instances, the actor is still liable for any actual harm caused by his conduct.)

In some states, there is also a self-help abatement privilege, provided that the actor (1) first complains to the defendant and waits for the defendant to refuse to remedy the condition (but this requisite may be discarded where the request probably would be futile), and (2) uses only such force as is reasonably necessary to terminate the condition. Here, B made no demand, and there was at least a possibility that A would have taken care of the problem. Indeed, B never bothered to notify A of his action, even after he disconnected the sewer line.

On the issue of public necessity, B probably is *not* liable to A for trespass, although, by never telling A what he had done, B himself may have created a public health hazard on R/A.

A's action against Clyde ("C"):

Generally, an easement appurtenant passes with the transfer of the dominant estate unless there is an agreement to the contrary. Here, however, the dominant estate is not being transferred but is instead being subdivided. It appears from the facts that only B's part of the dominant estate directly benefits from the easement; B had to grant C an easement to put in a sewer line across G/A to reach B's existing sewer line. C might contend that since his land is part of G/A, A cannot successfully preclude C from using B's sewer line. However, A could argue in rebuttal that (1) while subdivision of an easement may ordinarily be permitted, the new burden upon the servient estate dramatically exceeds that which was reasonably anticipated by the original parties; and (2) the terms of an express easement may not be exceeded. Because the grant was made solely to B for the purpose of accommodating his apartment house, it appears that allowing C to add his apartment house to the sewer line does significantly increase the original burden to the servient estate and exceeds the terms of the existing easement. Thus, A should prevail on this question, and she should be able to prevent C from attaching his sewer line to B's existing line.

Answer to Question 6

Is T liable for rent from September 1, 2002, through November 30, 2002?

Assume that T did not pay rent for this period.

There is a division of authority about whether the landlord or the tenant is obligated to eject a holdover tenant from the premises. If this jurisdiction follows the rule that a landlord's only obligation is to deliver legal (as opposed to actual) possession, T would be liable for rent during X's hold-over period. Assuming, however, that this is a jurisdiction in which L had a duty to deliver actual possession, L would have violated this obligation by refusing to take any action to oust X even though T persistently asked L to do so. In response, L would contend that T waived L's breach of this obligation by accepting possession of the premises on December 1, 2002. Generally the acceptance of the leased premises after the time when the landlord was supposed to deliver possession does not waive tenant's right to damages suffered prior to tenant's acceptance of possession. T could argue that he could not obtain another apartment easily or that he had adequate reasons for wanting this particular apartment (for example, it was near his place of employment and was within his budget), in which case L's contention should fail. Thus, for the three-month period during which X was in possession, T probably can recover from L any damages he incurred as a result of X's holdover, such as higher rent payments to another landlord while X was in possession.

Did L breach an implied warranty of habitability as to the premises and furniture?

No warranty of habitability existed at common law; the position taken was "tenant beware." Since most all states now impose some type of implied warranty of habitability on landlords of residential property, the implied warranty likely applies here. Where furnished premises are leased for a short period of time (i.e., one year or less), many courts have implied a covenant of habitability into the lease that both the premises **and the furniture** are fit for use at that time. If this jurisdiction adheres to the foregoing view, L probably did breach the implied warranty and would be liable for T's injuries. T would be able to recover for the injuries he sustained when the bedroom chair collapsed, even though L was not aware of the defective construction of the chair and was not negligent. In the absence of such a rule in this jurisdiction, L probably would have no liability for T's injuries.

Rights of L against T:

Whether T is liable to L for the $50 per month difference in rent would depend upon a resolution of the following issues.

(a) Is T relieved of liability for rent after March 1, 2003, because of the provision in the lease allowing him to terminate possession?

T would contend that since the roof began to leak badly and deteriorated (through no fault of his), the premises had become "damaged so as to be uninhabitable." Consequently, he would be entitled to give up possession of the apartment and to terminate his liability for rent. L would argue in rebuttal, however, that the ordinary meaning of the word "damaged" would cause T to be relieved of liability only if the premises were destroyed or impaired by reason of some external force (e.g., fire, destruction by the intentional or negligent conduct of a third party, flood), rather than the deterioration of the premises due to some latent defect. L would also argue that, even if the clause in the lease did apply, (a) the premises had not become uninhabitable (there is no indication that the leak was so extensive that T could not live there); and (b) T had waived L's breach of that clause, as evidenced by the fact that T had not actually given up possession since he (rather than L) relet the premises to Y. One cannot give up possession of premises and simultaneously do an act, such as reletting, that evidences a continuing authority over the premises. While T might argue in rebuttal that, given L's refusal to accept the surrender, T simply had helped L to relet the apartment for T's account, L's argument that T had waived L's breach of the clause in question probably will be successful. Instead of reletting the premises himself, T should have simply referred Y to L so that L could have entered into an agreement with Y. Consequently, T probably is not relieved of liability for the rent differential after March 1, assuming that he turned over to L the $200 he received from Y each month.

(b) Has a constructive eviction ("CE") occurred?

A CE occurs when the tenant is deprived of his use and enjoyment of the premises by reason of some cause or condition for which the landlord is responsible. However, L could probably successfully contend that this doctrine does not apply because (1) at common law, the tenant was responsible for repairs to the premises (and therefore T would be responsible for repairing the leaky roof); and (2) to assert the CE doctrine, the tenant must ordinarily have vacated the premises. T would have a hard time asserting two seemingly inconsistent positions: that he relet the apartment to Y for the remainder of the lease and that he was no longer in possession of the premises for purposes of a CE. Consequently, L probably would prevail on the issue of CE.

(c) A general implied warranty of habitability:

In recent years, a significant number of courts have implied a covenant into residential leases that requires the landlord to make whatever repairs are necessary to prevent the premises from becoming uninhabitable. Assuming a breach of this implied warranty of habitability, most jurisdictions permit the tenant to terminate the lease and recover damages or else, after appropriate notice to the landlord, to repair the defect and deduct the cost of the repairs from the rent. Again, there would be a question about whether T has in fact terminated the lease as a consequence of *his* reletting the premises to Y, but whoever had the roof repaired (either T or Y) probably could recover the cost of the repairs from L.

Answer to Question 7

To advise L of his rights against T, it is necessary to first determine if T can successfully assert any defenses against L. Since there was a signed lease, there is no Statute of Frauds problem even though the period of the lease exceeded one year.

Duty to deliver possession:

Under the English rule, a landlord has the obligation to assure the incoming tenant that no other party will be in possession of the premises when the lease term commences. T might assert that L breached his duty since R was still in the apartment when T's lease term began. However, even assuming this jurisdiction adheres to the rule that the landlord has an obligation to evict holdover tenants, T probably has waived L's breach of this obligation by taking possession of the premises after R moved out. Still, T can refuse to pay any rent attributable to the period R remained in the apartment—from June 1 through June 15, and can seek to recover any damages T suffered during this period. If the American rule is followed in this jurisdiction, L has a duty only to deliver *legal* possession, not actual possession. Here, T obtained legal possession on June 1 when the lease began, so R would be T's problem.

Constructive eviction ("CE"):

A constructive eviction occurs if there is a substantial interference with a tenant's right of use and enjoyment, due to a cause for which the landlord is responsible, and the tenant vacates the premises within a reasonable time thereafter. T might argue that a CE occurred by reason of (i) the noise caused by the Pebbles, (ii) the broken windowpane and warped floor, and (iii) the stove's malfunction.

In response, however, L could assert the following arguments. First, with respect to the noise caused by the Pebbles, L would claim not to be responsible for the activities of other tenants. In some states, where the lease contains a provision permitting the landlord to evict lessees who are disturbing other tenants, the landlord is given responsibility for noisy tenants. However, there is nothing in the facts provided that indicates such a clause exists here. Second, even assuming the Pebbles's noise persisted from June 16 through July 15 (the date three band members were arrested), L would argue that this did not constitute a substantial deprivation of T's right to the beneficial enjoyment of the premises. The noise occurred during daylight hours, not in the evening when other tenants would be home or trying to sleep. Finally, L could probably successfully argue that T waived the right to assert a CE by waiting 45 days after the noise had ceased before vacating the premises.

As to the broken windowpane and warped floor, L could argue that, at common law, it is T's duty to make repairs; thus T cannot complain about being deprived of the beneficial enjoyment of the premises when the condition that made them unsuitable was not L's fault. With respect to the broken stove, L could argue again that this was T's responsibility and that T apparently never even advised L about this problem, thus depriving L of the opportunity to remedy that particular problem.

The implied warranty of habitability:

Many states recognize an implied warranty of habitability that leased premises will not become uninhabitable by reason of the landlord's failure to make repairs attributable to the natural deterioration of the premises. (A few jurisdictions limit this doctrine to situations involving housing code violations.) T might argue that defects vital to the use of the premises existed in the form of the broken windowpane and subsequent warped floor and the broken stove.

Since the warping was the result of the failure to repair the broken window, whoever was responsible for repairing the window would be liable for the warped floor. L could argue that the window should have been repaired by T since (1) the pane was broken by a third party (e.g., children playing ball), as opposed to the natural deterioration of the premises; and (2) a broken window is not a defect that causes premises to become uninhabitable. With respect to the nonfunctioning stove, L could argue that the stove would not cause the premises to fall below minimal living requirements and that L was never told about the broken stove, if such is the case.

In response, T would argue that a broken window should fall within the phrase "natural deterioration" since it is to be expected that a window might break at some time through no fault of the tenant's, particularly if one lives in a neighborhood with children, and that a broken window would cause the premises to become unsafe and thus uninhabitable. In addition, T would argue that a broken stove impinges upon a very basic living requirement — the ability to cook one's own food in one's own kitchen — and thus T would contend that the premises did fall below minimal living requirements. T should contend, though, that she did not inform L about the stove because she was at wit's end. Despite T's contentions, it is likely that L would prevail against T on this issue, too.

Surrender:

T probably will also argue that L's acceptance of the keys to the apartment constituted a surrender, and therefore T is not liable for any rent accruing after August 31. However, the mere fact that L accepted the keys, without more, probably does not demonstrate a willingness to allow T to avoid her prospective obligations under the lease.

Advice on the extent of L's recovery:

(Assume that rent was payable monthly and that the lease did **not** have an accelerated rent or liquidated damages clause.)

L should be able to recover both T's unpaid rent for the June 16 through August 31 period and for the future months' rent payments as they become due. However, L should be advised to actively seek a new tenant for the premises; many states require a landlord to mitigate a tenant's liability, and it may be difficult for L to recover any judgment against T (even if one were obtained). Finally, L should be advised to notify T that if a sublet occurs, it is being done for T's account. This would preclude T from successfully contending that subletting the apartment constituted a surrender of the premises.

Answer to Question 8

O v. T (rent):

O would contend that S and T were tenants in common since O consented only to "add" S to the lease, without prejudice to O's rights against T. Therefore, when S held over at the end of the lease term by not removing the dry cleaning equipment, O was entitled to renew the lease for an additional term. In some jurisdictions, the new term is limited by statute to one year, regardless of whether the original lease was for a longer period of time. T, however, could make several arguments in rebuttal to O's assertion.

First, T might contend that leaving the equipment in the building did not constitute sufficient "possession" of the premises to justify applying the holdover tenancy doctrine. However, since dry cleaning equipment is probably large enough to have prevented O from reletting the premises, O should prevail on this issue.

Second, the holdover tenant must be notified that the landlord is renewing the lease. Thus, T might next contend that he never received actual notice of O's election to renew the original tenancy. The success of this argument would depend upon whether notice in this jurisdiction is defined by a properly stamped, addressed, and deposited envelope or by actual receipt by the addressee. O might also argue that notifying one co-tenant constitutes constructive notice to all co-tenants. The facts are silent about T moving to a new address or why the note was not forwarded, but given the fact that T had reserved the right to reenter the premises if S failed to pay the rent, O probably would be successful on this issue.

T could next contend that the original lease arrangement was merely a periodic tenancy (rather than one for a fixed term) because the precise date upon which the term would conclude was apparently *not* stated in the written lease. T would assert that the applicable term in this instance is month-to-month since the rental payments were made monthly. Because S notified O on April 10, 2004, that he was no longer liable for rent, S and T would argue that their liability to O under the lease ended as of May 31, given that termination of a periodic tenancy takes effect at the conclusion of the term following the one in which notice is given. However, O could argue in rebuttal that the concluding date of the lease was easily calculable (i.e., January 31, 2004) in that the lease referred to both an aggregate rental amount and a constant monthly amount.

Indeed, a court probably would conclude that the original lease was for a fixed term of two years and that there was a renewal for one year.

T could next contend that even if the lease was renewed, O materially breached the contract on February 15, 2004, by not permitting S to sublet the premises to Z based on Z's ethnic origin. (The contract specifically stated that the lessor's consent to an assignment or sublease shall not be "unreasonably withheld" and assume that when S was "added" to the lease, all terms between O and T applied to S, too.) Thus, T would assert that he is not liable for rent accruing after that time. However, O could probably successfully argue in rebuttal that even if her conduct constituted a material breach, this breach was waived by S's failure to remove his equipment immediately thereafter.

T could argue that a constructive eviction ("CE") occurred on April 1. A CE occurs where a tenant is deprived of the beneficial enjoyment of the leased premises because of some occurrence or condition for which the landlord is responsible. T could contend that a CE occurred when O's security guard negligently caused the fire that gutted the premises. O would attempt to counter this assertion by claiming that, in the lease agreement, the Lessees waived any acts of negligence by O or her employees. However, T could probably successfully argue in rebuttal that (1) the provision exculpates only acts of negligence, not gross negligence (smoking near highly flammable cleaning fluid would constitute gross negligence); and (2) the clause in question pertains only to lawsuits for negligence asserted by the Lessee, not to the assertion of a CE as a defense to the payment of rent by the Lessee. T should prevail and therefore probably would *not* be liable to O for rent accruing after April 1, 2004, but would remain liable for the rent during February and March.

O v. T (fixtures):

O could contend that as a result of S's failure to comply with the lease provision to maintain insurance, O sustained a loss in the amount of $7,000, the value of the destroyed fixtures and equipment. However, T could argue in rebuttal that (1) the Lessee was obligated to keep only the fixtures insured (not the equipment) and only the fixtures belonged to the Lessor at the end of the lease, so he is not liable for the equipment; and (2) the phrase "fixtures required for operation of a retail clothing store" is too vague to be enforceable (since one could presumably operate a retail clothing store without any fixtures, those installed by T were not so "required"). While the first argument probably would succeed, the second one would not. A court probably would rule that the fixtures T installed were "required" regardless of whether one could hypothetically operate a retail clothing store without them; therefore, T would be liable to O for the value of the fixtures destroyed in the April 2004 fire.

O v. S (rent and fixtures):

S could contend that he has no liability to O since (1) he never expressly agreed to be liable under the lease (O merely agreed with T that S could be added to the lease); and (2) there was no privity of estate with O since S was merely a sublessee (rather than an outright grantee of T's leasehold interest), as evidenced by the fact that T reserved the right to reenter the premises if S defaulted. However, O could argue in rebuttal that (1) S, in effect, agreed to be liable under the lease since the latter was presumably aware of O's written statement to T; and (2) because T transferred his rights under the lease to S, S should also be deemed to have assumed T's duties thereunder. Thus, O would be a third-party beneficiary between T and S, and it is likely that O would prevail on each of the foregoing contentions. Even though no privity of estate existed, S probably would be liable to O for any obligations arising under the lease.

If S had assumed T's obligations under the lease, he would assert the defenses described above under *O v. T* (except for the notification issue).

Summary:

S and T are liable to O for rent from February 1, 2004, through April 1, 2004 (when the CE occurred), as well as for the $2,500 value of the fixtures.

Answer to Question 9

(1) Lisa ("L") v. Tom ("T"):

If L were to sue T for the rental payments remaining under the lease, T probably would raise the following issues.

Is T relieved of his obligations under the mutual mistake doctrine?

Where there is a mutual mistake of fact existing at the time an agreement is made, and the mistake goes to the essence of the transaction, the adversely affected party can avoid the contract (provided the risk of the mistake was not borne by her). T could contend that since the weakness in the floor existed at the time the lease was made and the premises were specifically limited to being used as a dance studio, there was a mutual mistake of fact that went to the essence of the agreement. Even though L could contend in rebuttal that neither party actually contemplated the strength of the floor and this should be deemed to be a risk borne by T (who could have inspected the floor before entering into the lease), T should prevail on this issue. Thus, T should not be liable to L for rent after Alice ("A") vacated the premises.

Assuming, however, that L prevails on the preceding issue, all additional potential theories will be discussed.

Was T relieved of liability under the frustration of purpose doctrine?

Where one of the parties has a special purpose for entering into the contract and the other party knows this, if that purpose is subsequently frustrated by an unforeseeable event, the first party's obligations are discharged if the frustrating event is permanent. T could contend that since the premises were leased only for the special purpose of a dance studio, this purpose was frustrated when T and L later discovered that the floor was not strong enough to serve as a dance studio. L would argue in rebuttal that no post-contract event occurred because the defect (weak floor boards) already existed when the lease was made. In addition, L would assert that it was not "unforeseeable" that a floor in a commercial building would not be able to withstand constant dancing. Nevertheless, T should prevail since he would not be expected to continue using the premises for an activity that posed a risk of serious injury. In addition, if L wants to argue that this problem was not unforeseeable, then T could probably argue successfully that L should have investigated whether the floor could be used (safely) for a dance studio before renting the space specifically for that use.

Did L materially breach the agreement by permitting Charles to use the basement for an aerobic exercise class?

Where one of the parties materially breaches an agreement, the other side is excused from her prospective obligations. T will contend that when L leased the basement premises to Charles, she violated the anticompetition clause of their lease. Since aerobic exercises are ordinarily done to music, he would argue that it is an activity that is sufficiently similar to dancing to constitute a breach of the anticompetition clause. L, of course, would contend in rebuttal that dance lessons and exercising are sufficiently dissimilar to *not* violate the anticompetition clause. L should prevail on this issue.

Was T discharged from his obligations under the lease by reason of the constructive eviction ("CE") doctrine?

A CE occurs where there is a substantial interference with a tenant's use and enjoyment of the premises due to a cause for which the landlord is responsible, and the tenant vacates within a reasonable time after such condition arises. T could contend that a substantial interference with his use and enjoyment of the premises, due to L's failure to provide sufficiently strengthened floor boards, has made it impossible for him to continue his business. L will contend in rebuttal that at common law the tenant had the sole obligation to make necessary repairs to the premises, so T, rather than she, had the duty to strengthen the floor.

It is unclear from the facts whether the necessary strengthening could be done without breaking through to the fourth floor and whether the affected fourth floor area is a common area. These facts may be important because, even where the common law view is followed, most courts hold that repairs to a common area must be made by the landlord.

In addition, L would contend that T did not vacate the premises within a reasonable time since a six-month interval expired between the dance student's injury and the time the key was mailed back to L. (It is not clear from the facts whether A wrote to L immediately or allowed time to pass.) T would contend in rebuttal, however, that six months is not unreasonable given that (1) it is often difficult to find new premises for such an activity, and (2) A might have had outstanding contracts with students that extended through the end of June. Although these are both close issues, it is likely that even if L would not prevail on the first question (substantial interference with use and enjoyment), L probably would prevail on the second one (vacating within a reasonable time).

Can T avoid the lease under a breach of the implied warranty of habitability/suitability doctrine?

T could contend that the premises ceased to be habitable because of (1) the risk of another person being injured, and (2) L's refusal to strengthen the floor boards. However, L could probably successfully contend in rebuttal that (1) to date, in most jurisdictions, this doctrine has ordinarily been limited to residential as opposed to commercial premises; and (2) this theory is most often applied to situations involving housing code violations, which is *not* the case here.

There is a minority view that follows the position taken in the Restatement (First) of Property (§5.4), which permits a tenant to vacate without liability where the premises have ceased to become *suitable* because of a condition that occurred through no fault of the tenant's. If such a view were followed here, T probably would prevail because the premises were no longer suitable for a dance studio and the weak floor boards were not T's fault. However, relatively few jurisdictions adhere to this doctrine, and the Restatement (Second) of Property abandoned the minority view and takes no position on the issue.

Summary:

In light of the conclusion above that T would prevail under either the mutual mistake or frustration of purpose doctrine, L probably could not successfully sue T for the balance of the rent that remains under the lease term. If, however, L prevailed upon all of the foregoing issues, T would be liable only for the rent as it became due (unless there was a clause or statute permitting L to accelerate the rentals due under the remaining term of the lease).

(2) L v. A:

In addition to all of the arguments discussed above involving T, A would contend that she was not in privity with L. However, when a contract is assigned by one party to another and the assignee does not expressly refuse to assume the assignor's obligations under such agreement, the assignee is ordinarily deemed to have assumed the assignor's duties. Thus, L would contend that she was a third-party beneficiary of the agreement between T and A, and therefore she could sue A directly for any breaches under the lease. However, as discussed above, probably neither T nor A would have any liability to L under the lease.

Answer to Question 10

(1) Specific performance action:

If Tom ("T") sues Omar ("O") for specific performance, O probably would raise the defenses of Statute of Frauds ("SOF") and anticipatory repudiation ("AR").

According to the SOF, contracts for the sale of land must be embodied in a writing that contains the essential terms and is signed by the party against whom enforcement is sought. Even assuming the verbal understanding between O and T was sufficiently definite as to its material terms, O could contend that since his agreement with T to sell the land was not in writing, it is unenforceable. T could argue in rebuttal that where a grantee has done acts that are "unequivocally referable" to the existence of the alleged oral contract, the SOF is overcome. This standard is ordinarily deemed to be satisfied when the grantee has entered upon the grantor's land and made valuable improvements thereto. Although T was already on O's land as the operator of the gas station, he could argue that in the absence of a contract to purchase the land, it would be illogical for him to expend $18,000 on improvements *after* his lease term had expired, and the fact that O did not demand rent in February and March indicated that their relationship was changing. The facts are silent about whether the new equipment could be removed by T without incurring great expense and creating substantial damage to the premises. The more difficult and expensive it would be to remove the equipment, the greater is the likelihood that T would be successful on this issue. While O could contend that making the improvements described above could be explained by T's *expectation* that a contract for sale would be arranged subsequently (rather than by the existence of an actual agreement), T should prevail on this issue.

Even assuming that T prevailed on the SOF issue, O could contend that T made an AR of the contract when he advised O that he was moving out and was no longer interested in purchasing the land. (An AR occurs when one party unequivocally advises the other that she will not perform her prospective contractual obligation.) Retraction of an AR is not possible once the innocent party has relied upon it to his detriment. Since, in the interim, O entered into a nine-month lease with Jill and a contract to sell the land to Samuel (and therefore would be liable for damages if he were to complete the transaction with T), it is unlikely that T would be permitted to retract his repudiation at this point. Thus, T's action for specific performance should fail.

(2) T's liability for rent:

O could initially contend that T was a holdover tenant, thereby entitling O to renew the lease for a period of time equal to the original lease term or, presumably, for any shorter period of time. (Many states have enacted legislation that limits this renewal period to one year.) However, T could probably successfully contend in rebuttal that a landlord is required to notify the tenant of such an election, and since O failed to notify T of the renewal before March 15, 2005 (the date T advised O that he would be moving out), O's attempted renewal of the first term was no longer possible. T's arrangement with O probably would be characterized as a month-to-month tenancy since, under the lease, T paid rent on a monthly basis.

Assuming a month-to-month tenancy existed, T's notice of termination must be given prior to the month at the conclusion of which the lease is to be terminated. Consequently, O could argue that the March 15 notification would not take effect until May 1 (i.e., termination of a periodic tenancy takes effect at the conclusion of the term following the one in which notice is given), and T would be liable for rent for February and March, as well as for the $200 difference in April.

T, however, could make several counterarguments. First, T could contend that O had agreed that no further rent would be required of him, and thus T had been released from any further obligation to make rental payments. However, O could probably successfully contend in rebuttal that (1) since this understanding was an integral part of their land sales contract, evidence of it is inadmissible under the SOF (discussed above); and (2) this understanding (even if admissible) was impliedly conditional upon T purchasing the land within 90 days. O should be successful with respect to the second argument, and therefore T would not be released from paying rent.

T could next contend that he was relieved of his rent obligation under the lease by reason of O's failure to repair the premises after the March 5 mudslide. However, since a landlord of commercial premises ordinarily has no obligation to make repairs unless she was somehow responsible for the condition or occurrence that caused the damages, this argument will also probably fail. Even in the few jurisdictions that do recognize a landlord's obligation to maintain leased commercial premises, this duty is ordinarily *not* extended to repairs required by acts of providence.

Finally, T could probably successfully contend that a surrender by operation of law occurred when O relet the premises to Jill. While a surrender will *not* be presumed where the landlord notifies the prior tenant that the reletting has been done for the latter's benefit, no such statement was made by O in this instance. O merely informed T that T would be held responsible for rent in February and March, as well as for the rent differential through December 31.

In summary, O probably can recover rent only for February and March (an aggregate amount of $2,000).

Answer to Question 11

(1) Can Xavier ("X") prevent Annie ("A") from building the service station?

To answer this question, two issues must be analyzed: (1) whether the covenants that Owen ("O") made to X runs with the land (i.e., binds A), and (2) whether X can enforce the promise that O made to him against A.

Does the burden of the covenant run with the land?

Since X is seeking an injunction (i.e., equitable relief), O's promise to X should be analyzed as an equitable servitude ("ES"). For the burden of an ES to run with the land, (1) the original parties must have intended it to run, (2) it must touch and concern the burdened land (and, in some jurisdictions, the benefited parcel, too), and (3) the burdened parcel owner must have been on notice of the promise.

Since the deed between O and X stated that O had covenanted for his "heirs, successors and assigns" also, there seems to be little doubt that the covenant was intended to run with the land. Also, the promise touches and concerns the burdened land (Lots 3–8), since the use that A may make of her land is restricted by the requirement that at least 500 parking spaces will be available.

There is a minority view that follows the position taken in the Restatement (First) of Property that for the burden to run, both the benefit and burden of the covenant must meet the "touch and concern" test. The Restatement (Third) of Property §3.2 rejects this view. Indeed, the Third Restatement advocates eliminating the "touch and concern" element altogether. However, if this is a jurisdiction that requires that the benefited parcel also be "touched and concerned" by the restriction, X will contend that the covenant touches and concerns his land, too, since the unavailability of the parking area will render X's planned use of Lots 1 and 2 virtually ineffective. X will also contend that such unavailability would arguably diminish the value of the land since prospective department store customers would simply choose to shop at a more convenient establishment. A would argue in rebuttal that (1) the covenant does not affect X's use of its land since X is not required or restricted from doing anything with respect to it, and (2) X's fear that the value of the land will be diminished because potential shoppers will be discouraged is only speculation. X likely will prevail because the value of his land probably would be affected by the significantly reduced amount of available parking.

X will next contend that A was either on constructive or inquiry notice of the parking area covenant. In some jurisdictions, a subsequent grantee is deemed to be on constructive notice of **all** prior recorded conveyances within the county made by her grantor (even if they were not directly within the grantee's chain of title). This is because a prospective grantee, in searching the typical grantor/grantee index, would ascertain the point at which the grantor obtained the land being conveyed. The grantee would then inspect all subsequent grants made by the grantor. In such jurisdictions, A presumably would have discovered the deed that O had delivered to X and therefore would have notice of O's promises in that deed. However, some jurisdictions consider a grantee to be on notice only of promises made by the grantor that are contained in the grantee's direct chain of title. Since A, searching through the grantor/grantee index for information about Lots 3–8, would not discover the promises that O made to X involving Lots 1 and 2, A would **not** be on constructive notice of O's promise. Since most states do **not** require a prospective grantee to scrutinize every real property transfer made by a grantor within the county (but rather, only transactions involving the parcel that the grantee is about to obtain), A probably would **not** be considered to be on constructive notice of O's promises to X.

However, X might be able to contend that A was on inquiry notice (i.e., where there are facts or circumstances that would lead a prospective grantee to believe that the land that she is acquiring may be subject to some unrecorded interest or claim, she is charged with whatever notice a reasonable inquiry would have revealed). Here, the facts are silent as to how A became aware of O's covenant to X concerning the sale of tires and petroleum products. X might contend, however, that since A was aware that O had promised X no tires or petroleum products would be sold on Lots 3–8, A should have asked X whether O had made any other promises involving the same lots. X should prevail on this argument, and therefore A probably would be deemed to be on notice of O's promise to X concerning the parking area.

Should the court enforce the ES?

Since equitable relief is always discretionary, even if the burden of an ES does run with the land, the court may elect to deny X's request for an injunction.

A could contend that upon a balancing-of-hardships analysis, the construction of the service station should not be prevented since (1) A is leaving 90 percent of the stipulated, nonexclusive parking spaces that were to be available to X (O had promised X there would be at least 500 parking spaces, and here 450 spaces would remain); (2) any lost profits to X from the decreased parking are purely speculative; and (3) the inconvenience to X is outweighed by the definite financial loss that A believes she will incur by her inability to build a service station (this assumes that the service station will be profitable, which is also speculative). However, X probably could argue in rebuttal that (1) the inability to prove damages is precisely why an injunction should be permitted (money damages will not suffice since X could never show with reasonable certainty the number of potential department store customers who went elsewhere because of insufficient parking); and (2) since the construction of the service station would violate a covenant of which A clearly had notice (i.e., that no tires or petroleum products may be sold on the premises), A does not have "clean hands." Again, X should prevail unless there is evidence of an abundance of parking spaces in the surrounding area, with little likelihood of growth there. Consequently, A probably will not be able to build her service station.

(2) Assuming that A was permitted to build the service station, can the municipality enforce the zoning ordinance?

A might contend that the zoning ordinance is invalid because it represents an improper use of the police power (i.e., the statute in question appears to be concerned exclusively with aesthetics). However, the municipality can probably successfully argue in rebuttal that the ordinance is a safety measure and thus is reasonably related to the health and welfare of its citizenry. It presumably would enhance driver visibility and thereby reduce the possibility of vehicular accidents.

Assuming the ordinance was passed *after* A acquired her interest in Lots 3–8, A might contend that the imposition of the ordinance results in a deprivation of property (i.e., A's right to make the most profitable use possible from her land) without due process of law. However, to constitute a "taking" for Fifth Amendment purposes (applicable to the states via the Fourteenth Amendment), the restriction on the owner's use of her land must be substantial and result in a significant diminution of the owner's economic expectations with respect to that land. Since the curtailment on A's use of Lots 3–8 is relatively minor (the shopping center can still be maintained, and that asset presumably represents the bulk of A's economic return from the land), the municipality should prevail. In addition, even if an inverse condemnation was found to have occurred, the statute probably would not be deemed to be null and void. Instead, A probably would have only the right to compensation equal to the diminished value of her land.

Of course, if the ordinance had been passed before A acquired Lots 3–8, then she would have virtually no possibility of success. In such a case, she would be held to have recognized that the land must be used in a manner consistent with the ordinance.

Answer to Question 12

Adverse Possession ("AP"):

One obtains title to real property by AP where, under a claim of right, one enters upon and exclusively occupies another's land in an open, notorious, and hostile manner throughout the requisite statutory period. Danny ("D") could claim that by remaining at Sweetholm after the sale to Alicia ("A") without A's explicit permission, the "claim of right" and "hostile" elements are satisfied. In addition, D would argue, having a separate mailbox and putting out a welcome sign that bore his name would meet the "open" and "notorious" requisites. Finally, D's occupation of the guest house continued for a period of time in excess of the 10-year statute of limitations. Thus, D could claim ownership to the guest house (along with an easement to get to it) under AP, but his claim may not be persuasive.

In a minority of jurisdictions, the claim of right requirement is not satisfied unless the adverse claimant went upon the land with the belief that he was entitled to possess it. If this were such a jurisdiction, D's claim of AP would fail. In most states, however, the claim of right element is satisfied merely by the adverse possessor being in possession of land without the owner's permission. A knew, when she bought the property, that D was already living in the guest house. If this jurisdiction adhered to the latter view, A could contend that Jennifer ("J") had presumably advised D of her statement that it would be "all right" for D to remain on Sweetholm. If it could be shown that J had so informed D, A should prevail on this issue.

A alternatively could claim that D's occupation of the guest house was *not* "hostile." While this element is usually satisfied by the claimant's use of the land in an "open and notorious" manner, an exception to this rule exists where the rightful owner would not necessarily recognize that the adverse possessor's occupation of the land is hostile to her ownership interest, even though she is aware of it. In such situations, the adverse claimant must communicate (via clear words or actions) that the land is being held in derogation of the legal owner's rights thereto. For example, holdover tenancies often constitute such a situation, since a holdover tenant is usually deemed to be occupying the premises with the landlord's implicit permission.

A could contend that D should be viewed as having been either her guest (i.e., a continuation of the relationship that D enjoyed with J) or a tenant at sufferance. In either event, D would have been obliged to (1) inform A that his occupation of the guest house was hostile to A's claim of ownership thereto, or (2) act in a manner that clearly communicated this view (e.g., prevented A from entering the structure, built a fence around it). The mailbox would not suffice since A could have presumed that while D had felt comfortable in permitting J (D's cousin) to receive his mail, he would not have the same trust in a stranger. Finally, A would assert that the doormat was not adequate to inform her that D was claiming superior title to the guest house.

A probably would prevail upon the "hostile" issue, and therefore it is unlikely that D would prevail upon his claim of AP.

If, however, D's claim of AP were successful, he would have a right of action against A for evicting him. D probably would be entitled to recover the reasonable rental value of the land during his eviction, as well as any other costs and expenses that resulted from the interference with his right to possession.

Injunction sought by Trivers ("T"):

T might first contend that A had granted an express easement to Wilson ("W") permitting animals involved in the experiment to roam throughout Sweetholm, and that easements will automatically run with the benefited estate. A would respond that the right given to W was a license, not an easement. An easement is ordinarily described as the right of one person to make a particular use of another's land. A license, however, is usually defined as the right to do a particular thing on another's land. A could assert that no right was granted to W to *use* her land. Rather, A merely indicated that W's wolves could wander freely over Sweetholm. Thus, A would contend that the grant made to W was a license and such interests are (1) ordinarily *not* assignable, and (2) revocable at any time by the licensor (subject to the licensee's right to recover for monetary damages resulting from the revocation). However, T could argue in rebuttal that being engaged in an experiment whereby the wolves wandered onto A's land, W (and now T) was actually *using* the land for a particular purpose (i.e., to record the results of an experiment). A court likely would conclude that W had a mere license.

Even assuming the grant to W was an easement, A could contend that it was an easement in gross (rather than an appurtenant easement), and that such easements are ordinarily not assignable. Easements in gross are those that *personally* benefit the holder thereof (as opposed to easements appurtenant, which primarily benefit the holder's *land*). The grant in question appears to have been made for the purpose of facilitating W's experiment (rather than enhancing the use or accessibility of Laurel Hill). While T could argue that the use of Laurel Hill is enhanced by having the right to permit animals involved in the experiment to cross onto adjoining land, this probably would not be persuasive, and A's grant probably would be characterized as an easement in gross.

T might contend, however, even assuming the grant to W was deemed to be an easement in gross, that it should be viewed as being "commercial" in nature. Such interests have been deemed to be irrevocable where, for example, a severe disruption to a utility (e.g., telephone or sewer lines) would occur. Although T could contend that maintenance of the fence by A would disrupt an experiment that has been carried on for a 14-year period, it is unlikely that T's easement in gross would be considered "commercial." Thus, A probably would prevail on this question.

Finally, T might argue that A's written statement to W, whereby A had agreed that she would take no action to prevent W's animals from coming onto Sweetholm, constituted a covenant that ran with the benefited land. Since T is seeking an injunction, the covenant must be analyzed as an equitable servitude ("ES"). For the benefit of an ES to run against the covenantor: (1) the original parties must have intended it to run, and (2) it must touch and concern (affect the value or use) of the burdened land (and, in some jurisdictions, the benefited parcel, too). Although there was no "successors, heirs and assigns" language, some courts take the view that where the promise touches and concerns the burdened parcel, the original parties probably intended for the covenantor's promise to run with the benefited land. The value and use of Sweetholm is arguably diminished by the fact that wild animals could roam free on a portion of the land. However, A could probably successfully contend in rebuttal that there was no intent that the promise run with the land since the promise was given specifically to *W* for the purpose of permitting him to complete *his* experiment.

Thus, T probably *cannot* obtain an injunction against A.

Ownership of Sweetholm:

Richard (Ludwig's sole heir) could contend that the conveyance by Vladimir to Josiah was a fee tail (since the grant to him was followed by the words "and the heirs of his body"). Therefore, when Josiah died without issue (J was merely his niece, rather than a lineal descendant), Sweetholm became the property of Ludwig and his heirs.

A could argue in rebuttal that in many states the fee tail has been abolished entirely and in the majority of states it is viewed as a fee simple absolute. Thus Josiah would have been entitled to transfer the property to J. In some jurisdictions, however, the failure to have issue results in the estate terminating upon the death of the originally designated party. Under the latter view, Ludwig's heirs (Richard) would obtain title to Sweetholm upon Josiah's death. However, in such instance, A could probably claim superior title to Sweetholm through AP. While it is not clear when Josiah died and J succeeded to possession of Sweetholm, the facts do indicate that A has apparently occupied the realty for 11 years and paid taxes on it. Having purchased the land from J, A presumably went into possession of Sweetholm under color of title. It therefore appears that A could defeat any claim of Richard to the property. (Richard has a vested remainder, so it is not subject to the Rule Against Perpetuities.)

Josef could, however, contend that there was a fee simple determinable or fee simple subject to a condition subsequent with respect to the deed provision pertaining to animals, and that the triggering event occurred when D retained one of the animals for a two-week period. However, A could contend in rebuttal that any future interest held by Josef is unenforceable because implicit in the grant was that the *grantee* (rather than some other person who undertook such conduct without the owner's knowledge or consent) would not "keep" animals on Sweetholm. A should prevail on this argument, and therefore it is unlikely that Josef could presently claim paramount title to Sweetholm.

Answer to Question 13

The language in the deeds appears to be a covenant (as opposed to an easement).

(1) Can Alex ("A") prevent Dave ("D") from building as planned on Lot 16?

The covenant A seeks to enforce was made to Owen ("O") by the original grantee of D's lot. O's remaining land (including the parcel now owned by A) was benefited by the covenant. Since A is a subsequent transferee of a portion of the land benefited by the covenant, the first inquiry is, *Did the benefit of the covenant made to O by the original grantee of Lot 16 run with the land?*

A desires to enjoin D from building upon Lot 16. To be considered an equitable servitude ("ES") to run with the land, (1) the original parties must have intended the benefit of the covenant to run with the land; (2) the burden of the covenant must touch and concern the burdened parcel; and (3) in some jurisdictions, the benefit must also touch and concern the benefited parcel.

Assume that the original Lot 16 deed did **not** expressly state that it was binding upon the successors and assigns of each party; if it did, then this inquiry would almost certainly be resolved in A's favor. Notwithstanding the foregoing assumption, most courts will conclude that restrictions of this type were intended to run with the benefited land. This is so because it is presumed that the developer/covenantee will ultimately sell all of the lots, and therefore the restrictions that she required could be enforced only by her subsequent grantees.

Since the covenants in question restrict the use by D of his land, there is little doubt that the "touch and concern" condition is satisfied with respect to the burdened parcel.

D might contend that the covenant does not touch and concern A's (the benefited) land, since the construction of a two-story home might actually enhance the value of adjacent land (presumably, subdivisions within which two-story houses can be built are more valuable than those within which only one-story homes are permitted). However, A could probably success-fully argue in rebuttal that permitting deviations from a uniform develop-ment plan within a subdivision could ultimately lead to no restrictions at all, which in turn would diminish the value of each landowner's parcel. Thus, the "touch and concern" requirement with respect to the benefited parcel is probably also satisfied.

Since D was not the original grantee of Lot 16, the next inquiry is, *Did the burden of the covenant run with the land?* The burden of an ES runs with the land when (1) the original parties intended it to run with the land, (2) the burden of the ES touches and concerns the burdened parcel, and (3) subsequent grantees of the land were on notice of the covenant. The discussion above with respect to the first two conditions would apply equally here. Since the facts state that all deeds were recorded, D would be on constructive notice of the restrictions agreed to by the initial grantee of Lot 16. Thus, the burden of the ES would also run with the land.

Based upon the foregoing, both the benefit and the burden of the ES ran with their respective parcels of land.

Should the court enforce the ES?

D could contend that equitable relief should not be granted in this instance because (1) A has not come into court with "clean hands" (i.e., she never agreed to the covenant that she is attempting to enforce, and she has violated the restrictions by erecting the 20-foot wall); and (2) using a balancing-the-hardships analysis, any diminution in value to A's land would be outweighed by (a) D's inability to construct what he considers to be a comfortable home on his land and (b) the decreased value of D's land (a two-story home is presumably worth more than a single-story residence). In rebuttal, however, A could argue that (1) she built the 20-foot wall only to dissuade D from breaching the restrictions, and she would remove it if D is enjoined from deviating from the restrictive covenants; (2) she has observed, in fact, all the restrictions (except for the 20-foot wall, which she is willing to remove when D agrees to comply with the restrictions); (3) D should not be allowed to repudiate a promise of which he had knowledge; and (4) it is entirely possible that A's land would be significantly devalued if D is permitted to ignore the restrictions since a potential buyer of A's land would be uncertain about whether the covenants pertaining to the subdivision were enforceable.

A should prevail, and therefore a court probably would require D to build in accordance with the restrictions, conditioned upon A removing the creosote wall (which probably constitutes a nuisance — discussed below).

(2) Can O prevent D from building as planned?

A covenant is enforceable only by persons who own land that was intended to be benefited by the promise. The promise that the original grantee of Lot 16 made to O was to the owner of the remaining unsold parcels. There was no indication that the original parties intended any land outside of O's subdivision to be benefited by the covenant that the original grantee of Lot 16 made to O. It is therefore unlikely that O, no longer the owner of any benefited property, could prevent D from building as planned (even though O presently resides immediately adjacent to the subdivision).

(3) Does D have any rights against A?

Assuming O did not expressly covenant to D that all parcels in the subdivision would contain similar restrictions to those contained in D's deed, an implied reciprocal covenant would have to be implied into the deed that O delivered to the original grantee of Lot 16. In addition, A would have had to be on at least inquiry notice that such a reciprocal covenant might be implied into the original deed given by O pertaining to Lot 16.

To imply reciprocal covenants by the developer/grantor into earlier deeds within a subdivision, there ordinarily must have been some justification for the earlier covenantees to have expected subsequent deeds in the subdivision to be bound by similar restrictions (i.e., a plat map evidencing a common scheme or plan, verbal representations by the developer, statements in advertising literature, etc.). The facts do not indicate that O advised any of the original grantees that subsequently sold parcels would be similarly burdened. Thus, there does not appear to have been a plan or scheme of development at the time the original grantee of Lot 16 acquired the land.

In addition, even if a covenant by the developer/grantor were implied into earlier deeds within the subdivision, there would be no reason for A to be on notice of it (Lots 14 and 16 were undeveloped at the times he purchased Lot 15). Thus, there is little likelihood that D would have the right to assert an implied reciprocal covenant against A.

D, however, probably could require A to remove the wall under a nuisance theory. A nuisance occurs when the defendant has, in a nontrespassory manner, caused a substantial and unreasonable interference with the plaintiff's use or enjoyment of the latter's land. Since the motivation for the fence was unreasonable (i.e., it was erected exclusively for the purpose of making D uncomfortable), and darkened surroundings and odor emanating from the wall would constitute more than minor inconveniences to D, a nuisance would be found. Therefore, a court probably would require A to remove the creosote wall.

(4) Can A recover from Commercial Bank ("Bank")?

Most jurisdictions recognize an absolute right by a landowner to recover from an adjoining landowner where the failure by the latter to laterally support her land had caused the former's land in an unimproved condition to slide. While the excavating that caused A's prize flower bed to slide onto Lot 14 was done by Baker, Bank (as the legal owner of Lot 14) nevertheless had a two-month period to provide lateral supports vis-à-vis Lot 15. Thus, Bank is probably liable for the actual damages suffered by A and will be required to artificially support A's land.

Answer to Question 14

(1) Can Cullom ("C") enjoin Bayard ("B") from excavating without providing lateral support?

A landowner ordinarily must provide whatever lateral support is required to prevent an adjacent neighbor's unimproved land from sliding as a consequence of excavation undertaken by the former. B, of course, will contend that this obligation has been waived by reason of the original agreement to this effect with Albright ("A"). However, C could assert several theories as to why A's promise to B is unenforceable.

Statute of Frauds ("SOF"):

Most jurisdictions hold that promises that pertain to an interest in real property must satisfy the SOF (i.e., must be embodied in a writing that describes the interest involved and is signed by the party against whom enforcement is sought). C will contend that since A's promise to B was not contained in A's deed to B, it cannot be enforced by B. However, B could contend in rebuttal that (1) A's promise was merely collateral to the sale of an interest in land and so was not subject to the SOF, (2) C (as A's assignee) should be promissorily estopped from asserting the SOF since B detrimentally relied upon A's promise in deciding to purchase his lot, and (3) there has been substantial performance of the original contract by B's accepting A's deed and going into possession of the land. B's contentions would be persuasive, and thus, the promise by A to B, though verbal, should be enforceable.

Length of agreement:

Assuming the SOF is avoided, C could next contend that implicit in A's promise to B was that B would begin and conclude his construction of the commercial building within a reasonable period of time. Since a reasonable period of time appears to have passed and A no longer owns the adjoining parcel, the period of time envisioned by A and B during which the promise would be effective has expired.

B, of course, would contend that no time limitation was placed on the original promise. While C should prevail on this issue, the remaining arguments will be considered in the event the issue is resolved in B's favor.

Did the burden of A's promise run with Lot 2?

Since C would be attempting to enjoin B from beginning the excavation without providing lateral support (rather than seeking monetary damages), A's promise must be analyzed as an equitable servitude ("ES"). For the burden of an ES to run with the land (1) the original parties must have intended it to so run, (2) the promise must touch and concern the burdened parcel and (3) the subsequent grantee of the burdened parcel must have had (actual, inquiry, or constructive) notice of the promise.

There is no indication that A and B intended A's promise to be binding upon subsequent transferees of the land (there was apparently no "successors and assigns" language). B could contend that many courts take the view that any promise that touches and concerns the burdened land must have been intended to run with the property. However, C could probably successfully contend in rebuttal that A's promise to B was predicated upon B's intention to build a commercial structure upon Lot 1 in the *immediate* future. It is therefore unlikely that the parties intended the promise to burden subsequent purchasers of Lot 2.

The "touch and concern" requirement is usually deemed to be satisfied where the promise affects the use or value of the burdened land, although there is a minority view that finds this element satisfied only where the use of land is affected. B could probably successfully contend that this condition is satisfied because Lot 2 is rendered less valuable if the lateral support requirement normally imposed upon Lot 1 is no longer extant (in fact, Lot 2 might almost be worthless until B's construction is completed). Therefore, B should prevail on the "touch and concern" issue.

The facts do not indicate whether C had notice of A's original promise to B. The promise was *not* contained in A's deed to B; nor would there be inquiry notice since viewing Lot 1 would *not* have suggested to C that A had agreed to waive the lateral support requirement.

Thus, since the "intent to run" and "notice" requirements are absent, A's covenant to B would *not* be enforceable vis-à-vis C, even though the "touch and concern" requirement has been met.

(2) Can C enjoin B from removing the sewer line?

C could contend that the sewer line constitutes an easement across B's property and is therefore not removable by B. C would argue that this easement arose by implication or, alternatively, by necessity.

Easement by implication:

An easement by implication arises where (1) the servient tenement was used for the purpose for which the easement is now being claimed before the severance of the dominant and servient parcels, (2) such use was reasonably apparent and continuous at the time of the severance, and (3) the easement is reasonably necessary to the enjoyment of the dominant tenement. B will contend that the "reasonably apparent" element is absent since the sewer line was not discovered until he had razed the house on his lot. However, C could probably successfully contend in rebuttal that most jurisdictions find the "reasonably apparent" element satisfied if the easement would have been discovered upon a reasonable inspection of the lot. Because a reasonable inspection of a home would include the crawl space beneath the floor, the element should be deemed satisfied. In addition, since the cost of an alternative sewer line would be prohibitive, the "reasonably necessary" element is also met.

Although some jurisdictions are reluctant to find an easement by implication where the alleged easement was retained by the party who transferred the servient tenement (the rationale being that the grantor could have explicitly reserved an easement over the grantee's land if he desired to do so), we'll assume that this state does not adhere to such a view.

Easement by necessity:

An easement by necessity arises if the necessity for the easement existed at the time the dominant and servient tenements were severed and the easement is strictly necessary. B might argue that since it was at least possible for C to run the sewer lines across other land, there is no strict necessity and therefore this theory should fail. However, C could probably successfully contend in rebuttal that since the cost of a new outlet for the sewer would be prohibitive, the "high degree" of necessity required in most states is satisfied. Therefore, under either theory (by implication or necessity), an easement in favor of C probably exists. C may keep the sewer pipe and enjoy a permanent easement across B's property.

Answer to Question 15

Reciprocal covenants:

Phil ("P") and the other subdivision landowners ("Other Lot Owners") could contend that the language in the deeds that Vera ("V") gave to Lot Owners 1–5 and 7–10 ("To preserve high quality within this development") indicates an implied promise by V that all subsequently sold parcels would also contain a similar "residential purpose" restriction. Since P and the Other Lot Owners probably would want to enforce this covenant against Barb ("B") in equity (i.e., obtain a permanent injunction requiring B to use her parcel for residential, not commercial, purposes), it is necessary to analyze V's implied promise as an equitable servitude ("ES"). An ES ordinarily will run with the land where (1) the original parties intended it to be binding upon the covenantor's grantees, (2) it touches and concerns (i.e., affects the value or use of) the burdened parcel, and (3) the covenantor's grantee (in this instance, B) had notice of the covenant.

Express covenant by V:

B could first contend that the words "To preserve high quality within this development" do not constitute a promise by V to restrict the remainder of the subdivision to residential dwellings. If this is what the earlier purchasers desired, they could have easily insisted upon clear language to that effect (e.g., "V hereby promises that all parcels within the development shall be restricted to residential dwellings"). P and the Other Lot Owners will argue in rebuttal that they reasonably understood the language in question to be a covenant by V to limit the subdivision to residential use because this is the only means by which "high quality" could be preserved. However, without a plat map or similar document indicating that a uniform or comprehensive development scheme of residential housing was envisioned by V, B should prevail.

Assuming, however, that P and/or the Other Lot Owners prevail on the foregoing issue, B might next contend that since there was no "successors and assigns" language in the deeds given to the Other Lot Owners, there was no intention by the original parties that the ES run with the land. However, the plaintiffs could probably successfully argue in rebuttal that where a covenant affects the value or use of real property, most jurisdictions will presume that the original covenantor and covenantee intended it to be enforceable against subsequent possessors of the land.

In some states, a grantee is deemed to be on notice of all prior grants made by his grantor within the county. In such jurisdictions, B would be deemed to be on notice of the deeds pertaining to Lots 1–4 and 7–10 (and therefore would be on notice of V's purported promise to restrict subsequently sold parcels to residential uses). In other states, however, a grantee is only deemed to be on constructive notice of documents contained in his direct chain of title. In the latter type of jurisdiction, B would *not* be charged with knowledge of V's promise to the Other Lot Owners.

Finally, B could contend that P should not be permitted to enforce the alleged express covenant by V since he was (or should have been) aware, at the time he purchased Lot 5, that B was not using her parcel for residential purposes. Therefore, he should not be heard to complain now about B's use of Lot 6 for commercial purposes. P might have presumed, however, that since a zoning ordinance requiring single-family residential dwellings had been passed three months before P purchased Lot 5, B's compliance with the ordinance would be imminent. P reasonably could have assumed that B would not simply ignore the ordinance.

Implied reciprocal covenant:

If the language in question was deemed to be too ambiguous to constitute a covenant by V for residential use with respect to the rest of the subdivision, the Other Lot Owners could contend that a reciprocal covenant (limiting land in the rest of the subdivision to residential use) by V should be implied into the deed that B received. However, there would be little likelihood of success on this theory since, except for the language that appeared in the deeds themselves, the facts are silent as to any indicia that suggest that there was a common scheme pertaining to the development (i.e., a plat map, verbal statements made by V to purchasers of the lots, etc.).

Assuming there was an explicit restrictive covenant and P or the Other Lot Owners could enforce it, B could also contend that it had been waived by reason of the inaction of the Other Lot Owners. B has been engaged in her business for three years, and even P had purchased his lot one year ago. B could also argue that P and the Other Lot Owners should be estopped from asserting the covenant now because P has purchased additional land from Farmer. B would seem to have a good chance of prevailing upon these arguments.

Even if an ES restricting the land to residential uses was found and was deemed to run with the land, equitable relief is always discretionary with the courts. Thus, B could argue that her use of Lot 6 as a nightclub should not be enjoined because (1) of laches (the facts discussed above with respect to waiver and estoppel would apply equally with respect to this theory);

(2) on a balancing-of-hardships analysis; the economic loss that B would incur far outweighs any inconvenience that P and the Other Lot Owners would be forced to endure; and (3) B's use of Lot 6 as a nightclub is consistent with the newly designated "commercial" rezoning of Lot 6. P could contend in rebuttal that the equities weigh against B since (1) she had used Lot 6 for commercial purposes at a time when to do so was completely contrary to the zoning ordinance, and (2) the discomfort suffered by P and the Other Lot Owners outweighs the financial loss that will be suffered by B. However, it is unlikely that B would be obliged to convert her parcel into a residential dwelling at this late date.

Nevertheless, assuming a covenant for only residential use was found to exist and it ran with the land, P and the Other Lot Owners may be able to enforce B's promise as a real covenant. In such event, they would be able to recover monetary damages equal to the diminished value of their land resulting from B's failure to conform to the restrictions.

Nuisance:

A nuisance occurs where the defendant has, in a nontrespassory manner (Restatement (Second) of Torts §821B), caused a substantial and unreasonable interference with the plaintiff's use and/or enjoyment of his land. P and the Other Lot Owners could contend that B's nightclub is causing them discomfort and inconvenience due to the loud music late at night and B's customers throwing empty bottles onto their lawns adjoining the easement. B could contend in rebuttal that the nightclub should not be considered a nuisance because (1) she is using the land in a manner authorized by the applicable zoning ordinance (although this fact ordinarily is not, *per se*, dispositive with respect to whether a nuisance is occurring); and (2) at least with respect to P, the fact that he purchased Lot 6 after B had established the nightclub would militate against a successful finding in P's favor or on P's behalf. The facts are silent as to precisely how loud the music from B's nightclub becomes and how late into the evening it can be heard. However, if it is played late into the evening (i.e., after 10 p.m. on weekday nights or 11 p.m. on weekend nights), at a volume sufficiently high to annoy a person of ordinary sensibilities, it is likely that P or the Other Lot Owners would prevail (especially given the low utilitarian value of B's activity). The occasional bottles thrown by B's customers are probably too trivial and irregular to constitute a nuisance.

Even assuming that B's nightclub constituted a nuisance, an additional question exists as to what remedies are available to the plaintiffs. While

P and the Other Lot Owners probably would desire a permanent injunction, given the facts that (1) to preclude B from using her land as a nightclub probably would result in substantial economic loss to her (especially since she has already purchased additional realty from Farmer), and (2) B has been using Lot 6 in the complained-of manner for three years without any litigation being commenced, it is likely that a court would enjoin B only from playing music at unreasonable hours and restrict her to acceptable noise levels. Also, P and the Other Lot Owners should be able to recover damages equal to the decreased value of their land.

Spot zoning:

Zoning ordinances must be made in accordance with a comprehensive plan. Amendments that do not comply with such a plan are illegal (such ordinances are sometimes referred to as "spot zoning"). Since the County Commissioners advised P that Farmer's land was a likely shopping center site, they apparently have not prepared a comprehensive plan. P and the Other Lot Owners therefore could contend that changing Lot 6 to "Commercial" was an invalid act and that Lot 6 should be returned to "Single Family Residential" use. However, most jurisdictions permit the appropriate governmental entity to develop the plan through a series of disconnected zoning ordinances. Since this is probably what is occurring in this instance, this attack by P and the Other Lot Owners will probably *not* be successful.

Scope of B's easement:

P and the Other Lot Owners could contend that B will exceed the scope of her express easement since it was merely for the use and benefit of Lot 6; it will now be used by persons parking on the additional acre that B purchased from Farmer. In addition, the volume of cars that will be using the easement vastly exceeds the original parties' expectations. B, however, could argue in rebuttal that (1) the easement is not being used by different parcel owners, but merely by additional guests of Lot 6; and (2) unless explicitly limited, easements can ordinarily be given for a use that arises from the normal, foreseeable development of the dominant estate where this would not impose an unreasonable burden on the servient estate. Given that (1) the easement has been used by B's patrons for three years without formal complaint about the increased vehicular flow; (2) the misconduct by B's present customers appears to be isolated instances that are more properly dealt with by police authorities, rather than prejudicing B;

and (3) the rock stars' funerals presumably would be relatively rare occurrences, B probably would prevail on this issue.

Summary:

It is unlikely that P or the Other Lot Owners could impair B's business operations, except that unreasonably loud music played late into the night probably would be restrained.

Answer to Question 16

(1) The quiet title action between Baker ("B") and Charles ("C"):

Priority to the tavern will depend upon the type of recording act, if any, enacted in this jurisdiction.

In a pure race jurisdiction, the first to record a clean chain of title from the grantor prevails, and B would have priority to the tavern because she was the first to record.

In a pure notice jurisdiction, a subsequent transferee who acquires title to the land for value and without notice of the earlier conveyances has priority over earlier grantees. B could contend that C was on inquiry notice since a conveyancing document that states only that the grantor is conveying her "right, title and interest" is usually construed to be a quitclaim deed, and in a few jurisdictions, acceptance of a quitclaim deed charges the recipient with whatever facts would have been obtained from asking the grantor as to the validity of title to the land. However, C could probably successfully argue in rebuttal that (1) the majority view is that a quitclaim deed does *not* put the recipient on notice of any defect in the grantor's title to the land; and (2) even if he had asked Olga ("O") why only a quitclaim deed was being tendered, O probably would have not answered his inquiry honestly (i.e., since O was aware of her prior conveyance to B, she probably would have said she simply did not want to accept the risk of liability for a legal interest about which she was unaware). Assuming C is *not* deemed to have notice of B's interest by reason of his receipt of a quitclaim deed, C would prevail in a notice jurisdiction.

B probably would prevail in a race/notice state (a subsequent transferee for valuable consideration who has no notice of the prior conveyance at the time the deed is delivered to him and is the first to record a clean chain of title against the land in question has priority) because B recorded first.

Finally, the common law rule was that the first person to receive his *legal* interest in the land had priority ("first in time, first in right"), subject, however, in some jurisdictions, to a subsequent grantee having greater equities. In the unlikely event that this jurisdiction has not adopted a recording statute, B would contend that because she received her interest before C, and because both parted with valuable consideration (B gave up a right of action against O for payment for medical services), she should have priority to the tavern. However, C could successfully contend in rebuttal that B should be equitably estopped from asserting her interest in the tavern vis-à-vis C, based on the facts that B failed to record her deed for six-and-a-half months (which presumably could have been done quite easily), and that B allowed O to remain in possession of the premises (thereby making it possible for O to mislead a subsequent grantee of the land).

(2) May C reopen the tavern?

There are two bases upon which Waterbury ("W") can contend that a re-opening is prohibited: (1) while the zoning ordinance provided for continuation of any existing nonconforming use, since the tavern was closed at the time the ordinance became effective, the nonconforming use was not "in existence" on July 1, 1998, and therefore the tavern's subsequent re-opening was unlawful; and (2) because of the nine-month liquor license suspension, C's decision to close the tavern would constitute an "abandonment" within the meaning of the zoning ordinance.

As to the first contention, C would argue that (1) closing the tavern temporarily due to an injury did not cause it to cease existence, especially since the merchandise and fixtures remained intact; (2) the equitable doctrine of laches applies, since W's failure to enforce the ordinance for three-and-a-half years resulted in substantial prejudice to C (C obviously would not have purchased the tavern if he had any reason to believe that its operation would violate a three-and-a-half year old ordinance); and (3) W's construction of the statute would violate O's (and thereby derivatively C's) due process rights under the Fourteenth Amendment since it would amount to a taking of property (a substantial and unexpected diminishment of the value of land) without compensation. Because W does not appear to have a viable response to these arguments, C should prevail on W's first theory.

As to W's second theory (closing the tavern during the nine-month suspension would constitute an "abandonment"), C could (1) contend that the word "abandon" is ordinarily associated with a voluntary relinquishment of property, and therefore the word "voluntary" should be implied into the ordinance prior to the word "cessation"; and (2) assert the due process argument described above. However, W would argue in rebuttal that (1) the plain meaning of the statute is clear, and there is no qualification of the word "cessation"; and (2) assuming the suspension procedure satisfied due process, there has been no "taking." Rather, C himself is responsible for the loss of the nonconforming use if he does not continue to operate the tavern (e.g., selling coffee and soft drinks) during the liquor license suspension. It is not clear at what point in the nine-month suspension this question is being asked. If less than six months has passed since C closed on January 19, 2002, C should be advised to reopen the tavern and sell something other than liquor to preserve the commercial use of the tavern. It is unknown whether C will again be able to serve liquor at the end of the nine-month license suspension, but at least C would not have lost all commercial rights. If, however, the nine-month suspension has already expired, W probably would prevail, based on the second theory discussed above, and it would be unlikely that C could legally reopen the tavern.

Answer to Question 17

(1) Rights of Baker ("B") in the land ("Land"):

The facts indicate that the statute of limitations period for real property actions in Myth is 10 years. Thus, B could contend that he acquired title to the Land by adverse possession ("AP"). The elements for AP are satisfied where the adverse possessor exclusively occupies the land under a claim of right (i.e., without permission), and in an open, notorious, and hostile manner throughout the requisite statutory period. In a few jurisdictions, the adverse possessor must also have paid the real property taxes pertaining to the land during the applicable period of time, but we'll assume that this additional element is not required in this state. Nonetheless, in many jurisdictions, paying the taxes can strengthen the adverse possessor's claim. Thus, B would assert that the combination of building a fence around the entire 400 acres, planting and harvesting crops on the Land and paying the real estate taxes for 7 of the 11 years he was on the Land constitutes open, notorious, and hostile conduct.

Able's daughter could argue that (1) in many jurisdictions, "claim of right" means that the adverse possessor entered the land with the belief, even if erroneous, that he was lawfully entitled to occupy it (which B did not, as evidenced by his statement to Carla); and (2) B's nonpayment of real estate taxes for 4 of the 11 years is a fatal flaw. As to the first contention, most states adhere to the view that the "claim of right" element is satisfied as long as the adverse possessor is occupying the land without the owner's permission. If this view is not followed in this jurisdiction, B has not acquired title to the Land, and Able's daughter would still be the lawful owner. She would accordingly have a right against B for (1) *mesne* profits (i.e., the reasonable rental value of the land) for the period of time during which B grew crops on the Land; and (2) damages, to the extent that the Land has been diminished in value as a result of B's activities. The daughter's second argument, about nonpayment of taxes, would probably not be persuasive since B paid the taxes for the majority of the years in question, although the facts do not indicate whether the 4 years of nonpayment were consecutive or intermittent (perhaps this could be viewed as an important distinction).

(2) & (4) Rights to the oil and the slant-hole well:

The majority view is that a landowner has a right to extract oil that is underneath the surface of her property. If in doing so the oil is drained from beneath the surface of a neighbor's land, the neighbor has no recourse against the extractor (since there is always the possibility that oil could naturally seep into the adjacent land). In addition, it is often impossible to prove how much oil was extracted from beneath each party's real property. If this view is adhered to in Myth, neither B nor Carla ("C") has any rights against the other with respect to the oil they have each extracted from beneath their lands. However, B probably would have a right to recover damages from C to the extent that oil was obtained through the slant-hole well, since it encroached onto B's tract. In the slant-hole situation, C is deliberately withdrawing oil from beneath another's land interest (i.e., the oil is not merely "escaping" into C's land). Thus, C would have committed a trespass (an intentional intrusion upon, beneath, or above the surface of another's land) vis-à-vis B's right to the oil underneath B's land.

There is, however, a minority view whereby oil in its underground state is viewed as unowned, similar to an animal *ferae naturae*. In such a jurisdiction, oil becomes the property of anyone who has obtained possession of it without actually going upon another's land. If this view were followed here, B would have a right of action against C only for the oil obtained through the one well that encroached upon the substrata of B's tract, but would have no action against C for the oil obtained through those wells that do not trespass on B's land.

(3) Rights of downstream owners against B:

There are three actions for which B may be liable in this instance. First, B appropriated 100,000 cubic feet per day from the river for the irrigation of his crops. Second, B created the dam that reduced the flow of water to the downstream riparian owners ("DROs"). Finally, he entered into the recent contract with City to sell it water from the water wells.

Under the "reasonable use" doctrine (which is probably the prevailing view in the United States), a riparian owner may make any reasonable use of a waterway abutting her land (including the sale of water to a nonriparian party) provided that (1) such use does not significantly interfere with a similar or more beneficial use of the water by DROs, and (2) there is no permanent depletion of the waterway (since public policy usually desires the preservation of existing streams, rivers and lakes). In deciding what constitutes a reasonable use, the courts distinguish between "artificial" and "natural" uses and also consider whether due regard has been given to the rights of other riparian owners. Here B used the river water to irrigate his crops on a large expanse of land, and this type of large-scale irrigation is generally held to be an artificial use. Thus, B would be required to share his artificial use of the water equally with those DROs whose use of the water would also be considered artificial. And B would not be allowed to take any water for artificial uses until the needs of those DROs requiring water for natural uses had been satisfied.

It is unclear from the facts whether the DROs who relied upon the waterway for manufacturing purposes were significantly injured by B's dam. However, given the above restrictions placed on B's artificial use of the water, the DROs probably could obtain an injunction requiring B to remove the earthen dam and they also probably could recover for damages resulting from B's action, particularly if the reduced flow rendered the DROs' businesses more expensive or less productive. On the other hand, since the facts seem to indicate that as much as six years have elapsed since B created the dam, B could argue, perhaps successfully, that there has not been a substantial interference with the DROs' operations. If this conclusion is accurate, then B may not have any liability for damages to the DROs as a result of the dam.

Finally, no liability would lie with respect to the diminution of the water table unless the DROs could show that the water wells constructed for City's benefit ultimately would result in depletion of the waterway. If such result could be shown to be inevitable, the DROs probably could enjoin B from performing his contract with City.

Under the "natural flow" doctrine (the second most popular doctrine), a riparian owner can use as much water as necessary for commercial purposes, except that (1) a DRO can restrain any use that results in a material diminution in the quantity or quality of water flowing to him (regardless of whether he is harmed), and (2) nonriparian uses are *not* permissible. Under this view, B would have no liability with respect to the water used to cultivate his crops. However, to the extent that B's dam has caused a material decrease in the river's flow to the DROs, the DROs could enjoin continued use of the dam without the necessity of showing financial loss. However, since the dam appears to have been in existence for six years apparently without any complaint by the DROs, the DROs may now have difficulty contending that the river's flow has been seriously diminished by the dam. The DROs, however, probably could prevent B from performing his contract with City, since nonriparian uses are not permitted.

Numerous western states follow the "prior appropriation" doctrine, whereby water rights (both riparian and nonriparian) are determined by priority of beneficial use, subject to an earlier user's right to compensation when her water flow is diminished by a subsequent, higher priority usage.

Under this theory, B would not be liable for water used to cultivate his crops since this conduct resulted in no diminution to the uses being made of the waterway by other parties. Both irrigation of a large tract of land and using water for manufacturing purposes would be classified as "commercial" uses, and therefore neither usage would have priority over the Land.

As to the reduced flow attributable to the dam, the DROs probably could obtain an injunction and recover for any financial loss that resulted to their prior operations. Whether the DROs could impede performance by B of his contract with City would depend upon whether (1) the court viewed the furnishing of water to City as a higher priority than manufacturing purposes, and (2) the DROs could prove that the water basin would eventually be depleted. In the absence of such proof, B probably would not be restrained from furnishing water to City. If providing water to City were deemed to be a higher priority than manufacturing, the DROs would be entitled to compensation for their inevitable loss. If the manufacturing processes, however, were deemed to constitute a more beneficial use, then (assuming it could be demonstrated that the water basin would eventually be depleted) the DROs probably could restrain B from performing the contract with City.

Finally, it should be noted that there are a few jurisdictions that overlay the "reasonable use" and "natural flow" theories with the "prior appropriation" doctrine (i.e., the rights resulting from the "natural flow" and "reasonable use" theories are subject to alteration when the water is necessary for a subsequent, but more beneficial, usage). In these states, the rights that were vested at an earlier point in time are entitled to compensation from the party whose use of the waterway has been given priority.

Answer to Question 18

(1) B v. D:

B will contend that D does not come within the description of the recording statute because (1) D was not a good faith purchaser, (2) D did not take for "valuable consideration." and (3) D was not the first to "duly record."

B's first contention is that D was not a "good faith" purchaser because she received a quitclaim deed from C. In some jurisdictions, receipt of a quitclaim deed automatically results in a denial of *bona fide* purchaser status ("BFP"). In others, it places the recipient upon inquiry notice (i.e., the grantee is charged with notice of whatever facts a reasonable inspection of, and inquiry at, the premises would have revealed). However, even had D gone to the premises, she would have learned nothing about B's purported interest in Blackacre ("B/A") since the tract of land was vacant. In addition, even had D searched the grantor/grantee indexes, she would not have learned of B's interest (since B did not record his deed until December 1). Thus, unless this is one of the minority jurisdictions that equates receipt of a quitclaim deed with knowledge of all prior interests in land, D would be deemed to have acquired her interest in B/A in "good faith."

B would alternatively contend that D had not acquired her interest in B/A for "valuable consideration" since D did not part with any new monetary value in obtaining title to B/A. However, D could probably successfully rebut this contention by pointing out the contemporaneous consideration of D relinquishing a prior claim against C in exchange for the deed to B/A. Thus, the fact that D acquired B/A in satisfaction of an antecedent debt would probably be deemed to constitute valuable consideration.

In addition, many states employ the "shelter rule." Under this theory, a purchaser or transferee from a BFP, in effect, steps into the shoes of the grantor. Since C received a warranty deed and paid a fair cash price for B/A, there appears to be no question that C is a BFP. Thus, if this jurisdiction adheres to the "shelter rule," D would also be a BFP.

B would alternatively contend that D did not "duly record" her deed to B/A first. B would claim that one has not duly recorded until she has perfected a clean chain of title involving the subject land. Although D recorded the deed she received from C on November 2, prior to the time B recorded his deed from A (December 1), D did not perfect her chain of title until February 1 of the following year (when D recorded the deed from A to C). Before February 1, D had what is often referred to as a "wild" deed in B/A.

(A search of the grantor/grantee index looking for transactions by A involving B/A would not have discovered D's interest therein because of the absence of the deed between A and C. In fact, to perfect the chain of title properly with respect to B/A, D would have to rerecord the C-to-D deed after having recorded the A-to-C deed on February 1.) D does not appear to have a good rebuttal to this argument, and B probably would have priority to B/A under the statute.

However, D might contend that B should be equitably estopped from asserting a superior interest in B/A because it was as a result of B's failure to promptly record A's deed that D was not able to discover B's prior interest in B/A. (Had C searched the grantor/grantee index immediately before receiving A's deed, B's interest would *not* have appeared.) However, B could probably successfully argue in rebuttal that despite B's delay in recording A's deed, D could have still protected herself by requiring C to have recorded A's deed before she (D) accepted C's deed. Therefore, D's loss of priority to B/A was not due to B's failure to promptly record the deed from A.

(2) Omission of last six words from statute:

Omission of the last six words from the recording statute would convert the enactment into a "notice" statute. Based upon the *B v. D* discussion above, D would prevail in this instance because the property was acquired by C (and D) in good faith, for a valuable consideration, and without notice of any prior interests in the land.

(3) B's recourse against A:

B might contend that the typical warranty deed contains covenants of warranty, quiet enjoyment, and future assurances (i.e., that the grantee will not be disturbed in his enjoyment of the land by anyone with superior title, and that in the event the grantee is evicted, the grantor will indemnify the grantee for attorneys' fees and costs expended in attempting to protect title to the land). However, A could probably successfully contend in rebuttal that these warranties protect against claims by third parties in existence on the date of the conveyance, and that D did not predicate her claim against the land upon an interest that arose before B acquired B/A. Thus, B would have no rights against A based upon the deed (even assuming B had given value to A).

A might nevertheless be liable to B under a negligence theory. It should have been reasonably foreseeable to A that, by conveying the property to a subsequent party such as C, a title dispute might result between the transferees. Thus, B should be able to recover for any actual losses occasioned by A's subsequent transfer of B/A to C.

Answer to Question 19

Marketable title:

Implicit in transactions for the sale and purchase of real estate is that the vendor will have, at the closing, marketable title to the land that is being sold. Marketable title means that which would be acceptable to a reasonably prudent buyer (i.e., free from reasonable doubt). Vendor ("V") could contend that since the purported grant to Daughter ("D") was verbal, it is unenforceable by reason of the Statute of Frauds (i.e., transfers of land must be embodied in a writing that contains the essential terms and is signed by the party against whom enforcement is sought). Thus, V would argue that he retained marketable title to the land.

Purchaser ("P"), however, could argue in rebuttal that, in many states, where a grantee does acts that are "unequivocally referable" to a transfer of the land by the grantor, the grantee is entitled to prove that a conveyance was made (despite the Statute of Frauds). Since D lived on the land for six years and made substantial improvements thereto, P would contend that the "unequivocally referable" standard is satisfied. The facts are silent as to whether D also paid the real property taxes with respect to the land. If she did, P's position would be strengthened. If D were V's only child, V could respond that D's conduct was *not* "unequivocally referable" to a transfer of the real property since D's actions could have been in anticipation of her likely inheritance of the land. In other words, D would have had reason to improve and maintain the land, even if a transfer had not occurred. However, it is likely that D would be asked to testify about the conveyance to her, and P probably would prevail on this issue.

P could also contend that V might be estopped to assert the Statute of Frauds as to D since D foreseeably and justifiably relied upon V's gift in making "substantial improvements" to the land at "considerable expense." While V could argue in rebuttal that since D had lived on the land for six years on a rent-free basis, she suffered no detriment, P probably would prevail on this issue.

Alternatively, P could claim that D might be able to assert ownership to the land by adverse possession (assuming the statute of limitations for real property actions is six years or less). This doctrine applies where the claimant occupied the land in question under a claim of right, and in an open, notorious, and hostile manner continuously throughout the requisite statutory period. P could contend that since D entered the land under a claim of right (i.e., with the belief that she was the lawful owner of it) and committed acts that were consistent with exclusive ownership (i.e., occupying and making substantial improvements), D has acquired title to the real property. This definition of "claim of right" exists in only a few jurisdictions. Even if this were one of those jurisdictions, since V gave D permission to live in the house and provided her the keys to the house, it is unlikely that D satisfies the "hostile" element so as to claim ownership by adverse possession.

Based upon the foregoing, it does not appear that V had marketable title to the land.

The facts are silent as to the type of deed that V was required to deliver to P at the closing. If it were a quitclaim deed, V could conceivably contend that he had promised only to convey to P whatever interest, if any, he might have in the land. However, even where the parties have stipulated to a quit-claim deed, most courts nevertheless imply an obligation to transfer marketable title (at least to the extent of any adverse interests of which the seller was aware).

Equitable conversion:

Assuming, for the sake of discussion, that V was deemed to be able to convey marketable title, P might contend that he is entitled to cancel the agreement based on the destruction of the house. However, the majority view is that risk of loss that is neither party's fault and that occurs after a contract has been signed rests with the vendee, subject to the obligation of the seller to reduce the purchase price by the amount of any insurance proceeds received as a result of the damage. If this view is adhered to here, the building's destruction would not be grounds for P to avoid the con-tract. There is, however, a minority view (sometimes referred to as the "Massachusetts" rule) that usually places the burden of loss upon the seller until legal title is conveyed. Thus, a contract for the sale of land is deemed to be cancelled when there is **substantial** damage to the land prior to the closing. V could also argue that since P had indicated his intention to raze the building anyway, the "damage" to P is insignificant. Because P is attempting to avoid the contract primarily because he wants to buy other land (rather than because of the house being destroyed), V should prevail under these facts even if the Massachusetts view is followed in this jurisdiction.

Remedies:

If V could prevail on both the marketable title and equitable conversion issues described above, he probably could obtain a judgment against P for the balance of the purchase price (conditional upon his delivery of a valid deed to the land when the full amount was tendered). In a number (not a majority) of jurisdictions, however, an aggrieved vendor is entitled to recover only his out-of-pocket expenses if the seller attempted to convey, in good faith, an unmarketable title. If the latter view is followed here, V would still prevail, only if P acted in bad faith; if a court decided that he acted in good faith, V would be able to receive only out-of-pocket expenses.

If V were not successful on the marketable title dispute, P would be entitled to cancel the agreement and recover his deposit (i.e., the failure of V to furnish marketable title is a precondition to sale, entitling P to rescind the contract). If the deposit could be located, P probably would be entitled to impose a constructive trust upon it since V would be unjustly enriched if he were permitted to retain it.

Finally, D could institute a successful "quiet title" action to require V to give her a deed to the land. If V refused to execute a deed, D probably could obtain a court order transferring ownership of the land to her.

Answer to Question 20

Estoppel by deed:

Charlie ("C") would first contend that Able ("A") has no interest in Greenacre ("G/A") because at the time Owens ("O") purported to transfer the land to A, O had no interest therein. (A could have protected himself simply by performing a title search.) Since the initial purported transfer to A was void, C would argue that he is the only party with an interest in G/A. However, A could probably successfully contend that most jurisdictions recognize the common law doctrine of estoppel by deed. Under this theory, where a grantor purports to transfer real property that he does not then own, but later acquires title to the property, his subsequently acquired title automatically operates to vest ownership in the earlier grantee. If this jurisdiction recognizes this doctrine, title in G/A would have passed to A immediately upon O's grandmother's death three years ago, when she left G/A to O in her will.

Recording statute:

Even if the estoppel-by-deed theory exists in this jurisdiction, C could contend that, under the recording statute, he still has priority to G/A because he is a subsequent taker for value and without notice. A could claim, however, that C does not satisfy the elements of the recording statute since (1) the prior conveyance to A was recorded, (2) C did not give new value to O at the time G/A was conveyed to him, and (3) C was not "without notice" because a purchaser of land is ordinarily charged with whatever notice a reasonable inspection of the property would have disclosed (in this instance, it would have revealed the metallic sign posted by Bank, indicating the summer home had been built by A). However, C could argue in rebuttal that (1) A's initial recording would not satisfy the statute since it was outside the chain of title under the grantor/grantee indexes and therefore should be deemed "unrecorded" for purposes of the legislation; (2) C gave O present value since O was relieved of an outstanding obligation to C; and (3) there was no inquiry notice because, even had C seen the sign that was posted by Bank, he would have assumed the cabin was built by A before it was transferred to O. Finally, it appears that A built the cabin 22 years ago, and thus it is possible that Bank's sign had become so obliterated over time that it would be impossible to read. If this were the case, then C may be able to use this fact to strengthen his assertion that he had no inquiry notice of A's prior claim.

Assuming the metallic sign was readable, A could argue in rebuttal that C should have asked O whether anyone else had an interest in G/A since A's name would not have appeared in the grantor/grantee indexes. However, C might have reasonably assumed that A was simply a prior lessee of the property. In addition, C could contend that even if he had asked O about other grantees, O would have denied A's interest in G/A since O conveyed a second deed to G/A with full knowledge of A's prior interest. C probably will be deemed to satisfy the recording statute and therefore would have priority to G/A on this basis.

Adverse possession:

Assuming C prevails with respect to the foregoing issues, A could alternatively assert priority to G/A under the adverse possession ("AP") doctrine. Under this theory, an occupier obtains title where he enters upon the land of another under a claim of right (in most jurisdictions, this means without permission, but the minority view defines it as the belief that he is the rightful owner) and occupies such land in an open, notorious, and hostile manner (i.e., indicating to the world that the occupant believes he is the owner) continuously throughout the applicable statutory period of time. (In a minority of jurisdictions, the possessor must also pay real estate taxes pertaining to the land, which A here has done.)

A obviously went upon G/A under color of title since O had given him a deed. Where a person enters under color of title, the claim of right and hostility requirements are met. If this jurisdiction has adopted the minority view, then A has satisfied this element. The open and notorious requisites of A's AP claim are satisfied by the fact that A undertook actions (building a summer home, paying the taxes) that evidenced to the world his exclusive ownership of the land. The requisite statutory period would appear to be satisfied since A has been in possession of the land for 22 years; the applicable period of time is ordinarily no longer than 21 years (and sometimes as short as 5 or 10 years). The fact that O's grandmother was unaware that A had constructed a summer home on G/A would not diminish A's assertion of AP.

C might contend, however, that the "open" and "notorious" elements are not satisfied because A occupied G/A for only one month each year. A could argue in rebuttal, however, that the "continuously" element is satisfied if the adverse possessor uses the land in a manner similar to that which would be made of it by the legal occupant. Since the parcel was located in a mountainous area that was inaccessible by road for six months of the year, the use of the land solely as a summer home would be appropriate. C might argue that a summer cottage should be occupied two or three months a year, but most people have a vacation period of, at most, only one month. A's occupancy of G/A for that period of time should be sufficient. It therefore appears that A should have priority to G/A despite the recording statute because A can claim to have obtained title to G/A as an adverse possessor.

Answer to Question 21

To advise Mark as to his rights in Greenacre ("G/A"), the following issues would have to be analyzed.

Did Henry ("H") make a transfer of G/A to Paula ("P") and Mark ("M") 12 years ago?

It must be assumed that this jurisdiction does not require conveyancing documents to be witnessed or acknowledged. If such steps were so required, the purported deed to P and M would be invalid, and M would have no interest in G/A. Many states have enacted legislation that cures the absence of witnesses or acknowledgments if no dispute arises over the document within a specified time after recordation. However, even if such legislation exists in this jurisdiction, it might not apply here because H's deed to P and M was not recorded until just recently.

An interest in land is ordinarily transferred through delivery by the grantor (completion of a valid conveyancing document, together with the grantor's intention that the writing be immediately operative) and acceptance by the grantee. Where the purported transfer is a gift, acceptance will ordinarily be presumed and relate back to the time of delivery, unless express objection is made by the grantee immediately upon being informed of the conveyance. To be valid, a deed must reasonably identify the land conveyed and the grantees. Ruth ("R") could contend that the deed was not valid since (1) there was not a sufficient description of the real property being transferred (it merely referred to unspecified land in Utopia), and (2) the last names of P and M were not stated. However, M could probably successfully contend in rebuttal that (1) the land that H owned in Utopia was easily identifiable (it would require only checking the county records of all counties within Utopia) since the grant extends to *all* of H's property within that state; and (2) assuming P and M were H's only niece and nephew with those first names, the precise grantees are certainly determinable. It therefore appears that H's transfer of G/A to M is valid.

R might next contend that delivery did not take place since it appears that H did not intend the deed to be immediately operative, as evidenced by the facts that (1) he handed the deed to JoAnn, a friend from whom H could presumably later recover the deed if he chose to do so; and (2) he later sold G/A to R (presumably, H would not fraudulently sell land that he did not own). The facts seem to indicate that H sold the land to R because he no longer wanted M to have it, but there is no indication that H ever communicated this to any third party. M could argue in rebuttal that (1) delivery to JoAnn was unequivocal (i.e., H did not attach any conditions to delivery of the deed to P and M or otherwise advise JoAnn that he might demand the deed back, and (2) the fact that H gave R a quitclaim deed demonstrates that his recognition that he might not have any further rights in G/A. Since H made absolutely no provision for reobtaining the deed from JoAnn, it is likely that the conveyance of a future interest to P and M had occurred (i.e., H gave a future interest to P and M while preserving a life estate in himself).

Assuming G/A was conveyed to P and M, did M become the sole owner of it when P died?

When a joint tenant dies, his interest passes automatically to the surviving joint tenants. M would contend that since G/A was conveyed to P and himself as "joint owners," they received a joint tenancy estate and, thus, M succeeded to sole ownership of G/A when P died. P's heirs or devisees (whoever succeeded to her interest in G/A) could argue in rebuttal, however, that there is a judicial preference to construe ambiguous grants as tenancies in common rather than joint tenancies. In fact, some jurisdictions will refuse to conclude that a joint tenancy was intended unless the words "with right of survivorship" are contained in the grant. However, where the grantees have a consanguinary relationship (M and P may have been siblings), many courts presume that the grantor would not have desired one grantee to be able to force the other to permanently share land with a complete stranger (as would be the case if the property were conveyed as a tenancy in common). Thus, M probably became the sole owner of G/A when P died.

Did R obtain a superior interest in G/A by adverse possession ("AP")?

It is assumed that Utopia is not a pure race state (i.e., the first to record a complete chain of title has priority to that parcel). If it were, then R would have a superior interest to G/A since she recorded her deed before M. If the jurisdiction adheres to a race/notice or notice recording statute, R could not claim priority to G/A since she had actual knowledge of the earlier grant to M and P. (The fact that R believed the transfer was invalid does not detract from her awareness of the earlier transfer.)

Assuming this jurisdiction has a relatively short statute of limitations for real property actions (seven years or less), R would contend that she has, under color of title, occupied G/A continuously for the requisite time in an open, notorious, and hostile manner. Building a home and living on land certainly would constitute open, notorious, and hostile possession of the land. However, where an AP claimant commences her occupation between the time a future interest has been given and the right of possession by such future interest holder vests, the AP period does not begin to run against the holder of the future interest (here M) until his estate becomes possessory. Since H died only three months ago, M presumably would be entitled to commence eviction proceedings against R. (No equitable argument in the nature of laches could be successfully asserted against M since he has learned only recently of his interest in G/A.)

What are M's rights against R?

Assuming M prevailed upon the foregoing issues, he could claim ownership of G/A (including the home that R has constructed) and sue R for *mesne* profits (i.e., the reasonable rental value of G/A throughout the period the land was occupied by R). In many jurisdictions, however, where one in good faith (i.e., believing the land belongs to her) enters upon real property belonging to another and makes improvements thereon, the latter may be required to make restitution to the former for those improvements. Given R's belief that she owned the land, a court probably would allow R to offset the reasonable value of the home she constructed (and possibly also the taxes she paid on that property) against any rent due to M.

Answer to Question 22

The rights of Elk Mortgage Co. ("E") are derivative through Cap ("C"). Thus, E's rights turn upon whether C would have priority to Goldacre ("G/A") vis-à-vis Art ("A") and Bill ("B").

This answer assumes that all deeds to which the question refers were properly completed.

Was there a conveyance to A?

(If no conveyance occurred, then A never acquired any rights in G/A.)

A conveyance occurs when there has been a delivery (completion of a valid deed together with the grantor's intention that the instrument be immediately operative) and acceptance by the grantee. A will argue that (1) when the deed transferring G/A was handed to him subject to an oral condition that was not contained in the deed ("If I die before you"), there was a valid delivery and thus the oral statement is of no effect; (2) there is a presumption that if a deed is manually tendered to a grantee, the grantor intended it to be immediately operative (the fact that one's *possessory* interest in land will not vest until some point in the future does not prevent a delivery from having occurred if the grantor has relinquished any right to withdraw the grant); and (3) the statement by Ollie ("O") should be construed as a condition subsequent (i.e., A had a future interest in G/A subject to the condition that he survive O). However, B and C could contend in rebuttal that (1) extrinsic evidence is admissible for the purpose of showing that the grantor did *not* intend the deed to be immediately operative, and O's statement in this instance indicates clearly that the purported transfer was *not* effective unless A survived O; and (2) even though O did not expressly reserve the right to revoke the deed, O obviously did *not* intend the conveyance to be immediately operative since she subsequently changed her mind and gave deeds pertaining to G/A to B and C (which she would not have done if she believed that she no longer had any interest in G/A). However, A would contend in rebuttal that O's subsequent purported transfers of G/A are insignificant because O (a layperson) did not recognize that she no longer had any interest in G/A. A probably will prevail on this issue because O's statement did not establish her right to revoke the deed.

Was there a conveyance to B?

B will also contend that O intended the deed to him to be immediately operative. E, C, and A would argue in rebuttal that (1) since O kept the deed (she only showed it to B but did not give it to him), there is a presumption against delivery; (2) B was not to obtain physical possession of G/A until O died (which suggests that O intended the transfer to be effective only at that time); and (3) O would not have sold G/A to C if she believed that she no longer had any interest in G/A. B could probably successfully respond that (1) since he had the combination to the safe (with O's blessing), the deed was virtually in his possession; (2) the words by O ("I am *now* giving Goldacre to you") evidence an intention that the deed be immediately operative; and (3) as contended by A above, when O subsequently deeded G/A to C, O probably did not understand that she had already conveyed her interest in G/A. In short, O probably made a present conveyance to B and simply retained a life estate in G/A.

Was there a conveyance to C?

There seems to be little doubt that O intended the deed to C to be immediately operative, as evidenced by the fact that she accepted "valuable consideration" for the sale of G/A to C. However, C may have the most difficult substantive problems to resolve, as discussed below.

(1) Acceptance:

There appears to be no question that all of the possible grantees accepted their deeds. Acceptance is ordinarily presumed where no objection is made by the grantee when he learns of the delivery.

(2) Who has priority to G/A?

Priority to G/A would depend upon which type of recording statute is applicable in Lotus.

If this is a pure race state (the first to record a clean chain of title has priority), then C (and through C, E) would prevail because C was the first party to record a deed from O.

If Lotus is a pure notice jurisdiction (a subsequent grantee who acquires title to land for value and without notice of any prior grantees has priority over the prior grantees), A probably would have priority to G/A. This is because B would have been on constructive notice of A's prior recordation, and C had actual notice of A's and B's prior interests since C was present when O purportedly made a transfer of G/A to B and since O told C she had revoked her deeds to A and B. C might contend that since O specifically told him that she had revoked the deeds to A and B, he believed that his interest was superior to either of theirs. However, B could probably successfully argue in rebuttal that C was at least upon inquiry notice to (1) ask A and B what interest, if any, either claimed in G/A; and (2) verify independently that O was capable of revoking her prior deeds. Had C done this, he would have learned that O had already conveyed G/A both to A and to B.

If Lotus is a race/notice jurisdiction (a subsequent transferee for value, who has no notice of conflicting claims at the time of the conveyance and is the first to record a clean chain of title against the land, has priority vis-à-vis earlier grantees), the result would be the same as in a notice jurisdiction. Since C is deemed to have had notice of both A's and B's prior interests in G/A at the time of the conveyance to him, his interest would be subordinate to both A's and B's (even though C was the first to record his interest). B's interest would not succeed against A's interest because A recorded his deed first; under the race/notice statute, the subsequent grantee must be the first to record a clean chain of title.

Answer to Question 23

What, if any, rights does Peter ("P") have in Goldacre ("G/A") vis-à-vis Atwell ("A")?

In a race/notice state, a subsequent purchaser for value has priority over previous grantees where the former (1) acquires the land for valuable consideration without notice of any prior interests, and (2) is the first to record a complete chain of title with respect to her interest in the land. Since a search of the grantor/grantee indexes would have revealed the warranty deed that A recorded on July 5, 2002, there would appear to be little doubt that P was on constructive notice of A's interest in G/A. Thus, even though the initial recording between Oscar ("O") and A may have been a nullity (because the contract was notarized by a clerk whose commission had expired and this defect was apparent on the face of the document), P would probably still be deemed to have had constructive notice of A's interest in G/A. Thus, P took G/A subject to the conveyance of one-half of the minerals to A.

Was the interest of Baker ("B") divisible?

P might next contend that the interest held by B was a profit in gross (the right to come upon another's land and take something from it); in some jurisdictions, profits in gross are assignable in full but not divisible. Thus, P could argue that while B had the right to assign his entire interest in O's land to P, B did not have the right to make a partial transfer of it to A. Therefore, the purported conveyance to A was invalid. However, A could probably successfully argue in rebuttal that this rule has not been applied where the profit in gross allows the original grantee to take *all* of a particular substance from the land. In such instances, the grantor obviously expects the grantee to remove the entire quantity of such minerals, and so the grantor's estate is not unexpectedly burdened or depleted when the grantee extends his rights to other entities. Since the grant from O to B was in fee simple as to "all the minerals" in G/A, A should prevail on this issue.

Do A and P own their interests as a tenancy in common?

Where two parties concurrently hold indivisible, possessory interests in the same property, they are ordinarily deemed to be tenants in common. B had already conveyed one-half of the minerals in G/A to A at the time of B's conveyance to P, and it would (presumably) be impossible to determine at what point one-half of the minerals had been extracted from beneath a particular parcel of land. Therefore, A and P probably will be deemed to be tenants in common. A tenant in common must ordinarily account to other co-tenants for the permanent depletion of mineral resources from land. Thus, if P carries out a full mining operation, P probably would be obliged to deliver one-half of any net profits to A unless some contrary arrangement were made.

Assuming P decided to proceed with mineral extraction, can he move in heavy equipment and build roads?

Although there is fee simple language in the granting document to B, it is qualified by the additional wording "all the minerals in and under G/A." Thus, the interest conveyed to B was absolute with respect to the mineral rights on G/A. While it could possibly be contended by O that he did not expressly give B the right to build roads (which could lead to the permanent destruction of standing timber), it is ordinarily implied into the grant of a profit in gross that the grantee will have the right to do whatever is reasonably necessary to effectuate the purposes of the grant. Thus, P can probably successfully contend that to exploit the minerals it is necessary to use heavy equipment and to build roads capable of both supporting the transportation of this equipment onto G/A and carrying away the minerals that will be mined.

Answer to Question 24

Did Bob ("B") convey Blackacre ("B/A") to Joanne ("J") in July 1995?

(If B did not make a conveyance of B/A to J, she would have no rights in that land.) The answer assumes that all deeds were properly completed.

A conveyance occurs where there has been a delivery by the grantor (i.e., completion of a valid deed with the grantor's intent that it be immediately operative) and acceptance by the grantee (which is ordinarily assumed in the case of a gift). C would contend that B did *not* intend the deed to be immediately operative since he (1) continued to live at B/A and (2) believed that he could revoke the deed (as indicated in his letter to J). However, J would argue in rebuttal that (1) there is nothing in the deed or B's request that is inconsistent with the deed being immediately operative (J simply agreed that B would retain a life estate), and (2) the fact that B later attempted to revoke the deed is insignificant since B (a layperson) did not understand that he had already transferred B/A to J. J should prevail on this issue.

Who has priority to B/A?

Priority to B/A will depend upon which type of recording statute is applicable in this jurisdiction.

If B/A is located in a race jurisdiction (the first to record a clean chain of title to the property has priority), J probably will prevail. While C could argue that she recorded her particular deed first, there was no chain of title to C because B's deed to Frank ("F") had not been recorded at that time (C recorded B's deed to F in December 2002). J probably would prevail because she recorded her deed in October 2002.

If a pure notice statute is in effect (one who purchases for valuable consideration and without knowledge of earlier interests in the land has priority over prior grantees), C should prevail. Although C did not part with valuable consideration to obtain her interest in B/A, C would step into the position of F under the "shelter rule." J can be expected to contend, however, that F would not have had priority against her in a pure notice state because (1) F had received a quitclaim deed (in some jurisdictions, receipt of such a document puts the recipient upon inquiry notice that there may be a defect in the grantor's title), and (2) F should have asked B about the fact that George ("G") was occupying B/A at the time of the purported sale to F.

C can probably successfully refute J's arguments as follows: (1) in most jurisdictions, the mere receipt of a quitclaim deed is not deemed to place the recipient upon inquiry notice, and even if it did, it is unlikely that B would have told F about any defects in his title to B/A (since B apparently believed that his attempted revocation of the earlier deed to J was effective); and (2) G's possession of B/A was not inconsistent with B's ownership since B and G were related. Again, even if F had asked B about G's presence on B/A, B probably would have told F (accurately) that G would vacate B/A as soon as B asked G to leave. Therefore, F probably was not on inquiry notice of J's alleged prior interest. Since F parted with valuable consideration to obtain B/A, C (as F's successor in interest) would have priority to B/A under the typical pure notice statute.

In a race/notice jurisdiction (a subsequent purchaser for valuable consideration, who acquires her interest in land without notice of prior interests and is the first to record a clean chain of title, has priority over earlier grantees), J probably would prevail. As discussed above, while C would assume F's position with respect to the lack of knowledge of J's interest and the valuable consideration, J was the first to record a clean chain of title. The fact that she made her recording with actual knowledge of the purported transfer to F would be insignificant in a race/notice jurisdiction.

Conceivably, C might contend that J should be equitably estopped from asserting her priority to B/A since her failure to record the deed at the time it was physically tendered to her permitted B to sell B/A to F for $30,000 (i.e., had F seen J's deed in the chain of title, he would not have paid B for B/A). However, J could contend in rebuttal that (1) F could have protected himself (and thereby C) by promptly recording the deed that he had received from B, and (2) C (like J) did not part with valuable consideration to obtain her interest in B/A. Thus, it is unlikely that C would prevail against J under an equitable estoppel theory.

Can F recover the $30,000 he paid to B?

If C had priority over J to B/A, F's gift to C was effective and F could not recover the $30,000. If C did not have priority to B/A, then F could sue B in an attempt to recover the $30,000. B probably would contend that (1) B gave F a quitclaim deed, and therefore he was parting only with whatever interest (possibly none) he had in B/A; and (2) since F transferred his interest in B/A to C gratuitously, F suffered no damage if C is not entitled to possession of B/A. However, F could probably successfully contend in rebuttal that he has a right of restitution with respect to the money paid to B (i.e., B would be unjustly enriched if he were permitted to retain the $30,000, while C, F's transferee, received nothing). (C, of course, could assign back to F whatever interest F had conveyed to C.) Thus, if C were not deemed to have priority to B/A, F probably would be permitted to recover $30,000 from B.

Answer to Question 25

(1) Dale v. Art (quiet title action):

In an action by Dale ("D") to quiet title to Greenacre ("G/A") against Art ("A"), A can be expected to contend that Barb ("B") could not have conveyed G/A to D because no conveyance of G/A was made to B, and thus B had nothing to transfer to D. A transfer of land does not occur until there is delivery by the grantor (completion of a valid deed with the intention that it be immediately operative) and acceptance of the deed by the grantee. Where an escrow has been established, there is usually a presumption that the grantor intended the deed *not* to be operative until the conditions of the escrow have been satisfied. Since the condition precedent to the deed being operative (the payment of $5,000 by B) never occurred, B never acquired title to G/A that she could have transferred to D.

D, however, could contend that A should be equitably estopped from denying that the transfer to D was invalid. Some states have adopted the rule that where a grantee wrongfully acquires a deed from an escrow holder chosen by the grantor and then conveys the land to a *bona fide* purchaser ("BFP"), the grantor is estopped from denying the validity of the transfer against the BFP. Assuming D parted with present consideration to acquire G/A (the facts are silent on this point), D would seem to be a BFP (since the land was vacant, a visit to G/A would not have put D upon inquiry notice of A's ownership interest). Also, since A had prepared a warranty deed for B (as opposed to a quitclaim deed), D would have no reason to investigate B's title beyond a search of the grantor/grantee index.

Assuming D was a BFP, D would additionally contend that there is a maxim in the law that where one of two innocent parties must suffer, the loss should fall upon the more blameworthy person. Here, A is more blame-worthy because (1) A chose Carl, who mistakenly parted with possession of the deed; and (2) by giving Carl a "clean" deed (one with no conditions upon the face of it), A should have realized that it would be possible for B, if she ever obtained the deed from Carl, to "sell" G/A. A might contend in rebuttal that escrows are a common device for transferring ownership of land and that Carl, as a real estate broker, should have been well aware of the potential for harm if the deed left his possession. Assuming D paid value for G/A, D should prevail in her quiet title action against A (even though no actual conveyance took place).

(2) Art ("A") v. Carl ("C"):

A probably would sue C for breach of contract and negligence. With respect to the breach of contract claim, C could contend that he has no liability because (1) no contract ever arose between him and A (it appears that C did not receive any consideration); and (2) in any event, the Statute of Frauds (which pertains to the sale of land) was never satisfied (C never signed the statement prepared by A). However, it probably would be implied into the A-C arrangement that C would receive reasonable compensation for his efforts on behalf of A and B. In addition, equitable estoppel could probably be successfully asserted to overcome these contentions since A detrimentally relied upon C to act as escrow agent.

If C were found to have breached his contract with A, C might next assert that A's damages are limited to $5,000 (the amount he would have received if the escrow had closed), rather than the enhanced value of the land. However, A should be able to successfully argue in rebuttal that since the conditions for the close of escrow were never satisfied, he would have been able to recover the deed (there was never a valid contract between A and B for the sale of land). Therefore, A should be able to recover the present fair market value of G/A from C.

A would also contend that C, by agreeing to act as escrow agent, assumed a duty to A that he would not deliver the deed to B unless B gave C the $5,000 cash purchase price within a month. When C sent the deed to B (so that B allegedly could show the deed to a bank), C breached his duty to A and became liable to A for negligence. C might contend that he could only foresee damages of $5,000. A could probably successfully argue in rebuttal that C should have foreseen that, if B transferred the deed to G/A to another party without fulfilling the conditions of escrow, A would not be able to recover the deed and benefit from an enhanced market value of G/A.

Multiple-Choice Questions

1. Anna found a valuable tennis bracelet as she was entering a coffeehouse. She showed it to the manager, who told her to leave it with him so he could display the item in the hope that its owner would claim it. Several weeks later, Anna returned and asked about the bracelet. The manager told her that no one had claimed it, and that he had given it to his wife as a birthday present.

Based upon the foregoing, Anna's rights are best described as

A. superior to rights of the true owner, the shopkeeper, and his wife because the bracelet was lost.

B. superior to rights of the true owner, but inferior to rights of the shopkeeper and his wife.

C. inferior to rights of the true owner, but superior to rights of the shopkeeper and his wife.

D. inferior to rights of the true owner, the shopkeeper, and his wife.

2. Anna found a valuable tennis bracelet on the sidewalk as she was entering a coffeehouse. She showed it to the manager, who told her to leave it with him. He said he would display the item, hoping that its owner would claim it. Several weeks later, Anna asked about the bracelet. The manager told her that no one had claimed it, and that he had sold the bracelet to a customer for $200, the best offer he received. The bracelet's fair market value was actually $1,000.

Based upon the foregoing, it is most likely that Anna may

A. recover the bracelet from the customer who purchased it.

B. recover $1,000 from the shopkeeper, but not the bracelet from the customer.

C. recover $200 from the shopkeeper, but not the bracelet from the customer.

D. recover neither the bracelet, nor its true value, nor the consideration paid for it.

3. Cory took his radio to a local repair shop to have it repaired. The manager of the store gave him a receipt for the radio and told him to come back in a week. The receipt contained a provision that stated as follows: "Repair shop shall have no liability for damage to the item delivered, regardless of cause." When Cory returned to pick up his radio, he was told that a repairman had accidentally knocked it off a counter where it was being fixed and had broken it beyond repair.

Based upon the foregoing, if Cory seeks to recover the value of his radio from the repair shop, it is most likely that

A. the repair shop is liable to Cory since it was a gratuitous bailee.

B. the repair shop is liable to Cory if it failed to exercise ordinary care.

C. the repair shop is liable to Cory because it is an insurer of his property while the bailment exists.

D. the repair shop is not liable to Cory because it expressly limited its liability.

4. Anna wished to give some jewelry to her friend, Kate, who was on a trip through Asia. She telephoned her best friend, Gina, and asked her to come to Anna's house. When Gina arrived, Anna told her that she had some jewelry that she wanted to leave to her friend, Kate, but that she had never made a will. Anna asked Gina to take the jewelry and see that it was delivered to Kate upon Anna's death. Gina took the jewelry to her own home and kept it for Kate. When Anna died six months later, Gina delivered the jewelry to Kate. Anna was survived by her mother, who is her only heir.

Based upon the foregoing, if Anna's mother sues Kate to recover the jewelry:

A. Anna's mother should recover the jewelry because there was no completed gift.

B. Anna's mother should not recover the jewelry because there was a completed gift.

C. Even if the gift was complete, Anna's mother should recover the jewelry because the gift was *causa mortis.*

D. Anna's mother should not recover the jewelry because Anna's intent was clear.

5. Edward received an inheritance from his father. He wanted to retain access to the funds during his lifetime, but wanted the balance at his death to go to John, his son from a prior marriage. He deposited the funds in an account at First National Bank. The account was entitled "Edward, in trust for John." When Edward died recently, it was discovered that Edward's will left all of his property to his second wife, Emma, who is not John's mother. Emma has made claim to the funds on deposit at First National Bank.

Based upon the foregoing, it is most likely that

A. the funds pass to Emma because the account at First National Bank did not constitute a formal trust.

B. the funds pass to John because the account constituted a valid gift to John during his lifetime.

C. the funds pass to John because Edward manifested a testamentary intent that John have the funds at his death.

D. the funds pass to Emma because Edward retained control of the account until his death.

6. Ann and Maryellen bought adjoining tracts of land. Maryellen built a house on her property. The house encroached 12 feet onto Ann's land. Maryellen used the house sporadically as a vacation home. Since Maryellen worked and had an inconsistent vacation schedule, her visits were infrequent and sometimes as much as four to seven months apart. Ann discovered the encroachment 12 years after the house was built, when she had a new survey made of her property. She told Maryellen to move the house from her land, but Maryellen replied, "That house has been there for more than 10 years, and I'm not moving it."

Based upon the foregoing, in a jurisdiction which has a 10-year statute of limitations for the recovery of land, it is most likely that

A. Ann may force Maryellen to remove the house because Maryellen was not continuously in possession.

B. Ann may force Maryellen to remove the house because Maryellen was not exclusively in possession.

C. Maryellen will not have to remove the house since the house was built 12 years ago.

D. Maryellen will not have to remove the house if she built it in good faith.

7. Todd purchased a large residential lot from Barbara. The deed gave the boundaries of a tract of land that contained 1.7 acres. Unfortunately, the description in the deed mistakenly included .5 acres that Barbara did not own. The .5 acres belonged to Chad, who lived in another state and who had bought the property adjacent to Barbara's as an investment. Todd built a house on the parcel that he purchased from Barbara, but he also landscaped and gardened on the .5 acres owned by Chad. Todd has lived there for 15 years.

Based upon the foregoing, in a jurisdiction that has a 10-year statute of limitations for the recovery of land:

A. Chad can evict Todd since Todd's house did not encroach on the .5 acre tract.

B. Chad can evict Todd because Todd's claim occurred by a mistake and is therefore not "hostile."

C. Chad cannot evict Todd because Todd took possession of the land under color of title.

D. Chad cannot evict Todd because Todd has had hostile and continuous possession for the requisite statutory period.

Questions 8–10 are based upon the following fact situation:

O, the owner of Blackacre, conveyed the land in the following manner:

To A for life, remainder to B and his heirs, but if B ceases to use the property for residential purposes, to C and her heirs.

8. Following this conveyance, it is most likely that A's interest is

   A. a fee simple absolute.

   B. a fee simple determinable.

   C. a life estate determinable.

   D. a life estate.

9. Following this conveyance, it is most likely that B's interest is

   A. a vested remainder in fee simple determinable.

   B. a vested remainder in fee simple on condition subsequent.

   C. a vested remainder in fee simple subject to an executory limitation.

   D. a vested remainder in fee simple because the restriction on B's use of the property is unlawful.

10. Following this conveyance, it is most likely that C's interest is

    A. a contingent remainder in fee simple absolute.

    B. a contingent remainder in fee simple determinable.

    C. a shifting executory interest in fee simple absolute.

    D. a springing executory interest in fee simple absolute.

11. Gene was the owner of a large tract of land called Blueacre. He conveyed the land by deed "to my son, Bill, for life, then to my son's oldest surviving child and his heirs." At the time of this conveyance, Bill had no children.

    Based upon the foregoing, the most likely present state of title of Blueacre is

    A. Bill has a life estate, there is a contingent remainder in Bill's oldest child who survives Bill in fee simple absolute, and Gene has a reversion in fee simple absolute.

B. Bill has a life estate, there is a vested remainder in Bill's oldest child who survives Bill in fee simple absolute, and Gene has a reversion in fee simple absolute.

C. Bill has a life estate, and Gene has a reversion in fee simple absolute.

D. Bill has a life estate, Gene has a reversion in fee simple subject to executory limitation, and Bill's oldest child who survives Bill has a springing executory interest in fee simple absolute.

12. Toni conveyed 200 acres of land "to the Parks and Recreation District, its successors and assigns, so long as the property is used for park purposes."

Based upon the foregoing, it is most likely that

A. if the Parks and Recreation District uses the property for purposes other than a park, Toni must sue the District to recover title to the land.

B. if the Parks and Recreation District ceases to use the property for purposes other than a park, it is a trespasser and Toni may evict the District.

C. if the Parks and Recreation District ceases to use the property for purposes other than a park, Toni may not recover the land, but may sue it for damages.

D. the interest of Toni following this conveyance is a reversion in fee simple absolute. *possibility of reverter*

13. Sherri is the owner of Blackacre. She conveyed the land as follows: "To my daughter, Ann, for life; remainder to her eldest child, if such child reaches age 25." At the time of the conveyance, Ann had no children.

Based upon the foregoing, following this conveyance, Blackacre is most likely held in which manner?

A. Life estate in Ann; contingent remainder in Ann's eldest child; reversion to Sherri

B. Life estate in Ann; vested remainder in fee simple absolute in Ann's eldest child

C. Fee simple absolute in Ann

D. Life estate in Ann; reversion to Sherri in fee simple absolute

14. Arthur owned Greenacre. He devised it by will as follows: "To my son, Roger, for life; remainder to my grandchildren when they reach 21." At the time Arthur died, he had two sons, Roger and Ted. Roger

and his wife have two minor children who were alive at the time of Arthur's death.

Based upon the foregoing, following Arthur's death, Greenacre is most likely held in which manner?

A. Life estate in Roger; contingent remainder in Arthur's grandchildren; reversion in Arthur's heirs

B. Life estate in Roger; vested remainder in Arthur's grandchildren; reversion in Arthur's heirs

C. Life estate in Roger; reversion in Arthur's heirs

D. Life estate in Roger; contingent remainder in Arthur's grandchildren

15. Oliver, the owner of Blackacre, conveyed it to his to friends, "to Anna and Staci, equally." Soon afterwards, Anna conveyed "all my right, title, and interest in Blackacre to John." Thereafter, Anna died. Anna was survived by Staci and by Anna's mother, who is Anna's only heir.

Based upon the foregoing, Blackacre is most likely held in which manner?

A. Blackacre is owned by Staci by right of survivorship.

B. Blackacre is owned by John and Staci as tenants in common.

C. Blackacre is owned by Anna's mother by right of inheritance.

D. Blackacre is owned three-fourths by Staci and one-fourth by Anna's mother.

16. John owned a 200-acre tract of land. He devised this realty by will to "my sisters, Jeanne, Joan, and Jonni, as joint tenants, with right of survivorship." Jeanne conveyed her interest to her husband, Ted. Joan died survived only by her son, Bill.

Based upon the foregoing, it is most likely that the land is held in which manner?

A. Ted, Bill and Jonni are tenants in common.

B. Ted, Bill, and Jonni are joint tenants, with right of survivorship.

C. Ted and Jonni are tenants in common.

D. Ted and Jonni are joint tenants, with right of survivorship.

17. Moira and Colin owned Blackacre as joint tenants with right of survivorship. Blackacre consisted of 100 acres of land on which two houses were situated. Colin began farming the 100 acres. Moira moved into one of the houses and rented the other to Ian.

Based upon the foregoing, it is most likely that

A. Colin must pay Moira one-half of the reasonable rental value of the land he farmed, and Moira must pay Colin one-half of the reasonable rental value of the house she occupied.

B. Colin must pay Moira one-half of the reasonable rental value of the land he farmed; Moira must pay Colin one-half of the reasonable rental value for the house that she occupied and one-half of the rents she received from Ian.

C. Colin must pay Moira one-half of the actual profit he received from the land he farmed; Moira must pay Colin one-half the reasonable rental value of the house she occupied and one-half of the rents she received from Ian.

D. Moira must pay Colin one-half of the rents that she received from Ian.

18. John and Rita held title to Blackacre as joint tenants with right of survivorship. Each year, John made the mortgage payments out of his earnings and paid the taxes out of his savings account. Rita maintained the premises and made all necessary repairs to Blackacre at her own cost.

Based upon the foregoing, it is most likely that

A. John and Rita may seek immediate contribution from each other for a proportionate share of the expenditures made by the other.

B. John is permitted to seek immediate contribution from Rita for her proportionate share of the mortgage and tax payments; Rita is permitted to seek contribution only in an accounting for rents or partition.

C. John is permitted to seek contribution only in an accounting for rents or partition; Rita is permitted to seek immediate contribution from John for his proportionate share of the repairs.

D. Neither John nor Rita is permitted to seek immediate contribution from the other, but each may seek contribution in an accounting for rents or in partition.

19. Landlord leased a commercial building to Tenant for a term of three years. The lease commenced on August 1 and concluded on July 31 three years later. Rent was stated to be "$24,000 annually, payable in monthly installments, due on the first of each month, of $2,000." About one year after Tenant commenced occupancy, Tenant wrote to Landlord giving the latter 30 days' written notice of her intent to terminate the lease.

Based upon the foregoing, it is most likely that

A. since this is a month-to-month periodic tenancy, the notice terminated the lease at the end of the succeeding month.

B. since this is a year-to-year periodic tenancy, one year's notice is required to terminate the lease.

C. since this is a year-to-year periodic tenancy, six months' notice is required to terminate the lease.

D. since this is a term of years tenancy, notice is ineffective to terminate the lease.

20. Landlord leased her home to Tenant for one year. The lease commenced on January 1 and concluded on December 31, with rent being payable monthly. On January 1 following the end of the term, Tenant was still in possession and tendered to Landlord a check for one month's rent. Landlord refused to accept the check and sued to evict the Tenant.

Based upon the foregoing, it is most likely that

A. Landlord may evict Tenant and recover the reasonable rental value of the property for the time of Tenant's holdover.

B. Landlord may evict Tenant and recover the rent stipulated in the original lease for the time of Tenant's holdover.

C. Landlord may evict Tenant and recover the reasonable rental value of the property for the time of Tenant's holdover, or hold Tenant to an additional one-year's term.

D. Landlord may evict Tenant and recover the rent stipulated in the original lease for the time of Tenant's holdover, or hold Tenant to an additional one-year term.

21. Landlord leased an apartment to Tenant on a month-to-month basis for $1,000 per month. When the lease commenced on June 1, Tenant attempted to move into the premises, but was prevented from doing so by the previous occupant, who was wrongfully holding over.

Based upon the foregoing, it is most likely that

A. if the so-called English rule is followed in the jurisdiction, Tenant may sue Landlord for breach of the lease agreement and may also recover damages arising out of the lease, but Tenant may not sue the holdover tenant to evict him.

B. if the so-called American rule is followed in the jurisdiction, Tenant may sue Landlord for breach of the lease agreement and may also recover damages arising out of the lease, but Tenant may not sue the holdover tenant to evict him.

C. if the so-called English rule is followed in the jurisdiction, Tenant may sue Landlord for breach of the lease agreement and may also recover any damages arising out of the lease; Tenant may also sue the holdover tenant to evict him.

D. if the so-called American rule is followed in the jurisdiction, Tenant may sue Landlord for breach of the lease agreement and may also recover any damages arising out of the lease; Tenant may also sue the holdover tenant to evict him.

22. Landlord leased an apartment to Tenant for $500 per month. Landlord orally explained to Tenant that he normally received $700 per month; but since there were "some problems with the place," he would reduce the rent if Tenant would take the premises "as is." Tenant agreed, and the written, signed lease so provided. Upon moving in, Tenant found that the toilets did not work, there was no hot water, and the apartment was infested with rats and cockroaches. Tenant requested that Landlord cure these deficiencies, but Landlord refused, citing their agreement.

Based upon the foregoing, in most jurisdictions (which imply a warranty of habitability into lease agreements), it is most likely that

A. Landlord is liable for these conditions since Tenant cannot waive the warranty of habitability.

B. Landlord is liable for these conditions since Tenant did not effectively waive the warranty.

C. Tenant is liable for these conditions since he accepted the premises in an "as is" condition.

D. Tenant is liable for these conditions since he accepted the premises in an "as is" condition for specifically agreed upon consideration.

23. Landlord leased an apartment to Tenant for $500 per month. Landlord explained to Tenant that he normally let the apartment for $700 per month; but since there were "some problems with the place," he would reduce the rent if Tenant would take the premises "as is." Tenant agreed. Upon moving in, Tenant found that the toilets did not work, there was no hot water, and the apartment was infested with rats and cockroaches. Tenant requested that Landlord cure these deficiencies, but Landlord refused, citing their agreement.

Assume that Landlord is responsible for the conditions on the premises and that Tenant has given Landlord reasonable notice.

Based upon the foregoing, it is most likely that Tenant's remedies are

A. Tenant may treat the lease as breached and move out.

B. Tenant may treat the lease as breached and move out, or Tenant may remain in possession and withhold rent.

C. Tenant may treat the lease as breached, move out, and sue for consequential damages; or Tenant may remain in possession and withhold rent.

D. Tenant may treat the lease as breached, move out, and sue for consequential damages; or remain in possession without any further liability for rent.

24. Landlord leased a house to Tenant for 10 years commencing on January 1. Rent was payable in advance annually on January 1 of each year. Two years later, Tenant transferred possession of the house to Ben "for a period of two years from the date hereof" at a stated annual rental payable in advance to Tenant on January 1. (You may assume that Ben was not aware of the Landlord/Tenant lease.) Ben paid the first year's rent, but failed to pay rent for the second year. Tenant did not pay any rent to Landlord for two years.

Based upon the foregoing, under real property principles, it is most likely that

A. Landlord may hold Tenant and Ben jointly and severally liable for the unpaid rent for the two-year period.

B. Landlord may hold Tenant liable for the unpaid rent for the two-year period, but may not hold Ben liable for the rent.

C. Landlord may hold Ben liable for the unpaid rent, but may not hold Tenant liable for the rent.

D. Landlord may hold Tenant liable for the rent for the two-year period, but may hold Ben liable only for one-year's unpaid rent.

25. Landlord leased an apartment to Jill for two years with an annual rental payable in monthly installments. The lease agreement provided that Jill could not "assign the lease without the prior written consent of Landlord. Any such assignment is void and entitles Landlord to terminate Tenant's interest in the premises." Jill recently has been transferred to another city and wishes to transfer the balance of the lease (less one month) to a co-worker.

Based upon the foregoing, it is most likely that

A. the agreement is enforceable as written, and Jill may not put another tenant into possession.

B. the agreement is unenforceable as written, and Jill may put another tenant into possession.

C. Jill may sublease the apartment, but not assign the lease to another tenant.

D. Landlord would be able to enforce the agreement against an assignee from Jill, whether or not the Landlord acted reasonably.

26. Albert, the owner of Blackacre, approached Brad, the owner of Whiteacre, to request that Brad allow Albert to cross Whiteacre in order to get to a public road that bordered Whiteacre. Brad told Albert that Albert could cross Blackacre "anytime you want." Three years later, Brad decided to fence his land and, in doing so, closed off Albert's access to Whiteacre. Albert sued Brad to establish his right to cross Whiteacre.

Based upon the foregoing, it is most likely that

A. Albert has an easement across Whiteacre, and Brad cannot block Albert's access.

B. Albert has an easement across Whiteacre, but Brad may block Albert's access.

C. Albert has an easement by necessity across Whiteacre, which Brad may not block.

D. Albert has no easement across Whiteacre, and Brad may block Albert's access.

27. Okie, the owner of Blackacre, a 200-acre tract of land, sold the back half of Blackacre to Purchaser. Okie retained the front half, which abutted the county road. The back half of Blackacre was surrounded by other tracts of land owned by persons other than Okie or Purchaser, and was thus landlocked.

Based upon the foregoing, it is most likely that

A. Purchaser has an easement by necessity that will exist only so long as the necessity exists; Okie may decide the location of the easement.

B. Purchaser has an easement by necessity in perpetuity; Okie may decide the location of the easement.

C. Purchaser has an implied easement based upon prior use; but Purchaser may decide the location of the easement.

D. Purchaser has no right to an easement since the land was presumably purchased with knowledge of its condition.

28. Jim owned Tract A on which he operated a used car lot. He obtained from Ken a written easement "for purposes of ingress and egress" across Tract B, which abutted Tract A on its west side. Subsequently, Jim expanded his business by purchasing Tract C, which abutted Tract A on its east side. He then moved the used car business to Tract C and built a repair shop on Tract A.

Based upon the foregoing, it is most likely that

A. Jim may continue to use the easement for ingress and egress to Tracts A and C.

B. Jim may continue to use the easement for ingress and egress to Tract A.

C. Jim may not continue to use the easement for ingress and egress to Tract A.

D. Jim may not continue to use the easement for ingress and egress to Tracts A or C.

29. April owned a one-acre tract of land. After some negotiation, Barbara granted, in writing, to April a specific easement across Barbara's land for ingress and egress to April's one-acre tract. However, this writing was not recorded. Several years later, April divided her tract of land into two half-acre tracts, built houses on each, and sold one lot to Chris and the other to Colleen. The road that April had used runs solely to the land now owned by Chris. However, Chris is willing to permit Colleen to cross his land to have ingress to, and egress from, her house.

Based upon the foregoing, it is most likely that

A. Chris may use the road, but Colleen may not since Colleen's house is located on a nondominant estate.

B. Neither Chris nor Colleen may use the road since neither one owns a dominant estate.

C. Neither Chris nor Colleen may use the road since the easement was given to April and not to Chris or Colleen.

D. Both Chris and Colleen may use the road since both own dominant estates.

Questions 30–31 are based upon the following fact situation:

Staci and Shelley owned adjoining lots. They both wanted to build rather expensive single-family dwellings on their lots, but were concerned that the other might convert her lot to a different use. They entered into a written agreement in which each promised the other that her property would be devoted exclusively to a single-family residential dwelling, and that no structure inconsistent with that use would be erected. This agreement was not recorded, but each retained a copy of it.

30. Assume that Staci built a single-family home on her lot, but that Shelley sold her lot to Bill after telling him about the agreement. Assume, also, that Bill commenced construction of a commercial building on his tract.

Based upon the foregoing, it is most likely that

A. Staci may not enforce the covenant by injunction against Bill because the agreement was not recorded.

B. Staci may enforce the covenant by injunction against Bill, even though the agreement was not recorded.

C. Staci may not enforce the covenant by injunction against Bill because the agreement was not recorded, but may sue Bill for damages.

D. Staci may not enforce the covenant against Bill by either injunction or damages.

31. Assume that Shelley had not sold her home to Bill, but that she herself began construction of a commercial building on her tract.

Based upon the foregoing, it is most likely that

A. Staci may enforce the covenant by injunction or recover damages against Shelley.

B. Staci may enforce the covenant by injunction, but may not recover damages, against Shelley.

C. Staci may recover damages, but not secure an injunction, against Shelley.

D. Staci may not enforce the covenant against Shelley because there is no horizontal privity.

32. Rod owned a commercial building in which Lon was a tenant under lease for a term of 15 years. The lease contained a provision that stated as follows: "Tenant covenants and agrees that Tenant will not use the leased premises for an auto repair business." The lease was recorded. Three years after the date of the lease, Lon transferred "all my right, title, and interest in and to the premises leased from Rod" to Sarah for "a term of 5 years from date hereof." Sarah neither requested nor was given a copy of the Rod-Lon lease. Sarah immediately began using the premises for an automobile repair business.

Based upon the foregoing, if Rod commenced an action against Sarah, it is most likely that

A. Rod may sue Sarah for damages or for an injunction since there is both horizontal and vertical privity, and Sarah took with notice.

B. Rod may sue Sarah for damages or for an injunction, without regard to whether Sarah had notice.

C. Rod may not sue Sarah for damages or for an injunction since there was no horizontal or vertical privity.

D. Rod may not sue Sarah for damages, but may sue for an injunction.

33. Chad owned a house and lot that he orally agreed to sell to Lynn for $230,000. Lynn paid Chad a deposit of $25,000. After several weeks of unsuccessfully trying to find a lender who would loan her the balance of the money to buy the house, Lynn finally called Chad and said: "The deal is off. Send my deposit back." Chad refused to do so.

Based upon the foregoing, if Lynn sued Chad to recover her $25,000 deposit, the most likely result will be that

A. Chad must repay the $25,000.

B. Lynn will not be able to compel Chad to return the $25,000 since there was an enforceable agreement.

C. Lynn will not be able to compel the return of the $25,000 since the agreement is enforceable because of part performance (i.e., her down payment to Chad).

D. Lynn cannot compel the return of the $25,000, but can recover her actual damages.

34. Kyla owned a house and lot in a residential neighborhood. She entered into a written contract with John to sell him the house for $200,000. The contract provided that Kyla would deliver "marketable title" to John on the closing date. In examining title, John discovered that the property was covered by residential restrictions that were also imposed on the other houses in the subdivision. He thereafter refused to perform the agreement.

Based upon the foregoing, the most likely result will be that

A. Kyla may compel specific performance of the agreement or sue for damages since the restrictions presumably enhance the property's value.

B. Kyla may sue for damages since the restrictions benefit the property, but may not compel specific performance.

C. Kyla may not compel specific performance or sue for damages since the title is not marketable.

D. Kyla may not compel specific performance since the title is not marketable, but may sue for damages.

35. Bob purchased a vacant residential lot. He built a house on the lot that violated a municipal ordinance setback requirement of 3 feet from adjoining side lot lines. After building the house, Bob contracted with Carol to sell her the house and lot for $150,000 and to deliver "marketable title, but subject to all covenants, conditions, and restrictions of record." Subsequently, Carol had a survey made of the property and discovered the violation of the setback ordinance. She refused to complete the purchase of the house.

Based upon the foregoing, if Bob commences an action against Carol, it is most likely that

A. Bob may compel specific performance of the contract or sue for damages.

B. Bob may compel specific performance of the contract or sue for damages without regard to the marketability of title since Carol agreed to accept the land subject to restrictions of record.

C. Bob may not compel specific performance of the contract or sue for damages since the mere existence of a setback ordinance makes his title unmarketable.

D. Bob may not compel specific performance of the contract or sue for damages since violation of the setback ordinance makes his title unmarketable.

Questions 36–37 are based upon the following fact situation:

Amy owned a house and lot that she contracted to sell to Jennifer for $200,000. Jennifer made a $20,000 deposit at the time the contract was signed and took possession of the house. While Jennifer was examining the title and arranging for financing, lightning struck the house and burned it to the ground.

36. In a majority of jurisdictions,

A. the risk of loss was upon Amy.

B. the risk of loss was upon Jennifer.

C. the risk of loss was upon Jennifer because she had taken possession of the house.

D. the risk of loss is allocated 10 percent to Jennifer and 90 percent to Amy since Jennifer has paid 10 percent of the purchase price.

37. Assuming Amy had an insurance policy that covered the house against risk of loss by fire for $180,000, it is most likely that

A. the risk of loss is allocated to Amy since she had insured the premises.

B. the risk of loss is allocated to Jennifer, and Amy may keep the insurance proceeds.

C. although the risk of loss is allocated to Jennifer, Amy must credit the insurance proceeds against the purchase price.

D. the risk of loss is allocated to Jennifer, but Amy must rebuild the house to the extent permitted by the insurance proceeds.

38. Ted purchased Blackacre from Olivia. He paid $20,000 of the $200,000 purchase price in cash, and gave Olivia a promissory note for $180,000. The note was secured by a first mortgage lien on Blackacre. Ted then sold his interest in Blackacre to Mary for $30,000. Although Mary advised Ted that she would satisfy the first mortgage, she failed to pay the mortgage, and Blackacre was conveyed to her "subject to an outstanding indebtedness in favor of Olivia in the amount of $180,000, secured by a first mortgage lien on Blackacre." Mary subsequently defaulted on payment of the indebtedness due Olivia. There is still an unpaid balance of $180,000 under the promissory note. The property is now worth $150,000.

Based upon the foregoing, if Olivia forecloses, it is most likely that

A. Olivia may foreclose on Blackacre and hold Mary and Ted personally responsible for the difference between $180,000 and the foreclosure sale price.

B. Olivia may foreclose on Blackacre, but not hold Mary or Ted personally responsible for the difference between $180,000 and the foreclosure sale price.

C. Olivia may foreclose on Blackacre and hold Mary personally responsible for the difference between $180,000 and the foreclosure sales price.

D. Olivia may foreclose on Blackacre and hold Ted personally responsible for the difference between $180,000 and the foreclosure sales price.

39. Ron, the owner of Blackacre, executed a deed conveying Blackacre to his son, Ben, as a gift. The deed was not acknowledged and was not recorded. However, Ron immediately delivered it to Ben. Several months later, Ron told Ben that he (Ron) had received an excellent offer for Blackacre and would like to sell it. Ben retrieved the deed and handed it back to his father, saying, "Here, Blackacre is all yours."

Based upon the foregoing, it is most likely that

A. Blackacre is presently owned by Ron since no consideration was paid by Ben.

B. Blackacre is presently owned by Ron because Ron did not execute an acknowledgment to the deed.

C. Blackacre is presently owned by Ron since Ben returned the deed to him before it was recorded.

D. Blackacre is presently owned by Ben.

Questions 40–41 are based upon the following fact situation:

Norma owned Blackacre. She entered into a written contract with Nikki to sell Blackacre to the latter for $100,000. Nikki paid $20,000 down. The balance was due in cash upon closing. Norma executed a deed conveying Blackacre to Nikki and deposited it with an escrow agent, pending Nikki's payment of the balance of the purchase price. By mistake, the escrow agent mailed the deed to Nikki before the price was paid. Nikki promptly recorded it.

40. Based upon the foregoing, it is most likely that

    A. title to Blackacre is still in Norma, and she may sue to have the recorded deed set aside.

    B. title to Blackacre is vested in Nikki.

    C. title to Blackacre is vested in Nikki, but Norma has an equitable lien on Blackacre for the unpaid purchase price.

    D. title to Blackacre is vested in Nikki, but Norma has a cause of action against the escrow company for negligence.

41. Assume that Nikki went into possession of the land and then sold the property to her sister, Angela, for $80,000 cash. Assume that Nikki delivered a deed to Angela, who had no notice of Norma's interest and believed that Nikki had paid Norma in full.

    Based upon the foregoing, it is most likely that

    A. title to Blackacre is still in Norma, and she may sue to have both deeds set aside.

    B. title to Blackacre is vested in Angela.

    C. title to Blackacre is vested in Angela; however, Norma has an equitable lien against Blackacre for the unpaid purchase price.

D. Title to Blackacre is vested in Nikki since the conveyance to Angela was ineffective.

Questions 42–44 are based upon the following fact situation:

Shelley owned Whiteacre. She conveyed Whiteacre to Gary by general warranty deed for $20,000. Gary went into possession, but subsequently discovered that there was an outstanding mortgage on Whiteacre in favor of First National Bank. This mortgage had been recorded prior to the sale. Shelley has been making payments on the mortgage, so First National is not threatening foreclosure.

42. Based upon the foregoing, it is most likely that

    A. Shelley has breached the covenant of seisin.

    B. Shelley has breached the covenant against encumbrances.

    C. Shelley has breached both the covenant of seisin and the covenant against encumbrances.

    D. Shelley has not breached either the covenant of seisin or the covenant against encumbrances since there is no assertion by Bank of its right to foreclose.

43. Assume that Gary, prior to actually having notice of the outstanding lien, sold Whiteacre for consideration, by general warranty deed, to Randy.

    Based upon the foregoing, it is most likely that

    A. Randy may sue Shelley and Gary for breach of the covenant against encumbrances.

    B. Randy may sue Shelley, but not Gary, for breach of the covenant against encumbrances.

    C. Randy may sue Gary, but not Shelley, for breach of the covenant against encumbrances.

    D. Randy may not sue Gary or Shelley for breach of the covenant against encumbrances.

44. Based upon the foregoing, it is most likely that the measure of damages in Randy's suit against Gary will be

    A. the value of the property at the time Randy discovered the outstanding lien.

    B. restitution of the purchase price paid by Randy to Gary.

    C. the difference between the value of the property at the time of trial and the unpaid balance of the debt.

    D. the unpaid balance of the debt, plus accrued interest.

Questions 45–46 are based upon the following fact situation:

Louis owned Blackacre in fee simple absolute. He conveyed Blackacre to Tim by quitclaim deed several years ago. However, Tim did not record the deed or go into possession. Recently, Louis conveyed Blackacre to Marsha by general warranty deed. Marsha was aware of Tim's purported interest, but (as a consequence of cases covered in her Real Property class at Podunk Law School) did not believe that it was valid. Marsha promptly recorded her deed from Louis. Tim so far has made no claim to the land.

45. Based upon the foregoing, it is most likely that

   A. Louis has breached the covenant of seisin and the covenant of quiet enjoyment.

   B. Louis has breached the covenant of seisin, but has not breached the covenant of quiet enjoyment.

   C. Louis has breached the covenant of quiet enjoyment, but has not breached the covenant of seisin.

   D. Louis has not breached the covenant of seisin or the covenant of quiet enjoyment.

46. Assume that Marsha conveyed Blackacre to Amy by quitclaim deed, and that Amy then conveyed Blackacre to Laura by general warranty deed. All of the transferees had notice of Tim's purported interest. Tim then asserted his interest in the property.

   Based upon the foregoing, it is most likely that

   A. Laura may sue Louis, Marsha, and Amy for breach of the covenants of seisin and quiet enjoyment.

   B. Laura may sue Louis and Amy for breach of the covenant of seisin.

   C. Laura may not sue Louis for breach of covenants because of the quitclaim deed, but may sue Amy for breach of the covenants of seisin and quiet enjoyment.

   D. Laura may sue Amy for breach of the covenant of seisin, and Amy and Louis for breach of the covenant of quiet enjoyment.

47. Seller delivered a deed to Purchaser conveying Blackacre. The deed was not acknowledged by Seller before a notary, although acknowledgment is a requirement for recordation of deeds in the state where Blackacre is located. The recording clerk did not notice the lack of an acknowledgment and recorded the deed. Soon thereafter, Seller sold Blackacre again. This time, the sale was to Buyer. Buyer did not examine the record and had no actual notice of

Purchaser's claim. The state in which Blackacre is located is a "notice" jurisdiction (a purchaser who takes without notice of a prior claim is protected against it).

Based upon the foregoing, it is most likely that

A. Purchaser's interest is superior to that of Buyer since the recording of the deed constituted notice of Purchaser's prior interest.

B. Buyer's interest is superior to that of Purchaser since Buyer had no notice of Purchaser's prior interest.

C. Purchaser's interest is superior to that of Buyer, without regard to whether Buyer had inquiry notice of Purchaser's prior interest.

D. Buyer's interest is superior to that of Purchaser, without regard to whether Buyer had inquiry notice of Purchaser's prior interest.

48. Abbot conveyed Greenacre to Bill, as a gift, by general warranty deed. Bill did not immediately record his deed. Abbot subsequently conveyed Greenacre to Cliff, for consideration, by general warranty deed. Cliff recorded his deed. Subsequently, Bill recorded his deed. Greenacre is located in a jurisdiction that has a "race-notice" recording statute.

Based upon the foregoing, it is most likely that

A. Cliff's interest is superior to Bill's; however, Abbot is liable to Bill for breach of the covenant of seisin.

B. Cliff's interest is superior to Bill's.

C. Bill's interest is superior to Cliff's, and Abbot is liable to Cliff for breach of the covenant of seisin.

D. Bill's interest is superior to Cliff's, and Abbot is liable to Cliff for breach of the covenant of quiet enjoyment.

49. Marlo conveyed Blackacre to Amy, for consideration, by general warranty deed. Amy did not immediately record her deed. Subsequently, Marlo conveyed Blackacre to Connie, for consideration, by general warranty deed. Connie did not record her deed. Then, Connie conveyed Blackacre to Debbie, for consideration, by general warranty deed. Debbie immediately recorded her deed. Finally, Amy recorded her deed. Blackacre is located in a jurisdiction that has a "race-notice" recording statute that protects subsequent purchasers who take in good faith and are the first to record their interest.

Based upon the foregoing, it is most likely that

A. Amy's interest is superior to that of Debbie; however, Connie is liable to Debbie for breach of the covenant of seisin.

B. Amy's interest is superior to that of Debbie; however, Connie is liable to Debbie for breach of the covenant against encumbrances.

C. Debbie's interest is superior to that of Amy since Debbie recorded first.

D. Debbie's interest is superior to that of Amy; however, Marlo is liable to Amy for breach of the covenant of seisin.

50. Ed conveyed Blackacre to Adam, for consideration, by general warranty deed. Adam did not immediately record. Subsequently, Ed conveyed Blackacre to Baker, for consideration, by general warranty deed. Baker had no knowledge of Adam's interest in Blackacre. Shortly thereafter, Adam recorded his deed. Baker then conveyed Blackacre, by general warranty deed and for consideration, to Carl. Carl promptly recorded his deed. Blackacre is located in a jurisdiction that has a "notice" recording statute. This legislation protects subsequent purchasers who take in good faith and without notice.

Based upon the foregoing, it is most likely that

A. Adam's interest is superior to Carl's, if Carl had actual knowledge of Adam's interest at the time Carl purchased.

B. Adam's interest is superior to Carl's since Carl had constructive notice of Adam's interest.

C. Adam's interest is superior to Carl's, without regard to whether Carl had actual or constructive notice of Adam's interest.

D. Carl's interest is superior to Adam's since Carl is treated as a *bona fide* purchaser without notice.

51. Steve conveyed a 200-acre tract of land to Elise, for consideration, by general warranty deed. He gave her an owner's policy of title insurance that stated that marketable title was in Elise. The policy contains an exclusion from coverage for the "rights of parties in possession that are not a matter of record." Prior to this conveyance, Joan had filed suit against Steve to quiet title to 15 acres of Steve's tract on the basis of adverse possession, but the suit had not yet been tried. When Joan added Elise as a defendant in the suit, Elise discovered Joan's claim for the first time.

Based upon the foregoing, it is most likely that

A. the title company is liable to Elise if Joan prevails in her suit to quiet title since Steve did not have title to the 15 acres at the time of conveyance.

B. the title company is liable to Elise for negligent examination of the title to the property, if Joan prevails in her suit to quiet title.

C. the title company is not liable to Elise, but Steve has breached the covenant of seisin if Joan prevails in her suit to quiet title.

D. neither the title company nor Steve is liable to Elise, if Joan prevails in her suit to quiet title.

52. Peter operated a small automobile repair business in the garage at his home. His home was located in a neighborhood zoned for residential use only. Peter was employed elsewhere during the day, and he repaired the automobiles at night. In making these repairs, Peter made significant noise, which disturbed his neighbors' sleep. When they complained to Peter, he responded: "A guy's gotta make a living."

Based upon the foregoing, if Peter's neighbors commence a nuisance action to compel him to discontinue his automobile repair business, it is most likely that

A. Peter is not liable for interfering with his neighbor's sleep since he did not make noise for the purpose of disturbing them.

B. Peter is not liable for interfering with his neighbor's sleep since his actions were not unreasonable.

C. Peter is strictly liable for interfering with his neighbor's sleep since his actions violated applicable zoning laws.

D. Peter is liable since he knew that his actions substantially interfered with his neighbor's sleep.

53. Rick owned a lot on which he intended to build a home. Lita purchased the adjoining lot. She began excavating her lot in order to build a house. In order to protect Rick's lot, she built a retaining wall on her property on the side adjacent to Rick's lot. However, the retaining wall did not hold, and a slide occurred. As a result, part of Rick's lot slid onto Lita's lot.

Based upon the foregoing, it is most likely that

A. Lita is strictly liable to Rick for damage caused by the failure of the retaining wall.

B. Lita is liable to Rick for damage caused by the failure of the retaining wall, only if Rick can prove Lita was negligent in the excavation of her lot.

C. Lita is liable to Rick for damage caused by the failure of the retaining wall since her withdrawal of lateral support to his land was negligent per se.

D. Lita is not liable to Rick for damage caused by the failure of the retaining wall, if she was making a reasonable use of her land.

54. Seller owned a residential lot that Buyer wanted to purchase. Since Buyer had a poor credit rating, Seller agreed to sell the lot to Buyer by an installment sales contract. They executed a written contract, which provided that Buyer had paid 5 percent of the purchase price and agreed to pay the balance due in equal monthly installments over a three-year period. The contract contained a provision that "in the event that Buyer shall default in the payment of the amount due hereunder, Seller has the right to forfeit Buyer's interest in this property and retain all amounts previously paid as liquidated damages." Buyer made one payment, but was then unable to make any further payments to Seller.

Based upon the foregoing, it is most likely that

A. Seller may forfeit Buyer's interest in the property and retain the amount paid as liquidated damages.

B. Seller must judicially foreclose upon Buyer's interest in the property.

C. Seller must give Buyer a reasonable period of time to pay the balance due on the contract and, if Buyer fails to do so, may forfeit Buyer's interest in the property and retain the amount paid as liquidated damages.

D. Seller must give Buyer a reasonable period of time to pay the past due amounts on the contract and, if Buyer fails to do so, may forfeit Buyer's interest in the property and retain the amount paid as liquidated damages.

55. Erin owns a restaurant in a relatively unpopulated area of City. She has operated the restaurant for almost seven years. City recently amended its general plan to provide that the area of City in which Erin's restaurant is located shall be "used for residential purposes only." In fact, the City Council recently enacted an ordinance that zones Erin's property for single-family residential use only.

Based upon the foregoing, it is most likely that

A. the City Council's action is a per se Fifth Amendment taking for which Erin must be paid just compensation.

B. the City Council's action will not be a Fifth Amendment taking, provided that it grants Erin the right to continue her nonconforming use indefinitely.

C. the City Council's action will not be a Fifth Amendment taking, if it grants Erin a substantial period of time in which to continue her nonconforming use.

D. despite the ordinances, Erin has the constitutional right to continue her preexisting use of the premises indefinitely.

56. Five years ago, Omar, the owner in fee simple absolute, conveyed Stoneacre, a 5-acre tract of land, to Church. The relevant words of the deed stated that the conveyance was to "Church [a duly organized religious body having power to hold property] for the life of my only child, Carla, and from and after the death of my said daughter, Carla, to all of my then living grandchildren, provided that Church shall use the premises for religious purposes only."

In an existing building on Stoneacre, Church immediately began to conduct religious services.

Last year, Church granted to Darin a right to remove sand and gravel from a one-half acre portion of Stoneacre in return for royalty payments. Since that time, Darin has regularly removed sand and gravel and paid the royalty to Church. Church has continued to conduct religious services on Stoneacre.

All four of the living grandchildren of Omar, joined by a guardian *ad litem* to represent unborn grandchildren, instituted suit against Church and Darin seeking damages for the removal of sand and gravel and an injunction preventing further acts of removal. There is no applicable statute. Which of the following best describes the likely disposition of this lawsuit?

A. The plaintiffs should succeed because the interest of Church terminated automatically with the first removal of sand and gravel.

B. Church and Darin should be enjoined, and damages should be recovered but impounded for future distribution.

C. The injunction should be granted, but damages should be denied because Omar and Carla are not parties to the action.

D. Damages should be awarded, but the injunction should be denied.

57. Alice conveyed Twinoaks Farm "to Barbara, her heirs and assigns, so long as the premises are used for residential and farm purposes, then to Charles and his heirs and assigns." The jurisdiction in which Twinoaks Farm is located has adopted the common law Rule Against Perpetuities unmodified by statute.

    As a consequence of the conveyance, Alice's interest in Twinoaks Farm is

    A. nothing.

    B. a possibility of reverter.

    C. a right of entry for condition broken.

    D. a reversion in fee simple absolute.

Questions 58–62 are based on the following fact situation:

Thirty years ago, Owen, owner of both Blackacre and Whiteacre, executed and delivered two separate deeds by which he conveyed the two tracts of land as follows: Blackacre was conveyed "to Alpha and his heirs so long as it is used exclusively for residential purposes, but if it is ever used for other than residential purposes, to the American Red Cross." Whiteacre was conveyed "to Beta and his heirs so long as it is used exclusively for residential purposes, but if it is used for other than residential purposes within the next 20 years, then to the Salvation Army." Twenty-five years ago, Owen died, leaving a valid will in which he devised all of his real estate to his brother, Bill. The will had no residuary clause. Owen was survived by Bill and by Owen's son, Sam, who was Owen's sole heir.

For the purpose of this set of questions, it may be assumed that the common law Rule Against Perpetuities applies in the state where the land is located and that the state also has a statute providing that "all future estates and interests are alienable, descendible, and devisable in the same manner as possessory estates and interests."

58. Twenty years ago, Alpha and Sam entered into a contract with Joan whereby Alpha and Sam contracted to sell Blackacre to Joan in a fee simple. After examining title, Joan refused to perform on the ground that Alpha and Sam could not give good title. Alpha and Sam joined in an action against Joan for specific performance. Their action for specific performance will be

    A. granted, because Alpha and Sam together own a fee simple absolute in Blackacre.

    B. granted, because Alpha alone owns the entire fee simple in Blackacre.

C. denied, because Bill has a valid interest in Blackacre.

D. denied, because the American Red Cross has a valid interest in Blackacre.

59. Twenty-nine years ago, the interest of the American Red Cross in Blackacre could best be described as

A. a valid contingent remainder

B. a void executory interest.

C. a valid executory interest.

D. a void contingent remainder.

60. Twenty-four years ago, the interest of Bill in Blackacre could best be described as

A. a possibility of reverter.

B. an executory interest.

C. an executory interest in a possibility of reverter.

D. none of the above.

61. Twenty-seven years ago, a contract was entered into whereby Beta and the Salvation Army contracted to sell Whiteacre to Yates in fee simple absolute. After examining title, Yates refused to perform on the ground that Beta and the Salvation Army could not convey a fee simple. Beta and the Salvation Army joined in an action for specific performance. Their action for specific performance will be

A. denied, because Beta and the Salvation Army cannot convey a fee simple without Owen joining in the deed.

B. granted, because Beta and the Salvation Army together own a fee simple absolute in Whiteacre.

C. granted, because the attempted restrictions on the use of White-acre are void as a violation of the Rule Against Perpetuities.

D. granted, because the attempted restrictions on the use of White-acre are void as a violation of the rule against restraints on alienation.

62. Twenty-nine years ago, the interest of Beta in Whiteacre could best be described as

A. a determinable fee.

B. a fee simple subject to a condition subsequent.

C. a fee simple absolute.

D. a determinable fee subject to an executory interest.

Questions 63–65 are based upon the following fact situation:

Al, who is in possession of and who owns Redacre in fee simple absolute, conveyed Redacre by deed "to my daughter, Bea, for so long as she may live, then to Carla, only child of my deceased son Sam, and her heirs, but if Carla should ever enroll in law school, then to the Legal Aid Society."

63. What interest has Al retained in Redacre?

   A. Reversion

   B. Possibility of reverter

   C. Executory interest

   D. Right of reentry

64. What interest has Carla received in Redacre?

   A. Remainder absolutely (i.e., indefeasibly) vested

   B. Vested remainder subject to complete divestment

   C. Executory interest

   D. Contingent remainder

65. What interest has the Legal Aid Society received in Redacre?

   A. Contingent remainder

   B. Fee simple subject to a condition subsequent

   C. Executory interest

   D. Vested remainder

Questions 66–69 are based upon the following fact situation:

Ten years ago, Alex paid for and received a deed to Flatacre from Steve, who, unbeknownst to her, was a swindler who did not own Flatacre. Alex immediately moved onto Flatacre, built a home, and resided there openly for the next three years. Alex then entered into a written lease of Flatacre with Bill. The terms of that lease gave Bill a one-year tenancy, and thereafter a month-to-month, all at an agreed rental. The agreement also gave Bill the option to purchase Flatacre during Alex's life at a price to be set following an appraisal by a mutually selected appraiser. Bill took possession of Flatacre and faithfully paid rent to Alex for 19 months. Bill then sent Alex timely notice of his desire to purchase Flatacre. However, unbeknownst to Bill, Alex had recently embarked upon a trip around the world and had left instructions with her neighbor, Norma, to receive and deposit rent checks for Alex. Norma received Bill's letter but misplaced it.

Six months later, having patiently awaited a response from Alex, Bill, who had paid no rent since sending the letter to Alex, became disgusted and vacated Flatacre, taking his belongings with him. When Alex returned one year later (six months after Bill left) and observed that Flatacre was vacant, she moved back in and has resided there to date.

Owen, the true owner of Flatacre, has just learned of both Steve's conveyance to Alex and that Alex and Bill had occupied Flatacre. He now seeks to recover possession of Flatacre. The applicable statute of limitations is five years, and there is no requirement concerning the payment of property taxes.

66. If Owen were to bring an action to eject Alex:

   A. Owen would prevail because Alex's right of adverse possession has not vested.

   B. Owen would prevail because he never was aware that Flatacre was being occupied by other persons.

   C. Alex will prevail because she has occupied Flatacre for more than five years.

   D. Alex will prevail because she may tack Bill's possession of Flatacre onto her own.

67. If the local school district were now to acquire title to Flatacre by eminent domain, to whom would the district be obliged to pay "just compensation"?

   A. Alex and Bill, in appropriate proportions

   B. Bill only

   C. Alex only

   D. Owen only

68. Assume for this question that Flatacre consisted of four acres of land and that only one acre (upon which the house was located) had been occupied by Alex and Bill. If Owen's ejectment action was **not** successful, Alex could claim ownership to

   A. none of Flatacre.

   B. the one acre of Flatacre that had been occupied.

   C. all of Flatacre.

   D. the house and an easement of ingress onto and egress from Flatacre.

69. Assume for this question that Owen was successful in his ejectment action against Alex. Bill would owe rent to

   A. no one, since Alex was an adverse possessor and Owen was unaware of Bill.

   B. Steve, since he was the original vendor of Flatacre.

   C. Alex, since their contract called for payment on a month-to-month basis.

D. Owen, because Alex never became owner of Flatacre under the adverse possession doctrine.

Questions 70–71 are based on the following fact situation:

Forty years ago, Owens, the owner in fee simple of Barrenacre, a large, undeveloped tract of land, granted an easement to the Water District "to install, inspect, repair, maintain, and replace pipes" within a properly delineated strip of land 20 feet wide across Barrenacre. The easement permitted the Water District to enter Barrenacre for only the stated purposes. The Water District promptly and properly recorded the deed. One year later, the Water District installed a water main that crossed Barrenacre within the described strip; the Water District has not entered Barrenacre since then.

Thirty-five years ago, Owens sold Barrenacre to Peterson, but the deed, which was promptly and properly recorded, failed to refer to the Water District easement. Peterson built her home on Barrenacre that year, and since that time has planted and maintained, at great expense in money, time, and effort, a formal garden area that covers, among other areas, the surface of the 20-foot easement strip.

Recently, the Water District proposed to excavate the entire length of its main in order to inspect, repair, and replace it, to the extent necessary. Peterson objected to the Water District plans.

70. Peterson asked her attorney to secure an injunction against the Water District and its proposed entry upon her property. The best advice that the attorney can give is that Peterson's attempt to secure injunctive relief will be likely to

   A. succeed, because Peterson's deed from Owens did not mention the easement.

   B. succeed, because almost 40 years have passed since the Water District last entered Barrenacre.

   C. fail, because the Water District's plan is within its rights.

   D. fail, because the Water District's plan is fair and equitable.

71. Assume that Peterson's injunction was not granted, and after the Water District had completed its work, Peterson sued for $5,000 in lost profits she suffered by reason of the disruption to her garden caused by the Water District's entry. Peterson's action probably will

   A. succeed, because her deed from Owens did not mention the easement.

   B. succeed, because of an implied obligation imposed on the Water District to restore the surface to its condition prior to entry.

C. fail, because of the public interest in maintaining a continuous water supply.

D. fail, because the Water District acted within its rights.

72. Bill, owner of Redacre, granted to Jane, owner of adjoining Blackacre, an easement for a right of way across Redacre. After Bill went to live in Europe for a while, Jane moved into possession of Redacre and used it openly and exclusively, paying the taxes, for 20 years. She did not use her easement during this period. Bill returned and tried to evict Jane from Redacre. The court held that Jane had acquired title to Redacre by adverse possession. Jane then sold Redacre back to Bill, who immediately put a chain across the easement. Jane has now brought an action to remove the chain. In most jurisdictions, Jane will

A. lose, because she had become the owner of Redacre.

B. lose, because she did not use her easement for the statutory period of 20 years.

C. lose, because it had become unnecessary to use the easement due to her possession of Redacre.

D. win, because mere nonuse of an easement does not extinguish it.

73. The following events took place in a state that does not recognize common law marriage. The state does recognize the common law estate of tenancy by the entirety, but has no statute on the subject.

Wade Sloan and Mary Jones, who were never married, lived together over a seven-year period. During this time, Mary identified herself as "Mrs. Sloan" with Wade's knowledge and consent. Wade and Mary maintained several charge accounts at retail stores under the names Mr. and Mrs. Wade Sloan, and they filed joint income tax returns using the same names. During this period, Wade decided to buy a home. The deed was in the proper form and identified the grantees as "Wade Sloan and Mary Sloan, his wife, and their heirs and assigns forever as tenants by the entirety." Wade made a down payment of $10,000 and gave a note and mortgage for the unpaid balance. Both Wade and Mary signed the note and mortgage as husband and wife.

Wade made the monthly payments as they became due until he and Mary had a disagreement and he left her and the house. Mary then made the payments for the next three months. She has now brought an action against Wade for partition of the land in question.

The prayer for partition should be

A. denied, because a tenant by the entirety has no right to partition.

B. denied, because Wade has absolute title to the property.

C. granted, because the tenancy by the entirety that was created by the deed was severed when Wade left Mary.

D. granted, because the estate created by the deed was not a tenancy by the entirety.

74. Lawnacre was conveyed to Celeste and Donald by a deed that, in the jurisdiction in which Lawnacre is situated, created a co-tenancy in equal shares with the right of survivorship. The jurisdiction has no statute directly applicable to the problems posed.

Celeste, by deed, conveyed "my undivided one-half interest in Lawnacre" to Paula. Celeste later died. In an appropriate action between Paula and Donald, in which title to Lawnacre is at issue, Donald will

A. prevail, because he must be the sole owner of Lawnacre.

B. prevail, if, but only if, the co-tenancy created in Celeste and Donald was a tenancy by the entirety.

C. not prevail, if he had knowledge of the conveyance prior to Celeste's death.

D. not prevail, because the conveyance by Celeste to Paula automatically caused a severance of Lawnacre.

75. Talbot and Rogers, as lessees, signed a valid lease for a house. Lane, the landlord, duly executed the lease and delivered possession of the premises to the lessees.

During the term of the lease, Rogers verbally invited Andrews to share the house with the lessees. Andrews agreed to pay part of the rent to Lane, who did not object to this arrangement despite a provision in the lease that provided that "any assignment, subletting, or transfer of any rights under this lease without the express written consent of the landlord is strictly prohibited, null and void." Talbot objected to Andrews moving in, even if Andrews were to pay a part of the rent.

When Andrews moved in, Talbot brought an appropriate action against Lane, Rogers, and Andrews for a declaratory judgment that Rogers had no right to assign the lease. Rogers's defense was that she and Talbot were tenants in common for a term of years, and that she had a right to assign a fractional interest in her undivided one-half interest. In this action, Talbot will

A. prevail, because a co-tenant has no right to assign all or any part of a leasehold without the consent of all interested parties.

B. prevail, because the lease provision prohibits assignment.

C. not prevail, because she is not the beneficiary of the nonassignment provision in the lease.

D. not prevail, because her claim amounts to a void restraint on alienation.

76. Ted agreed to rent a yogurt shop from Lin on a year-to-year basis beginning January 1, 2002, at an annual rental of $3,600, to be paid in advance.

On June 30, 2002, Ted sent a valid legal notice to Lin informing her that he was terminating his tenancy as of December 31, 2002. However, Ted did not actually vacate because the new space he had rented as of January 1, 2003, had been painted, and he didn't want to move in until the paint odor had dissipated.

Today is January 2, 2003, and Ted has just received notice from Lin that his annual rent of $3,600 is overdue. Is Ted liable for the sum in question?

A. Yes, because Ted held over after the original lease term had expired.

B. Yes, because Ted failed to give Lin prior notice of his temporary holdover.

C. No, because a holdover tenant is liable for rent only in monthly increments.

D. No, because a holdover tenant is liable for rent only on a pro rata basis.

77. Larry rented a one-bedroom apartment to Tina four months ago. The valid, written lease was for three years with a monthly rent of $250. It also contained a covenant to repair from Larry.

Tina's apartment is one of four within a large 50-year-old house. She has had plumbing problems ever since she moved in. Larry has been slow to respond when Tina complains about problems, and the repairs, even when made, fail to last.

Two weeks ago, Tina's plumbing went on the blink again. The faucets in both the kitchen and bathroom have discharged only lukewarm and cold water for an entire week. To date, Larry has done nothing to remedy the situation, although Tina notified him the day the problem arose.

Tina has been advised by an independent contractor that the plumbing problem could be rectified with a water heater that would cost $500 to purchase and install.

If Tina sued Larry for the $500 necessary to acquire and install the water heater, the theory upon which she would most likely be successful is

A. constructive eviction.

B. breach of contract.

C. breach of implied warranty of habitability.

D. frustration of purpose.

Questions 78–82 are based on the following fact situation:

A certain written lease was entered into, the total contents thereof being as follows:

Commencing November 1, 2001, Landlord rents his grocery store on Main Street in Crosstown to Tenant for four years. The rent shall be $100 per month, payable on the first day of each month.

/s/ "Landlord"

/s/ "Tenant"

On January 31, 2002, Landlord conveyed the grocery store and lease to Owner for consideration. Tenant had no notice of the conveyance and continued paying rent to Landlord until June 30, 2003, when he learned of the sale. That same day, Tenant assigned his entire interest in the lease to Assignee without Owner's knowledge. Tenant vacated the premises, and Assignee took over the premises, but paid no rent.

78. If Owner now sued Tenant for the rent due for the period February 1, 2002, to June 30, 2003, she would

A. collect, because the conveyance made her the landlord.

B. collect, if her conveyance had been recorded, because recording is notice to the world.

C. not collect, because the assignment by Tenant was made before Owner commenced the suit.

D. not collect, because Tenant did not receive notice of the conveyance.

79. If Owner sued Assignee for the rent due under the lease for the months of July, August, September, October, and November 2003, she would collect

A. because one can never occupy land without being obliged to pay the rightful owner for such right.

B. if Assignee had notice of the conveyance to Owner.

C. because they stood in privity of estate.

D. if the assignment by Tenant to Assignee was in writing.

80. In the absence of an applicable statute, the assignment of the lease by Tenant to Assignee was

A. effective, regardless of whether it was in writing.

B. effective, because the lease did not prohibit an assignment.

C. not effective, because leasehold interests cannot ordinarily be assigned.

D. not effective, because Tenant failed to give notice thereof to Owner.

81. Assume Assignee dies testate before the lease expires. Assignee's interest in the lease

A. is terminated, because a leasehold estate cannot survive the death of the lessee.

B. is terminated, unless the land is located in a state that has a statute abolishing the distinction between freehold and nonfreehold estates.

C. survives for the remaining portion of the term and is dealt with as a part of Assignee's estate.

D. reverts to Tenant for the remaining portion of the term.

82. For purposes of this question, assume that Tenant (1) transferred to Assignee his interest in the lease only for the next two years, and (2) reserved the right to reenter the premises if Assignee was in default under the lease. In the absence of an applicable statute, which of the following statements is most accurate?

A. Tenant could not enforce his sublease because it was not authorized by the lease.

B. Tenant could enforce the sublease because it was not prohibited by the lease.

C. Tenant's position would be the same as that of an assignee.

D. Assignee would be liable to Owner for rent because of his privity of estate with Owner.

Questions 83–86 are based on the following fact situation:

After Allen had built a four-story building on his own land, an accurate survey revealed that one of the eaves extended about 6 inches over the land of Bates, his neighbor. The gutters and spouts were constructed so that no water from the house fell upon Bates's land. Bates's land was unoccupied and unimproved at the time, but shortly thereafter Bates began to build a two-story building on her land. In doing so, she excavated several feet down — up to but not over the line between the two properties. Bates did not give Allen any advance notice of the excavation. The excavation was performed in a careful manner, except that no steps were taken to shore up Allen's building. As a result of the excavation, Allen's building settled and cracked and was seriously damaged before Allen knew about the excavation.

83. Bates sued Allen in trespass, praying for damages caused by the overhanging eaves. Judgment will likely be for

   A. Allen, because Bates has suffered no damages.

   B. Allen, because Allen was unaware of the overhang until after the building was completed.

   C. Allen, because the overhang does not interfere with any present or contemplated use of Bates's land.

   D. Bates, without regard to whether Bates is able to show any actual harm to herself.

84. Allen sued Bates for damages to his building as a result of Bates's failure to provide lateral support, but was unable to show that there would have been any settling of Allen's land if it had been in its natural condition without the weight of Allen's four-story building upon it. Judgment will likely be for

   A. Allen, because he is entitled as a matter of right to lateral support from adjoining lands.

   B. Allen, because of Bates's failure to give Allen notice of the excavation.

   C. Bates, because a landowner has no obligation to provide support to artificial structures on her neighbor's land.

   D. Bates, because her duty extends no further than to perform the excavation in a careful manner.

85. Assume for this question that in an action brought by Allen against Bates for damage to Allen's building as a result of Bates's failure to provide lateral support, it was shown that even if there had been no building on Allen's land, it would have subsided as a result of Bates's

excavation. This was because of an especially pliable clay soil condition of which Bates had no reason to be aware prior to the excavation. Judgment will likely be for

A. Allen, because he is entitled to support for his land in its natural condition.

B. Allen, because he is entitled to support for his land in its improved condition.

C. Bates, because she is not liable for the peculiar condition of the soil.

D. Bates, because there was no showing of malice or ill will toward Allen.

86. Assume, for the purposes of this question, that there was no settling or subsidence of Allen's land at the time of Bates's excavation. Because of a carefully designed drainage system upon Bates's land, water was drained from Allen's land. As a result, Allen's building settled and cracked. Allen sued Bates, claiming that Bates was strictly liable for the resulting damage. Judgment likely will be for

A. Bates, because Allen's building must have been constructed on an inadequate foundation.

B. Bates, because she has drained only water, not sand, silt, or other substance of the soil.

C. Allen, because Bates was strictly liable for her conduct.

D. Allen, because Bates was not legally entitled to improve her land in a manner that caused harm to the land of another.

Questions 87–88 are based on the following fact situation:

West is the owner and operator of an oil well on her ranch. West is now, and has been for the past year, dumping waste from the oil well into a slush pit about a quarter of a mile from East's property. East has just begun raising chickens commercially on his property. As the waste is dumped, it settles into the ground and eventually percolates into a small stream that runs through East's property. East had intended to obtain water from this stream for his chickens. If the pollution of the stream is not stopped, East will have to import water for his chickens at a substantial expense. Also, last year West erected bright lights around her oil well that go on at dusk and off at dawn to discourage people from stealing her oil. East lives near his chicken operation with his wife and five-year-old son.

87. West's activities are probably

A. a nuisance, because they have interfered with a commercial enterprise (East's chicken business).

B. a nuisance, because they unreasonably interfere with East's use of his property.

C. not a nuisance, unless she intended to cause injury to East's chicken business.

D. not a nuisance, because her activities preceded East's decision to raise chickens.

88. East's chances of obtaining judicial relief in court with regard to the slush pit would be LEAST aided by evidence that

A. West is wealthier than East.

B. others downstream also suffer hardships as a result of the stream pollution from West's slush pit.

C. West's well is an economically marginal operation.

D. West knew the waste material was percolating into the stream that ran through East's land.

89. Baker, the seller, authorized Smith in writing to sign a contract on her behalf for the sale and purchase of land. Arthur, the buyer, orally authorized Thomas to sign the contract for him. The contract adequately described the terms of the transaction. Smith and Thomas signed the contract: "Baker by Smith, her agent" and "Arthur by Thomas, his agent." Arthur refused to complete the purchase. Baker sued Arthur, who asserted that the contract is unenforceable by reason of the Statute of Frauds. Baker probably will

A. win, because the sales contract was signed by Thomas.

B. win, because her agency contract was in writing.

C. lose, because she did not sign the contract personally.

D. lose, because Arthur's agency contract was not in writing.

90. Jones, as seller, and Williams, as buyer, orally agreed to the purchase and sale of Jones's summer home. Without Jones's knowledge, Williams's wife moved into the house with a key given to Williams for inspection of the premises and spent substantial sums in renovating it. One month later, Jones refused to enter into a written agreement to convey the land or give a deed to Williams. Williams sued Jones for specific performance. Jones contended in rebuttal that evidence of the alleged oral agreement is inadmissible under the Statute of Frauds. The decision probably will be controlled by

A. the doctrine of part performance.

B. the fact that Williams has not tendered the agreed-upon purchase price to Jones.

C. Mrs. Williams's knowledge of the contract.

D. the fact that Mrs. Williams acted without Jones's knowledge.

Questions 91–92 are based on the following fact situation:

Sue owned a five-acre tract of land, one acre of which had previously been owned by Opal, but to which Sue believed she had acquired title by adverse possession. Sue contracted to convey the full five-acre tract to Peg, but the contract did not specify the quality of title Sue would convey.

91. Suppose that at the closing Peg paid the purchase price and accepted a deed. Subsequently, Sue's title to the one acre proves inadequate, and Opal ejects Peg from that acre. Peg sues Sue for damages. Which of the following statements is most accurate with respect to Peg's rights?

   A. Sue's deed was fraudulent, and therefore Peg is entitled to rescission.

   B. The terms of the deed control Sue's liability.

   C. The only remedy available is damages because 80 percent of the transfer was valid.

   D. Peg's rights are based on the implied covenant that title shall be marketable.

92. Suppose Sue's contract had called for the conveyance of "a good and marketable title." Pursuant to that contract, Peg paid the purchase price and accepted a quitclaim deed from Sue. Sue's title to the one acre subsequently proved defective and Peg was ejected by Opal. Peg sued Sue for the reasonable value of the one acre recovered by Opal. Which of the following results is most likely?

   A. Peg will win, because Sue's deed was fraudulent.

   B. Peg will win, because the terms of the deed control Sue's liability.

   C. Sue will win, because the terms of the deed control her liability.

   D. Sue will win, because a deed incorporates the terms of the contract.

93. Four years ago, Owen held Blackacre, a tract of land, in fee simple absolute. In that year, he executed and delivered a quitclaim deed to Price, which purported to release and quitclaim to Price all of the right, title, and interest of Owen in Blackacre. Price accepted the deed and placed it in his safe deposit box.

Owen was indebted to Crider in the amount of $35,000. Three months ago, Owen executed and delivered to Crider a warranty deed, purporting to convey Blackacre in fee simple to Crider in exchange for a full release of the debt he owed to her. Crider immediately recorded her deed.

One month ago, Price recorded her quitclaim deed to Blackacre and notified Crider that she (Price) claimed title. Crider contested Price's claim.

Assume that (1) there was no evidence of occupancy of Blackacre, and (2) the jurisdiction in which Blackacre is situated has a recording statute that requires good faith and value as elements of a subsequent grantee's priority. Which of the following is the best comment concerning the conflicting claims of Price and Crider?

A. Price cannot succeed because the quitclaim deed through which she claims title prevents her from being *bona fide* (in good faith).

B. The outcome will turn on whether Crider paid value within the meaning of the statute requiring this element.

C. The outcome will turn on whether Price paid value (a fact not given).

D. Price's failure to record until one month ago estops her from asserting title against Crider.

Questions 94–96 are based on the following fact situation:

Owen held Farmdale, a large tract of vacant land, in fee simple. The state in which Farmdale is situated has a statute that provides, in substance, that unless a conveyance is recorded, it is void as to a subsequent purchaser who pays value without notice of such conveyance. The following transactions occurred in the order given.

First: Owen conveyed Farmdale, for market value, to Allred by general warranty deed. Allred did not immediately record.

Second: Owen executed a mortgage on Farmdale to secure repayment of a loan concurrently made to Owen by Leon. Leon had no notice of the prior conveyance to Allred and duly recorded the mortgage promptly.

Third: Owen, by general warranty deed, gratuitously conveyed Farmdale to Niece, who duly recorded the deed promptly.

Fourth: Allred duly recorded her deed from Owen.

Fifth: Niece, by general warranty deed, conveyed Farmdale for value to Barrett. Barrett had no actual notice of any of the prior transactions and promptly recorded the deed.

94. Asserting that her title was held free of any claim by Barrett, Allred instituted suit against Barrett to quiet title to Farmdale. If Barrett prevails, it probably will be because

A. Allred's prior recorded deed is deemed to be outside Barrett's chain of title.

B. Barrett's grantor, Niece, recorded before Allred.

C. as between two warranty deeds, the latter one controls.

D. Barrett's grantor, Niece, had no notice of Allred's rights.

95. Asserting that her title was held free of any claim by Leon, Allred instituted suit against Leon to quiet title to Farmdale. Judgment should be for

A. Allred, because Leon is deemed not to have paid value.

B. Allred, because she gave value without notice of any competing interests to Farmdale.

C. Leon, because he recorded before Allred.

D. Leon, because he advanced money without notice of Allred's rights.

96. Assume for this question only that Niece had not conveyed to Barrett. After Allred recorded her deed from Owen, Allred asserted that her title was held free of any claim by Niece and instituted suit against Niece to recover title to Farmdale. Judgment should be for

A. Niece, because she had no notice of Allred's rights when she accepted the deed from Owen.

B. Niece, because she recorded her deed before Allred recorded hers.

C. Allred, because Niece was not a *bona fide* purchaser who paid value.

D. Allred, because she had paid value for Farmdale.

97. Vetter and Prue each signed a memorandum that stated that Vetter agreed to sell and Prue agreed to purchase a tract of land and that the contract should be closed and conveyance made and accepted "by tender of general warranty deed conveying a good and marketable title" on a specified date. The memorandum signed by the parties contains the elements deemed essential and necessary to satisfy the Statute of Frauds except that the purchase price to which they had agreed was omitted. Vetter has now refused to perform the contract, and in an action by Prue for specific performance, Vetter relies upon the Statute of Frauds as a defense.

If, in support of his claim, Prue offers evidence, in addition to the written memorandum, that the parties had agreed upon a purchase price of $35,000, Prue should

A. prevail, because Vetter is estopped to deny the existence of a contract.

B. prevail, because the law will imply a reasonable price where the contractual amount is not stated.

C. lose, because the price agreed upon is an essential element of the contract and must be in writing.

D. lose, because the evidence does not show that the price agreed upon is, in fact, the fair market value of the land.

Questions 98–99 are based on the following fact situation:

The owner of Newacre executed and delivered to Power Company a right-of-way deed for building and maintenance of an overhead power line across Newacre. The deed was properly recorded. Newacre then passed through several intermediate conveyances until it was conveyed to Sloan about 10 years after the date of the right-of-way deed. All intermediate deeds were properly recorded, but none of them mentioned the right of way.

Sloan entered into a written contract to sell Newacre to Jones. By the terms of the contract, Sloan promised to furnish an abstract of title to Jones. Sloan contracted directly with Abstract Company to prepare and deliver an abstract directly to Jones. Abstract Company did so. The abstract omitted the right-of-way deed. Jones delivered the abstract to his attorney and asked the attorney for an opinion as to title. The attorney signed and delivered to Jones a letter stating that, from the attorney's examination of the abstract, it was her "opinion that Sloan had a free and unencumbered marketable title to Newacre."

Sloan conveyed Newacre to Jones by a general warranty deed. Jones paid the full purchase price. After Jones had been in possession of Newacre for more than a year, he learned about the right-of-way deed. Sloan, Jones, Abstract Company, and Jones's attorney were all without actual knowledge that the right of way existed prior to the conveyance from Sloan to Jones.

98. If Jones sues Abstract Company for damages caused to Jones by the presence of the right of way, the most likely result will be a decision for

A. Jones, because he was a third-party beneficiary of the contract between Sloan and Abstract Company.

B. Jones, because the abstract prepared by Abstract Company constitutes a guarantee of Jones's title to Newacre.

C. Abstract Company, because it had no actual knowledge of the existence of the right of way.

D. Abstract Company, because Sloan, rather than Jones, retained its services.

99. If Jones sues Sloan because of the presence of the right of way, the most likely result will be a decision for

    A. Jones, because Sloan is liable for her negligent misrepresentation.

    B. Jones, because a covenant in Sloan's deed to Jones had been breached.

    C. Sloan, because Jones relied upon Abstract Company, not Sloan, for information concerning the title.

    D. Sloan, because she was without knowledge of any defects in the title to Newacre.

100. Venner, the owner of Greenacre, entered into an enforceable written agreement with Brier, which provided that Venner would sell Greenacre to Brier for an agreed price. At the place and time designated for closing, Venner tendered an appropriate deed, but Brier responded that she had discovered a mortgage on Greenacre and would not complete the transaction because Venner's title was not marketable. Venner said that he would pay the mortgage from the proceeds of the sale, and offered to put the proceeds in escrow with any responsible escrowee, for that purpose. The balance due on the mortgage was substantially less than the contract purchase price. Brier refused Venner's proposal. Venner began an appropriate legal action against Brier for specific performance.

    There is no applicable statute. Venner's best legal argument in support of his claim for relief is that

    A. as the seller of real estate, he has an implied right to use the contract proceeds to clear the title being conveyed.

    B. the lien of the mortgage shifts from Greenacre to the contract proceeds.

    C. under the doctrine of equitable conversion, title has already passed to Brier.

    D. no specific provision of the contract has been breached by Venner.

Questions 101–102 are based on the following fact situation:

Albert, the owner of a house and lot, leased the same to Barnes for a term of five years. In addition to the house, there was also an unattached, two-car brick garage located on the lot. Barnes earned her living working in a local grocery store, but her hobby was making small furniture. Barnes installed a work bench, electric lights, and a radiator in the garage. She also laid pipes connecting the radiator with the heating plant inside the house. Four years into the lease, Albert mortgaged the premises to Bank to secure a loan. Barnes was not given notice of the mortgage, but the mortgage was recorded. Six months later, Albert defaulted on his mortgage payments, and Bank began foreclosure proceedings. By this time, Barnes's lease was almost ended. Barnes began removing the equipment she had installed in the garage. Bank brought an action to enjoin the removal of the equipment mentioned above. Both Barnes and Albert were named as defendants.

101. If the court refuses the injunction, it will probably be because

  A. Barnes was without notice of the mortgage.

  B. the circumstances reveal that Barnes did not intend the items involved to become fixtures.

  C. in the absence of a contrary agreement, a residential tenant is entitled to remove any personal property she voluntarily brings on the premises.

  D. the Statute of Frauds precludes Bank from claiming any interest in the equipment.

102. If the equipment at issue had been installed by Albert, but the facts were otherwise unchanged, the effect on Bank's prayer for an injunction would be that the

  A. likelihood of Bank's succeeding would be improved.

  B. likelihood of Bank's succeeding would be lessened.

  C. likelihood of Bank's succeeding would be unaffected.

  D. outcome of the litigation would depend upon whether the mortgage expressly mentioned personal property located on the premises.

103. Chase, as seller, and Smith, as buyer, enter into a written contract for the sale and purchase of land. The contract is complete in all respects except that no reference is made to the type of deed to be conveyed. Which of the following will result?

  A. The contract will be unenforceable.

  B. Chase will be required to convey a marketable title.

  C. Chase will be required to convey only what he owned on the date of the contract.

  D. Chase will be required to convey only what he owned on the date of the contract plus whatever additional rights he might acquire in the land prior to the closing date.

104. Arthur owns a 500-acre farm on which his dwelling is situated. He enters into the following written agreement:

> I, Arthur, hereby agree to sell Walter my dwelling and a sufficient amount of land surrounding the same to accommodate a garden and lawn. Price: $20,000. Received: $1 on account.
>
> /s/ Arthur

Arthur now refuses to perform the agreement. Walter sues for specific performance. Judgment will likely be for

A. Arthur, because Walter did not sign the agreement.

B. Arthur, because $1 is too nominal to constitute consideration.

C. Arthur, because the agreement is ambiguous.

D. Walter, because valid contracts for the sale of land ordinarily are enforceable by specific performance.

Multiple-Choice Answers

1. C The finder of a lost article acquires rights superior to those of everyone except the true owner. The finder holds the lost property in trust or as bailee for the true owner, but may enforce her rights against everyone else. The facts are not clear, but if we assume Anna found the bracelet *outside* the coffeehouse, choice **C** is correct. Anna's rights are subordinate to the true owner's, but she has superior rights as against the shopkeeper and his wife. However, if she found the bracelet *after entering* the coffeehouse, then choice **D** may be the correct answer. When lost property is found on someone's premises, even by one invited to the premises, some courts hold the owner of the premises has rights superior to the finder's. Choice **A** is incorrect because the finder of lost property does not have rights superior to the true owner's. Choice **B** is incorrect for the same reason as choice **A**, and it is also wrong in those jurisdictions that prefer the finder to the owner of the premises.

2. B The facts make it clear that Anna found the bracelet outside the coffeehouse. This contrasts with the facts in Question 1. Anna's rights are therefore inferior to the true owner's, but superior to the rights of the coffeehouse. When she delivered the bracelet to the manager, she had voidable title to the bracelet. When property is acquired by means other than theft, such as by a finder or by voluntary delivery of possession, the possessor generally is held to have a ***voidable title***. When Anna gave the bracelet to the manager, she conveyed only her own voidable title. One having a voidable title may deliver good title to a purchaser who pays valuable consideration and who takes without notice of another person's interest. It is likely that Anna cannot recover the bracelet from the customer, who was a ***bona fide*** purchaser for value. As between Anna and the manager, however, because he converted Anna's property to his own use, he is liable to her for its fair market value. Choice **A** is incorrect. The shopkeeper had a voidable title that he delivered to the customer. Choice **C** is incorrect because Anna can recover the full value of the bracelet. Choice **D** is incorrect in that the shopkeeper is liable to Anna for the full value of the bracelet. The correct answer is choice **B**.

3. B The facts indicate that this was a bailment for mutual benefit. Generally, a bailee in a bailment for mutual benefit must use ordinary care to protect the bailed item while it is in his possession. The issue raised is whether the duty is modified by a blanket waiver of liability. Most courts do not allow bailees for mutual benefit to exempt themselves from liability for ordinary negligence, although they may allow reasonable limits on the extent of liability. Here, the repair shop attempted to remove all liability. Choice **A** is incorrect because the bailment is not gratuitous; it is for the mutual benefit of the bailor and bailee. Choice **C** is incorrect in that bailees are not absolute insurers of the goods delivered to them; ordinarily, they must exercise only ordinary care to protect the goods from damage. Finally, choice **D** is incorrect because the language of the waiver is too broad. It attempts to relieve the repair shop of all liability. The correct answer is choice **B**.

4. **B** A gift is the voluntary transfer of property from the donor to the donee without consideration. In order for a gift to be complete, there must be (1) delivery of the item or a writing that embodies the terms of the gift, (2) an intent to make a gift, and (3) acceptance by the donee. There is nothing in the facts to indicate that Anna made the gift in contemplation of death, so the gift is not a gift *causa mortis*. Choice **C** is therefore incorrect. Delivery of the jewelry was to a third party with instructions to deliver it at her death to a person who was then unavailable to Anna. Gina became the agent of Kate. Gina was acting as an independent person and was not acting as the agent for Anna alone. Therefore the surrender of the jewelry to Gina constituted delivery to Gina, and the gift was complete. The correct answer is choice **B**. Choice **A** is incorrect because there was a completed gift to Kate. Choice **D** is incorrect because intent alone, however clear, is not sufficient to create a valid gift. There must also be delivery and acceptance.

5. **C** The facts describe a bank account commonly referred to as a "Totten trust." The name derives from the case of *In re Totten*. Even though the arrangement does not meet the requirements of a formal trust (because the depositor retains full rights to the funds on deposit during his lifetime), it has been sustained as a trust so long as the donor had a donative intent. Choice **A** is incorrect. Totten trusts are recognized everywhere, though they do not meet the requirements of a formal trust. They are considered a poor man's substitute for a formal will or trust document. Choice **B** is incorrect. Even though Edward manifested his intent to dispose of the account to John, he did not intend to give John control of the funds until he died. The gift was not completed until Edward died. Finally, choice **D** is incorrect. Totten trusts are valid even though the donor retains control over the account until he dies. The correct answer is choice **C**.

6. **A** Because record title to the disputed property is in Ann, Maryellen must prove ownership by adverse possession. Adverse possession

requires possession that is (1) actual; (2) open and notorious; (3) exclusive; (4) continuous; and (5) "hostile," i.e., without the owner's consent; and that satisfies the requirements of the statutory period in that jurisdiction. In this case, the statutory period is 10 years. Although Maryellen's possession clearly satisfies the other three requirements, it appears doubtful that she has been in continuous possession. Her visits were sporadic and there were relatively large gaps in time when she was not in possession. Although the facts state that this was a vacation house, Maryellen's visits would seem too infrequent to satisfy the test of continuous possession. Choice **A** is the best answer. Choice **B** is incorrect on the facts. Maryellen was apparently in exclusive possession of the property upon which her house sat. Choice **C** is incorrect in that compliance with the statutory time requirement is not enough to create title through adverse possession. The three other elements must also be met. Finally, c hoice **D** is incorrect in that good faith is **_not_** an ingredient of adverse possession. Maryellen must prove that her entry upon Ann's land was exclusive (i.e., hostile), open, notorious, and continuous for the requisite statutory period.

7. **D** Adverse possession can ultimately confer good title even when it begins under a mistake as to a property boundary line. Under the majority view, a person who occupies his neighbor's land under the mistaken assumption that he is occupying his own meets the requirements of hostile possession. The interesting twist in these facts is that the land mistakenly occupied by Todd was not his grantor's, but a stranger to his title. Nevertheless, by building and occupying the house and by landscaping and gardening Chad's land, Todd's possession of Chad's half acre was open, hostile, and continuous. Choice **D** is the correct answer because Todd's possession for more than 10 years extinguished all other titles. Choice **A** is incorrect because it was not necessary for the house itself to encroach on Chad's land. Todd occupied Chad's land by landscaping and gardening on it. Choice **B** is incorrect because the majority view is that land occupied by mistake can be the subject of adverse possession. Finally, choice **C** is incorrect in that Todd did not occupy Chad's land under "color of title." Chad did not convey any land to Todd; and Barbara did not have the power to convey Chad's land. Todd's possession is the result of a mistake between two parties unrelated to Chad's title.

8. **D** A's interest is a life estate, pure and simple. There are no words of inheritance, A's interest is confined to his life, and provision is made

for a remainder following A's death. Choice **A** is incorrect because the gift to A is a life estate, not a gift in fee simple. A's interest is limited by the phrase "for life." Choice **B** is incorrect; if there is no fee simple, there is no fee simple determinable. Finally, choice **C** is incorrect in that no condition is attached to the life estate in A.

9. **C**   The interest of B is a remainder following A's life estate. It is a vested remainder because B is born and ascertainable, and there is no condition precedent to its becoming possessory except the close of A's life estate. It is a remainder in fee simple because the conveyance contained words of inheritance ("and his heirs"). However, the gift to B is limited by the restriction that B and his heirs continue to use the property for residential purposes. Restrictions of this kind create one of three categories of fees simple: *a fee simple determinable, a fee simple subject to a condition subsequent*, and *a fee simple subject to an executory limitation*. A fee simple determinable simply lapses on the failure of the restriction. Because the gift here provided for a gift over to C and his heirs, this is not a fee simple determinable. Choice **A** is therefore incorrect. A fee simple subject to a condition subsequent occurs when the grantor reserves the right to terminate the estate and reenter the property on failure of the condition. That is not the case here, and choice **B** is therefore wrong. The correct answer is choice **C**, which correctly states that this is a fee simple subject to an executory limitation. This occurs when the grantor provides for transfer of the property to a third person upon failure of the condition, rather than to himself. Finally, choice **D** is incorrect because the restriction providing for termination of B's interest is not unlawful. B's interest will continue so long as he observes the restriction.

10. **C**   C's interest will come into being only if B fails to observe the restriction imposed by the grantor upon B's remainder. It is not a remainder because it will not come into effect, if it comes into effect at all, by virtue of the *natural* expiration of the prior estate, but only because the prior estate has been disrupted by the failure of B to observe the restriction. Choices **A** and **B** are, therefore, both wrong. As we have seen, B's interest is a fee simple subject to an executory limitation. (See Answer 9.) C's interest is therefore a shifting executory interest in fee simple absolute. The correct answer is choice **C**. Choice **D** is incorrect because a springing executory interest springs from the grantor and divests the grantor of his

interest upon an event occurring in the future. (Example: A conveys "to B and her heirs when B marries.") A shifting executory interest (as in this question), on the other hand, divests another grantee, not the grantor.

11. **A** The conveyance to Bill is a life estate because it contains the words "for life." The interest of Bill's oldest child who survives Bill is a contingent remainder because it takes effect following Bill's life estate and the taker is neither born nor identified at the time of the conveyance. Gene's interest is a reversion since it was not certain at the time of conveyance that the contingent remainder would ever vest. Choice **B** is incorrect in that the remainder cannot be vested because Bill has no children and a remainder cannot be vested if the person who may take it is unborn. If it were vested, Gene would have no reversion. Choice **C** is incorrect in that the remainder in Bill's oldest child who survives Bill is a valid contingent remainder; this choice ignores the interest of a child of Bill who may be born and survive Bill. Finally, choice **D** is incorrect in that the interest of Bill's oldest child who survives Bill will vest at Bill's death, and is thus a remainder. Because it is a present contingent remainder, Gene's interest is a reversion, not a springing executory interest. A springing executory interest is a future interest in a grantee that springs out of the grantor at a date subsequent to the conveyance.

12. **B** The conveyance is a fee simple determinable because the words "so long as" are used to define the condition subsequent. When the grantor conveys all his interest, subject to a condition that may or may not happen, he gives a fee simple determinable. If the condition does occur, possession automatically reverts to the grantor, who then has an immediate right to possession and may immediately bring an action to evict the grantee, who is now a trespasser. The correct answer is choice **B**. Choice **A** is incorrect in that title automatically reverts to Toni upon occurrence of the condition subsequent. Toni may have to sue to evict the District, but not to recover title. Choice **C** is incorrect in that title automatically reverts to Toni. She may recover the land in an action to evict. She is not limited to a suit for damages. Finally, choice **D** is incorrect in that Toni's interest is a possibility of reverter, not a reversion. In a possibility of reverter, the grantor gives a determinable interest with the same quality as his own; in a reversion, the grantor gives a lesser interest than he has; he will recover possession when that interest terminates (e.g., "to A for life," with nothing more).

13. D Ann's interest is a life estate; this is established by the use of the words "for life" in the grant to her. The remainder in Ann's eldest child is a contingent remainder that is invalid under the Rule Against Perpetuities. The Rule states that an interest must vest, if at all, not later than 21 years following a life in being at the date of the conveyance. In these facts, because Ann had no children at the time of the conveyance, there is no certainty that a child born to Ann will have reached the age of 25 within a period of 21 years following the deaths of both Ann and Sherri. For example, suppose that Ann had a child, and then Sherri and Ann both die. The child, who was not a life in being at the time the interest were created, could gain title more than 21 years after Ann and Sherri's deaths (the two lives in being at the time the interest was created). Choice **A** is incorrect because the contingent remainder to Ann's eldest child is void under the Rule. Choice **B** is incorrect because the remainder is void under the Rule and because it cannot be deemed vested in any case because no child of Ann is ascertainable. Following the life estate, there is a reversion to Sherri. Finally, choice **C** is incorrect in that the grant to Ann was clearly limited by the phrase "for life" and is thus a life estate. Choice **D** is the right answer because it correctly reflects the fact that the conveyance to Ann's eldest daughter is void, resulting in a reversion to Sherri following Ann's life estate.

14. C The life estate in Roger is created by Arthur's will; the remainder in Arthur's grandchildren is contingent. Even though two grandchildren were alive at Arthur's death, neither of them has reached the age of 21; and it is possible that neither of them will. The contingent remainder is invalid under the Rule Against Perpetuities. Remember that under the common law, the validity of the gift must be construed as of the time it is created. At the time of Arthur's will, it was not certain that the remainder in his grandchildren would vest within 21 years after lives then in being. It was possible for Arthur to have another child whose children might not become 21 within the requisite period, viewed from the date of Arthur's will. The interest of Arthur's grandchildren is therefore void. Because the interest of the grandchildren is void, the reversion in Arthur's heirs will take effect following Roger's life estate. The correct answer is choice **C**. Choice **A** is incorrect. The remainder in Arthur's grandchildren is void under the Rule Against Perpetuities. Choices **B** and **D** are incorrect because the contingent remainder in the grandchildren is void.

15. **B** There is nothing in the conveyance to indicate that Oliver intended a right of survivorship in Anna or Staci. The modern view is that any ambiguity in a conveyance as between a joint tenancy and a tenancy in common will be resolved in favor of the latter. The conveyance to them will therefore be construed as creating a tenancy in common. A tenancy in common is an estate shared by two or more people at the same time. However, there is no right of survivorship in a tenancy in common. Any of the tenants is able to convey his undivided interest in the property to another, and Anna's gift to John transferred all her interest as tenant in common to John. The correct answer is therefore choice **B**. After Anna's death, the property was owned as tenants in common by Staci and John. Choice **A** is incorrect because as one of two tenants in common, Staci does not have a right of survivorship. Choice **C** is incorrect. John takes Anna's share as a result of the conveyance from her during her life. Following the conveyance, Anna had no interest to bequeath or convey. Finally, choice **D** is incorrect in that Anna had the power to convey her one-half interest to John. John owns an undivided one-half interest, and Staci continues to own only her original one-half interest.

16. **C** The conveyance to Jeanne, Joan, and Jonni created a joint tenancy with right of survivorship. Because they took their interests at the same time and from the same instrument, they have equal ownership interests and equal rights of possession. When Jeanne conveyed her interest to Ted, the joint tenancy was severed as to her interest, and Ted became a tenant in common with Joan and Jonni. Joan and Jonni remained joint tenants as to each other after Jeanne's conveyance to Ted. When Joan died, her interest passed to Jonni by right of survivorship. Thus, Jonni and Ted became tenants in common. However, Ted's interest was as to one-third of the property and Jonni's as to two-thirds. Tenants in common may have unequal shares. The correct answer is choice **C**. Choice **A** is incorrect in that Bill acquired no interest. Joan's interest was extinguished at her death and taken by Jonni by right of survivorship. Choice **B** is incorrect because Ted's interest was not as joint tenant but as tenant in common and Bill took no interest at all. Finally, choice **D** is incorrect because Jeanne could not convey her right of survivorship to Ted. Because Ted did not acquire his interests at the same time or by the same instrument as Joan and Jonni, he cannot be their joint tenant.

17. D As joint tenants, Moira and Colin have equal rights to occupy the premises, subject to the equal rights of the other. Here, the two have reached a reasonable accommodation. Colin is farming the land, and Moira is in possession of the two houses. Normally, a co-tenant has no duty to account to his co-tenant for his use of the property. Colin does not have to account to Moira for the income from his farming, nor does Moira have to account to him for the rental value of the house she occupies. However, when one co-tenant leases all or part of the property to a third person, a different rule applies. The co-tenant now has a duty to account for the rents received. Thus, Moira has a duty to account to Colin for the rents she receives from Ian. The correct answer is choice **D**. Choices **A** and **B** are incorrect in that each co-tenant has a right to possession of the premises and has *no* duty to account for profits produced from occupation of the land or for the fair rental value of his or her occupancy. Choice **C** is incorrect for the same reason.

18. B Each co-tenant has a duty to pay her share of taxes and payments due on mortgages. A tenant who pays a mortgage or taxes is entitled to reimbursement from his co-tenant(s) and can compel contribution from the other cotenants (although if the tenant is in sole possession of the property, he will receive reimbursement only for the amount that exceeds the rental value of the property). John can seek contribution from Rita for the taxes and mortgage. Rita probably cannot seek immediate contribution from John for the cost of necessary repairs. Although courts are split on whether the co-tenant who makes necessary repairs can compel contribution, the majority view is that she can, provided she has notified the other co-tenant of the need for repairs. It does not appear, however, that Rita has notified John of the need for repairs. The correct answer is choice **B**. Choice **A** is incorrect because while John likely has a right to seek contribution, in most states Rita must provide notice before she can seek contribution from John. Choice **C** is incorrect in that John can seek immediate contribution for the mortgage payments and taxes. Finally, choice D is incorrect because John is entitled to seek immediate contribution.

19. D The lease in these facts has a fixed beginning and a fixed end covering a period of three years. It is therefore for a fixed period of time and is a tenancy for years. It is the usual practice, even in a long-term lease, to state the rent as an annual obligation payable in monthly installments. The correct answer is choice **D**. A term of years cannot be terminated by either party during the term. Tenant's notice of her intent to terminate has no legal effect. She is liable for the entire three-year term. Choice **A** is incorrect; this is not a month-to-month tenancy. Choices **B** and **C** are incorrect in two respects; this is not a year-to-year tenancy, and there is no fixed notice requirement for termination of a year-to-year lease — the notice requirement is usually fixed by the parties in the lease agreement.

20. **A** When a tenant wrongfully holds over following termination of the tenancy, the tenant becomes a ***tenant at sufferance,*** and landlord ordinarily has an election of remedies. The landlord may (1) evict the tenant and hold him responsible for the reasonable rental value of the premises during the period of holding over, or (2) hold the tenant to a new term under the original lease terms. Once the landlord makes an election, he may not subsequently choose another remedy. In this case, Landlord has elected not to accept the rent and to evict Tenant. He is entitled to recover possession of the premises and the reasonable rental value for the period of the holdover. The correct answer is choice **A**. Choice **B** is incorrect in that the recovery is not the rent stipulated in the lease, but the reasonable rental value of the premises, which may or not be the stipulated rent. Choice **C** is incorrect on these facts, which show that Landlord has already elected to evict Tenant; he may not repudiate that election. Finally, choice **D** is incorrect for the same reason, and for stating that the lease rent may be recovered in the eviction action, instead of the reasonable value of the premises for the holdover period.

21. **C** Statutes in most states follow the so-called English rule. Under the English rule, Landlord has a duty to deliver actual possession to Tenant. If the landlord fails to deliver possession, as in this case, tenant may terminate the lease and recover damages for the landlord's breach. Or, he may continue the lease and recover damages until either he or the landlord can evict the holdover tenant. Because Tenant has a superior legal right to the premises, Tenant may evict the holdover tenant. Choice **C** is the correct answer because it correctly states Tenant's remedies in a jurisdiction that observes the English rule. Choice **A** is incorrect because it misstates the English rule in that under the rule, Tenant may sue to evict the holdover tenant. Choice **B** is incorrect because it misstates the American rule. Under the American rule, the landlord has the duty only to deliver

the legal right to possession (which Landlord has done), not actual possession. Landlord has no obligation to evict the holdover; it falls to the Tenant to evict him. Finally, choice **D** is incorrect because Tenant cannot sue Landlord for breach or for damages under the American rule; his remedy is to evict the holdover.

22. B In recent decades, the courts have expanded the tenant's right to rely on the landlord's implied warranty of habitability, especially with respect to residential leases. On these facts, there would seem to be little question that the landlord has breached the warranty. Few courts would require that a tenant suffer a lack of toilets and hot water, or an infestation of roaches. Most courts now look unfavorably on a waiver of the warranty by the tenant, especially when the waiver is part of "boilerplate" language in the lease. On these facts, few courts would find a waiver by the tenant, not even in the light of landlord's statement that there were "some problems with the place." Even in those jurisdictions that follow the Uniform Residential Landlord and Tenant Act ("URLTA") in allowing a tenant to waive the warranty, the waiver must be set forth in a separate writing, signed by the parties, and supported by adequate consideration. On these facts. choice **B** is the correct answer. Choice **A** is incorrect in that the majority of states now do permit a tenant to waive the implied warranty of habitability, but only if the necessary formalities are observed. Choice **C** is incorrect in that Tenant did not effectively accept the premises in "as is" condition; in most jurisdictions, the "as is" clause will not be construed as a waiver; some jurisdictions will reject it altogether; and the majority will require compliance with the URLTA, which requires a separate writing supported by consideration to effectuate a waiver. Finally, choice **D** is incorrect in that the waiver, if any, was not in a separate writing nor for a separate, clearly described consideration.

23. C Upon breach by the landlord of the implied warranty of habitability, Tenant has several options: he may simply terminate the lease and move out; he may also recover damages for the landlord's breach; or he may remain in the premises and withhold part or all of the rent until the premises are repaired and made habitable. In some jurisdictions, he may even make the necessary repairs himself and deduct the cost from the rent. Choice **C** correctly describes the tenant's remedies. Choice **A** is incorrect in that it fails to describe all of Tenant's remedies; it omits his right to remain in possession and withhold all or part of the rent. Choice **B** is incorrect in that it is also incomplete; it omits Tenant's remedy of suing for consequential damages or of setting them off against any rent still owed. Finally, choice **D** is incorrect. If Tenant remains in possession, he is not unconditionally relieved of all further liability for rent; his credit against the rent will be calculated by the court in accordance with one of several alternative methods.

24. **B** When Landlord leased the premises to Tenant, Landlord and Tenant were in privity of contract and privity of estate. The transaction described in these facts is a sublease by Tenant, not an assignment of his interests. Tenant put his subtenant in possession only for a period of two years. Because he reserved the balance of his term, he did not make an assignment. Tenant therefore remains liable for the payment of rent unless and until released by Landlord. A sublessee has no privity of estate or contract with the Landlord. For this reason, Ben is not liable to Landlord for the payment of rent. Choice **B** correctly identifies the obligations of the parties. Choice **A** is incorrect in that Ben is not in privity of estate or contract with Landlord and is not liable for the payment of rent. Choice **C** reverses Landlord's remedies against Tenant and Ben, and therefore is incorrect. Choice **D** is incorrect. Landlord may hold Tenant for the entire lease; he may not look to Ben at all.

25. **C** Most provisions against assignment will also include a prohibition against subleasing. Because no such prohibition is contained here, the provision will be construed as only prohibiting assignment. In any event, although the parties may include a prohibition against assignment and subletting, the provision will be construed strictly against the landlord. Because the prohibition in this case is only against assignment, Jill can sublease the apartment to a subtenant for less than her remaining term. Choice **C** is the correct answer. Choice **A** is incorrect because the agreement will not be enforced to prevent Jill from subleasing the premises. Choice **B** is incorrect; the agreement is generally enforceable as written, but only to prevent assignments, not subleases. Finally, choice **D** is incorrect because a growing majority of jurisdictions now requires the landlord to act reasonably even when there is a blanket prohibition against assignment.

26. **D** An easement is an interest in the land of another, and the Statute of Frauds therefore requires that it be in writing. In this case, the right of Albert to cross Brad's land was created orally and did not comply with the statute. Because no easement was created, Brad may interfere with access by Albert at any time. The correct answer is

choice **D**. Choice **A** is incorrect because the easement is not in writing, as required by the Statute of Frauds. At most, Albert had a license that was revocable by Brad at any time. Choice **B** is incorrect in that Albert never legally acquired an easement. If he had, Brad could not now block Albert's access across Whiteacre. An express easement created by a writing that satisfies the Statute of Frauds is enforceable as an interest in land. Finally, choice **C** is incorrect because the facts do not indicate that Albert had no other access to his land. Also, there are no facts to suggest a former common ownership of Blackacre and Whiteacre, a requirement for an easement by necessity.

27. **A** Because both halves of Blackacre were originally owned by Okie and were divided by sale of the back half to Purchaser, Purchaser has an easement by necessity because he is landlocked. The easement arises even though the deed is silent. But an easement by necessity exists only so long as the necessity exists, and the owner of the servient estate may locate the easement so long as he acts reasonably. The correct answer is choice **A**. Choice **B** is incorrect. An easement by necessity does not exist in perpetuity. It is limited in duration to the period of necessity. Choice **C** is incorrect in that there are no facts that indicate that the front half was previously used for access to the back half; further, an easement by necessity does not need a showing of prior use. Finally, choice **D** is incorrect in that Purchaser has an easement by necessity because he is otherwise landlocked. There's nothing in the facts to indicate that Purchaser agreed to renounce the easement because he had found some other means of egress from his property.

28. **B** When an easement is created, the land that benefits from the easement becomes the dominant tenement, and the parcel that is burdened by the easement is called the servient tenement. Here, Tract A was dominant and Tract B servient. When Jim acquired Tract C, it represented additional property that is not part of the dominant tenement. It is therefore not entitled to the benefit of the easement. This is true whether or not the burden upon the servient tenement is increased. The best answer is choice **B**. Although Jim probably may continue his access across Tract B from Tract A, he may not do so from Tract C. (It should be noted that Jim may also have lost his easement through Tract B when he built a repair shop on Tract A. This may have increased the burden on Tract B unreasonably and constituted an unwarranted development of Tract B.) Choice **A** is incorrect because Tract C cannot use the easement owned by Tract

A. Choices **C** and **D** are incorrect in that Jim probably may continue to use the easement for ingress and egress to Tract A. It is still the dominant estate and the beneficiary of the easement.

29. **D** April's entire one-acre tract is the dominant estate. When a dominant estate is subdivided, each subdivided lot has a right to use the easements appurtenant to the dominant estate. (There is one exception to this general principle. If the burden upon the servient estate is substantially greater than at the creation of the easement, the easement will not be available to the subdivided lots. That would not seem to be the case here, in which only one lot is added.) Chris and Colleen may both use the easement, making choice **D** the correct answer. Because the easement is appurtenant to April's land, she may convey it to Chris and Colleen as against Barbara, who seems not to have conveyed her land to a *bona fide* purchaser. (Note: Consider what the result would be if Barbara had sold her parcel to a *bona fide* purchaser who had no notice of the easement.) Choice **A** is incorrect in that, following the sales by April, the easement became appurtenant to both parcels of land, which were carved out of April's one-acre tract. Choice **B** is incorrect in that both Chris and Colleen now own portions of the dominant estate, and a dominant estate may be subdivided so long as the burden on the servient estate is not increased unreasonably. Finally, choice **C** is incorrect because the easement is appurtenant to the land, not a personal right of April. Ownership of the easement passes to succeeding owners of the land.

30. **B** As between two adjoining landowners who have no horizontal privity (i.e., they do not have the relationship of grantor-grantee or other common source of ownership), covenants of the kind involved here are not ordinarily enforceable against the grantee from either of them. On these facts, Staci and Shelly have entered into an agreement that creates reciprocal burdens and benefits. Each is burdened by her promise not to build anything but a residence, and each has the benefit of the other's promise not to build. Under these circumstances, most jurisdictions would agree that the covenants are not enforceable at law as between Staci and Bill. However, if the covenant is a **negative covenant** (i.e., a covenant involving a restriction on building), it will be treated as an equitable servitude enforceable at equity by an injunction. In the case of equitable servitudes, horizontal privity is not required, and two adjoining landlords who are strangers to each other's title can enforce the covenant. Anyone who takes possession of the burdened property

from the original promisor and has notice of the restriction is bound to observe the covenant. Enforcement of an equitable servitude does not require either horizontal or vertical privity. The correct answer is choice **B**. It doesn't matter that the agreement was not recorded because Bill had actual notice of the covenant. Choice **A** is incorrect. Because Bill had actual notice of its terms, the agreement may be enforced against him in equity as an equitable servitude. Choice **C** is incorrect. Staci cannot sue Bill for damages because the covenant does not bind Shelly's grantees at law because of the lack of horizontal privity between Staci and Shelly. It may, however, be enforced in equity by injunction as an equitable servitude. Finally, choice **D** is incorrect because the covenant can be enforced in equity by injunction.

31. **A** The agreement between Shelley and Staci is an enforceable contract based upon mutual promises. It is enforceable at law in an action for damages, and, as between Staci and Shelly, by injunction, provided Staci can show she will suffer irreparable harm. A covenant running with the land is no different from any other contract, except with respect to the rights and duties of assignees from the original parties. Because there is no horizontal privity between Staci and Shelley, this contract is not a covenant running with the land, but an ordinary, enforceable contract between the contracting parties. The correct choice is choice **A**. Choice **B** is incorrect in that Staci may enforce her claim by an action for damages since Shelley is a party to the contract. Choice **C** is incorrect in that Staci may enforce the contract by an injunction, provided she proves that irreparable harm will result from the construction. Finally, choice **D** is incorrect in that horizontal privity is relevant only when enforcement is being sought at law against a grantee from one of the parties. That is not the case here.

32. **D** The transfer from Lon to Sarah was a sublease rather than an assignment because the interest conveyed was less than Lon's entire interest. There is therefore no horizontal privity between Rod and Sarah. However, Sarah took with constructive notice of the covenant in the lease between Rod and Lon because the lease was recorded. The covenant may be enforced by Rod as a equitable servitude; the restraints of privity are not applicable in an action for an injunction. Choice **A** is incorrect in that Rod may not sue Sarah for damages. The covenant does not run at law since there was no privity between Rod and Sarah. Choice **B** is incorrect for the same reason as choice **A**. Finally, choice **C** is incorrect in that Rod

may sue for an injunction without regard to whether there was horizontal or vertical privity since Sarah took with notice of the covenant contained in the lease.

33. **A** The best answer is choice **A**. The Statute of Frauds requires that contracts for the sale of land be in writing. A written memorandum is enough to satisfy the statute if it recites the basic terms and is signed by the party against whom enforcement is sought. One major exception to the statute's requirements is part performance, which recognizes that a party is entitled to enforce an oral contract if he has relied on it to this detriment. However, this exception usually requires acts that are unequivocally referable to the contract (such as taking possession and paying part of the purchase price, or taking possession and making valuable improvements to the property). Payment of a deposit is not usually enough without more. Choice **B** is incorrect because it begs the issue; on these facts, there was no enforceable contract. Choice **C** is incorrect because payment of a portion of the purchase price alone is not ordinarily sufficient to avoid the requirement of a writing. Finally, choice **D** is incorrect in that, because the contract is not enforceable, Lynn can recover her entire deposit.

34. **C** Privately negotiated use restrictions constitute defects in title, without regard to whether they benefit the property. Thus, John is justified in rejecting the title, and choice **C** is the correct answer. Choice **A** is incorrect in that the use restrictions are title defects without regard to whether they benefit the property. Choice **B** is incorrect in that Kyla, without regard to whether the restrictions benefit the property, cannot successfully sue for damages or compel specific performance (since the title is not marketable). Finally, choice **D** is incorrect in that Kyla may not sue for damages since her title is not marketable. To constitute marketable title, the property may not be affected by private use restrictions even if they benefit the property.

35. **D** Violation of a municipal ordinance may or may not make title unmarketable. The violation involved here constitutes a zoning violation. On these facts, most courts would find Bob's title unmarketable. The best answer is choice **D**. Bob cannot successfully seek specific performance or damages from Carol because his title is unmarketable. Choice **A** is incorrect in that Bob's title is unmarketable because there is an existing violation of a municipal zoning ordinance. Choice **B** is incorrect in that the term "restrictions of

record" usually refers to impairments in the record title, not to ordinances, which are *not* part of the title record. Choice **C** is incorrect in that the mere existence of the ordinance does not make title unmarketable. Title is unmarketable because the structure violates the ordinance, not because the ordinance exists.

36. B In a majority of jurisdictions, the risk of loss in the "gap" period between execution of the contract and the closing of title is on the purchaser, whether or not the purchaser has taken possession. The doctrine of equitable conversion treats the buyer as owning the property from the date the contract is signed. The correct answer is choice **B**. Choice **A** represents the minority view or "Massachusetts rule," which places the risk of loss upon the seller until the passing of title, even though the buyer is in possession. Choice **C** is incorrect in that the change of possession is not the basis for allocating the risk of loss in a majority of jurisdictions. The risk is on the buyer not because she is in possession but because she is the buyer. Finally, choice **D** is incorrect because no court would attempt to allocate the loss on these facts.

37. C In a majority of jurisdictions, the risk of loss is upon the purchaser. However, if a vendor has insured the premises, most courts give the purchaser the benefit of the vendor's insurance in order to prevent a windfall to the vendor, who would otherwise get both the insurance proceeds and the purchase price, leaving the purchaser with the full burden of the loss. The purchaser is given an abatement of the purchase price equal to the insurance proceeds. Choice **A** is incorrect. In the majority view, the risk of loss is not allocated to the vendor, whether or not she has secured insured. Choice **B** represents the minority or English rule, which allows the vendor to keep the proceeds on the theory that the insurance policy is a personal contract. However, there are exceptions to this rule, which are not applicable on these facts. Finally, choice **D** is incorrect in that the vendor has no duty to rebuild under either rule; her obligation under the majority rule is only to credit the insurance proceeds against the purchase price.

38. D In the usual transaction between seller and buyer in which the seller provides the mortgage financing, the buyer executes a promissory note as well as a purchase-money mortgage. The mortgage acts as security for the payment of the purchase price balance and is therefore recorded. The promissory note is the buyer's personal promise to pay the balance of the purchase price and subjects him to personal liability. The note is not usually recorded. When the buyer sells the property, if his buyer takes subject to the mortgage but does not assume it, there is no personal liability by the new buyer. The correct answer is therefore choice **D**. Olivia may hold Ted personally responsible for any deficiency since Ted signed the promissory note. Choice **A** is incorrect because Mary took "subject to" the indebtedness and did not assume it. Her statement to Ted that she would satisfy the mortgage is not enforceable because it was not in writing and is negated by the language in the conveyance. Choice **B** is incorrect because Olivia may hold Ted personally liable for payment of the deficiency. Finally, choice **C** is incorrect in that Mary is not personally liable. She took subject to the indebtedness, but did not assume it.

39. D To convey title to a parcel of real estate, it is only necessary to execute and deliver a deed. It is not ordinarily necessary to acknowledge or record the deed. When the deed was executed and delivered to Ben, title passed to him. Ben's title may not be divested, except by a formal conveyance from him The correct answer is choice **D**. Choice **A** is incorrect in that consideration is not required for an effective conveyance; property may be gifted by deed. Choice **B** is incorrect in that an acknowledgment by the grantor is not a necessary requisite to the validity of the deed. In some states, it is merely a prerequisite to recordation. Finally, choice **C** is incorrect in that Ben's return of Ron's deed is ineffective to return title to Ron. Ben must execute a new deed with the usual formalities.

40. A It is not unusual for a deed to be delivered to an escrow agent with instructions to surrender the deed only upon performance of specified conditions. Under these circumstances, title remains in the grantor until the conditions are satisfied. Here, Norma never intended to have the deed delivered until the payment of the balance on closing. Delivery of the deed was ineffective to pass title to Nikki The correct answer is choice **A**. Choice **B** is incorrect because title did not pass to Nikki. Choice **C** is incorrect for the same reason. Choice **D** is also incorrect. Title has not passed to Nikki, and Norma's remedy is to have the deed and recording nullified and set aside. She is not limited to an action in negligence.

41. B The assumptions in this question raise the issue of the rights of a *bona fide* purchaser. There is a conflict among the courts about the rights of a *bona fide* purchaser to receive good title from a seller who has recorded a deed mistakenly delivered to him by an escrow agent.

But all the courts agree that a *bona fide* purchaser from a grantee **who has taken possession** after mistakenly obtaining delivery of the deed and recording it does have priority over the original grantor. The correct answer is choice **B**. Title is in Angela, free of any interest in the property by Norma. However, Norma does have an action against the escrow agent and against Nikki. Choice **A** is incorrect. Because Angela was a *bona fide* purchaser without notice, Norma does not have title. Choice **C** is incorrect. Norma has no further interest in the property. Choice **D** is incorrect. Nikki transferred any interest she may have had in the property — if, indeed, she had any title interest at all — to Angela, a *bona fide* purchaser.

42. **B** A general warranty deed is said to contain six covenants of the grantor. One of these is the covenant of seisin. Another is the covenant against encumbrances. This covenant is a statement by the grantor that there are no mortgages, liens, easements, or covenants affecting the property. Clearly, Shelley has breached this covenant, and the correct answer is choice **B**. Choice **A** is incorrect in that the covenant of seisin does not apply to encumbrances. It states that the grantor owns an indefeasible estate in the quality and quantity she purports to convey. Here, the facts indicate that Shelley did own a fee simple absolute. Choice **C** is incorrect because Shelley did not breach the covenant of seisin. Finally, choice **D** is incorrect in that a covenant against encumbrances is breached when made if there is in fact an encumbrance, whether or not the terms of the encumbrance are being performed.

43. **C** A general warranty deed is said to contain six covenants, among which is a covenant against encumbrances. This covenant is breached, if at all, at delivery of the deed. It is considered a present covenant and does not run with the land. Breach of the covenant creates a chose in action that, at common law, was held to be non-assignable. The general warranty deed from Gary to Randy violated the covenant against encumbrances. The correct answer is choice **C**. Choices **A** and **B** are incorrect in that, under the majority view, Randy may not sue Shelley because the covenant in Shelley's deed does not run with the land. Finally, choice **D** is incorrect because Randy may sue Gary for breach of the covenant against encumbrances in the warranty deed given to Randy by Gary.

44. **D** The usual measure of damages for breach of the covenant against encumbrances is the cost of removing the encumbrance (presumably the unpaid balance of the debt), including accrued, but unpaid,

interest. This puts the grantee in the same position he would have enjoyed if the breach had not occurred. The best answer is choice **D**. Choice **A** is incorrect since this would give Randy a windfall equal to his equity in the property, plus the entire value of the property without encumbrance. Choice **B** is incorrect because it is illogical and does not measure Randy's damage; Randy is out the amount of the mortgage plus interest and the cost of remove it. Finally, choice **C** is incorrect because the value at trial is not what the parties bargained for.

45. **B** A general warranty deed contains six covenants, one of which is the covenant of quiet enjoyment. This states that the grantee will not be evicted by another party with superior rights. However, the covenant is deemed a future covenant, which is not effective against the grantor until the grantee is evicted or finds his possession disturbed. Therefore, Marsha cannot enforce the covenant of quiet enjoyment because Tim has not attempted to disturb her possession. Louis has breached only the covenant of seisin because he has misrepresented his capacity to convey free of Tim's interest. The correct answer is choice **B**. Choice **A** is incorrect in that Louis will not have breached the covenant of quiet enjoyment until Tim attempts to evict Marsha. Choice **C** reverses the correct and incorrect answers. Finally, choice **D** is incorrect in that Louis has breached the covenant of seisin but not the covenant of quiet enjoyment.

46. **D** Refer to Answer 45 above. The covenant of quiet enjoyment has now been breached by Tim's assertion of his interest in the property. The covenant of seisin has also been breached because neither Louis nor Marsha nor Amy owned the interest he or she purported to convey. However, Laura cannot sue Louis for breach of the covenant of seisin because the covenant of seisin is a present covenant, and present covenants do not run with the land to future grantees. She may sue Louis, however, for breach of the covenant of quiet enjoyment since that covenant does run to future grantees (despite the intervening quitclaim deed). Laura may sue Amy for breach of both covenants because Amy was the grantor to Laura. Choice **A** is incorrect in that Laura may not sue Louis for breach of the covenant of seisin for the reasons explained above, and she may not sue Marsha because Marsha's quitclaim deed contained no covenants. Choice **B** is incorrect in that Laura may not sue Louis for breach of the covenant of seisin for the reasons explained above. Finally, choice **C** is incorrect in that Laura may sue Louis for breach

of the covenant of quiet enjoyment, despite the intervening quit-claim deed, because the covenant contained in the warranty deed continues to run with the land to later grantees.

47. **B** A document that is not entitled to be recorded does not give record notice, even if the document is mistakenly accepted for recording. Here, the lack of an acknowledgment compelled the clerk to reject the deed. His failure to do so acted to prevent notice to subsequent purchasers. The correct answer is choice **B**. Choice **A** is incorrect in that the deed from Seller to Purchaser did not constitute notice to Buyer because it was **not** entitled to be recorded. Choice **C** is incorrect in most jurisdictions. Buyer was not put on "inquiry" notice because the facts tell us that Buyer did not examine the record. Even if he had, in most jurisdictions, he would not be required to inquire after a defective deed. In some jurisdictions, however, he would be considered placed on "inquiry" notice; if further inquiry showed the deed between Seller and Purchaser was effective, Buyer's title would be inferior to Purchaser's. Choice **D** is incorrect because we do have to consider whether Buyer was put on "inquiry" notice in those jurisdictions that consider it relevant.

48. **B** In jurisdictions that have "race-notice" recording statutes, the superior title goes to the first person to record an effective deed, provided he takes without actual notice of the prior conveyance. The facts do not indicate that Cliff had notice of the deed to Bill. Cliff is a subsequent purchaser without notice and is thus protected by the recording act and has priority to Greenacre. The correct answer is choice **B**. Choice **A** is incorrect in that Abbott owned the interest he purported to convey to Bill. Thus, he did not breach the covenant of seisin, which states that the seller has the interest he claims to convey. Finally, choices **C** and **D** are incorrect in that Bill's interest is **not** superior to Cliff's. Because this is so, Abbott is not liable to Cliff for breach of any covenant.

49. **A** In a race-notice jurisdiction, a subsequent purchaser can claim the protection of the recording act only if all instruments in her chain of title are recorded. Since the deed from Marlo to Connie was **not** recorded, Debbie cannot claim priority under the applicable recording act. A deed from Connie is a deed that is unconnected to the chain of title because there is no recorded deed from Marlo to Connie. Connie is liable to Debbie for breach of the covenant of seisin because the interest that Connie purported to convey to Debbie was actually owned by Amy. The correct answer is choice **A**.

Choice **B** is incorrect in that the covenant that was breached was the covenant of seisin, not the covenant against encumbrances. The covenant of seisin covers problems in title. The covenant of encumbrances provides against existing mortgages and liens. Finally, choice **C** is incorrect. Though Debbie recorded first, the conveyance to her from Connie was not in the chain of title. Choice **D** is incorrect for the same reason. Also, Marlo is not liable to Amy because Amy's title is protected by the recording system.

50. **D** In states that have "notice" statutes, a subsequent *bona fide* purchaser who takes without notice prevails over a prior grantee who fails to record. When Ed conveyed Blackacre to Baker, Baker took without notice of Adam's interest. Under the applicable "notice" statute, Baker's interest was superior to that held by Adam. Under the "shelter" concept, a subsequent purchaser from Baker (Carl) is treated as a *bona fide* purchaser, even though Adam's deed was recorded before Carl's. The correct answer is choice **D**. Choice **A** is incorrect. Even if Carl had actual knowledge of Adam's claim, he is protected by the superior title of his grantor, Baker, who was a *bona fide* purchaser without notice and was protected under the applicable recording act. Choice **B** is incorrect in that, under the applicable notice statute, Carl prevails. Constructive notice is no better than actual notice. Finally, choice **C** is incorrect in that Adam's interest is not superior to Carl's for the reasons explained above.

51. **C** Title companies insure only against matters disclosed in the record title. They do not go outside the record or make an inspection of the property. Unless Joan had filed a *lis pendens*— a document announcing that a suit affecting land has been started—the record would not disclose Joan's claim of adverse possession. Therefore, the title company is not liable to Elise since Joan's claim is based upon adverse possession (which is *not* a matter of record). The policy expressly excludes the claims of parties based upon possession that are not a matter of record. On these facts, the correct answer is choice **C**. The title company is not liable, but Steve has violated the covenant of seisin because Joan's claim does affect his title. Note, however, that in most states, Joan's attorneys would have filed a *lis pendens*. Choice **A** is incorrect in that, even though Steve may not have title to the 15 acres, Joan's claim is based upon adverse possession (which is not a matter of record in the absence of the filing of a *lis pendens*). Choice **B** is incorrect because title

companies do not inspect properties, and, as a consequence of the policy exclusion, the title company had no duty to determine the rights of parties in possession that were **not** a matter of public record. Finally, choice **D** is incorrect in that Steve may be liable to Elise for breach of the covenant of seisin (if Joan prevails in her suit) since Steve may not actually have owned the disputed 15 acres at the time he conveyed the tract to Elise.

52. **D** If an owner commits a nuisance in the use of his land by interfering with his neighbors' use and enjoyment of their land, he becomes subject to a suit for damages or an injunction. A nuisance occurs when the owner commits an intentional act that is unreasonable. Violation of a zoning ordinance is strong proof that the conduct is unreasonable. Here, Peter is conducting a noisy business in a residential district at night in violation of a zoning ordinance. It would be hard to conceive of a more persuasive case of nuisance. The correct answer is choice **D**. Choice **A** is incorrect. The fact that Peter did not create the noise for the purpose of his neighbors is irrelevant; he knew that auto repair was a noisy business and acted with unreasonable disregard for the sleep of his neighbors. Choice **B** is incorrect in that Peter's actions are unreasonable; they constitute a commercial use in a residential zone and interfered with the neighbors' use of their property, both of which he knew or should have known. Finally, choice **C** is incorrect in that there is no strict liability for nuisance. Plaintiffs must show that defendant's use of his property is a substantial and unreasonable interference with the use and enjoyment of their own property.

53. **A** The right of an owner to lateral support from his neighbor's land is absolute, so long as the former's land is in its natural state. Because the facts suggest that Rick's land was still in its natural state, Lita is liable to Rick, even if she acted with reasonable care in the excavation. The correct answer is choice **A**. Choice **B** is incorrect in that Rick does not have to prove negligence. Lita is strictly liable for failure to provide lateral support when she undertook to excavate her lot to build her house. Choice **C** is incorrect in that the basis for liability in lateral support cases is strict liability, not negligence. Negligence per se is a torts doctrine that is applied to impose liability when a defendant violates a statute that proscribes some act or conduct. Finally, choice **D** is incorrect in that, even if Lita was making reasonable use of her land, she is strictly liable because she undertook the excavation.

54. A However unsympathetic they may be to the concept of forfeiture, most courts will enforce an installment contract for the purchase of land unless the buyer has paid a substantial portion of the purchase price. Here, Buyer paid only 5 percent of the purchase price, an insubstantial amount, and the contract will be enforced as written. Seller may retain all the money as liquidated damages. The correct answer is choice **A**. Choice **B** is incorrect in that most jurisdictions do not require judicial foreclosure, unless the buyer has paid a substantial portion of the purchase price. Finally, choices **C** and **D** are incorrect in that most jurisdictions do *not* require a seller to give the buyer a reasonable period of time to cure arrears or to pay the entire balance prior to forfeiture, but will adhere to the terms of the installment contract.

55. C Although the City Council has the right to pass zoning ordinances that restrict the uses of property, an existing nonconforming user must at least be given a reasonable amount of time in which to continue the nonconforming use in order to protect her investment. Otherwise, a Fifth Amendment "taking" occurs, and the affected landowner must be compensated. Choice **A** is incorrect in that the City Council's action is not, without more, a per se taking; the Council can provided Erin with a substantial time in which to protect her investment. Choice **B** is incorrect in that the City Council is not required to continue Erin's nonconforming use indefinitely, but only to give her a reasonably significant time in which to protect her investment. The reasonableness of the period will depend on all the facts, among which is the fact that Erin's business has existed for seven years. Choice **D** is incorrect in that Erin has no constitutional right to continue her use indefinitely. Her rights are satisfied if City Council gives her a reasonable extension in which to continue her use.

56. B A life tenant may not permit or cause affirmative waste (i.e., permanent injury) upon the land that she is occupying. A condition subsequent is usually characterized by words such as "provided that," "on the condition that," "but if it should happen that" and so on. Where a condition subsequent occurs, the grantor must reenter the land and evict the grantee. Since the exploitation of natural resources constitutes a permanent injury to the land from which they are extracted, an injunction is proper. Damages may also be recovered for the net profits derived from the sale of the gravel and sand. Since Carla might have additional children, it would be proper to impound recovery of such damages for future distribution. Choice **A** is incorrect because even if the language in question requires Church to use the premises only for religious purposes, the plaintiffs would *not* automatically succeed to Stoneacre. Even if Church had a life interest (i.e., the life of Carla) subject to a condition subsequent, it would still be necessary to evict Church. Since there are no words addressing Omar's right to reenter in the event the land is used for other than religious purposes, the requirement might be deemed only a promise made by Church. Choice **C** is incorrect because Omar and Carla cannot possibly succeed to ownership of Stoneacre. Therefore, they would have no right to any damages resulting from the exploitation of natural resources upon the land. Finally, choice **D** is incorrect because the exploitation and extraction of natural resources constitutes a permanent injury to the land from which they are taken, so an injunction is proper. (Note that there is no Rule Against Perpetuities problem since, even if Omar were to have additional children and grandchildren, their interest(s) would vest, if at all, at Carla's death.)

57. **B** A reversion is the estate that remains in a grantor when the grantor (1) has conveyed less than a fee simple estate; and (2) has not, in the same conveyancing document, created a vested remainder in fee simple. A possibility of reverter is the future interest that remains in a grantor after he has made a grant of a fee simple determinable. A right of reentry is the future interest that remains in the grantor after he has made a grant of a fee simple subject to a condition subsequent. An executory interest is a future interest in land (held by someone other than the grantor) that either (1) divests the grantor of a possessory interest at a subsequent date, (2) divests a prior grantee of a possessory interest prior to its natural termination, or (3) becomes effective upon the termination of a fee simple interest (there cannot be a remainder after any type of fee simple interest). Under the Rule Against Perpetuities, no contingent remainder or executory interest is valid unless it will vest, if at all, within 21 years after an ascertainable life that was in being at the time such contingent remainder or executory interest was created or, in the case of a devise, became effective. The grant to Charles is void under the Rule Against Perpetuities since it is an executory interest that might vest outside of the 21-year period. Thus, the purported grant to Charles would be stricken from the conveyancing document. Since language normally associated with a fee simple determinable ("so long as") has been used, the interest held by Alice

would be a possibility of reverter. Choice **A** is incorrect because Alice, by law, has retained a possibility of reverter. Choice **C** is incorrect because language normally associated with a fee simple subject to a condition subsequent was not used in the conveyancing document. Finally, choice **D** is incorrect because Alice did not retain a reversion since a fee simple interest (a fee simple determinable) was granted to Barbara.

58. **C** An executory interest is a future interest in land (held by someone other than the grantor) that (1) divests the grantor of a possessory interest at a subsequent date, (2) divests a prior grantee of a possessory interest prior to its natural termination, or (3) becomes effective upon the termination of a fee simple interest (there cannot be a remainder after any type of fee simple interest). Under the Rule Against Perpetuities, no contingent remainder or executory interest is valid unless it will vest, if at all, within 21 years after an ascertainable life that was in being at the time such contingent remainder or executory interest was created or, in the case of a devise, became effective. A possibility of reverter is the future interest that remains in a grantor after she has made a grant of a fee simple determinable. The American Red Cross received an executory interest from Owen. Since this interest could conceivably vest more than 21 years after a life in being (presumably Alpha would be the measuring life), it is void under the Rule Against Perpetuities. Owen therefore retained a possibility of reverter because Alpha probably received a fee simple determinable (language associated with such a grant, "so long as," was used). Since there is a statute that specifically states that future interests are devisable, Owen's will properly devised Owen's possibility of reverter to Bill. Thus, Joan was justified in asserting that a fee simple was not being offered to her because Bill was not conveying his possibility of reverter in Blackacre. Choice **A** is incorrect because Alpha owns only a fee simple determinable, and Sam owns no interest whatsoever. Choice **B** is incorrect because Alpha owns a fee simple determinable (rather than a fee simple absolute). Finally, choice **D** is incorrect because the interest held by the American Red Cross is void under the Rule Against Perpetuities.

59. **B** An executory interest is a future interest in land (held by other than the grantor) that (1) divests the grantor of a possessory interest at a subsequent date, (2) divests a prior grantee of a possessory interest prior to its natural termination, or (3) becomes effective upon the termination of a fee simple interest. Under the Rule Against Perpetuities, no contingent remainder or executory interest is valid

unless it will vest, if at all, within 21 years after an ascertainable life that was in being at the time such contingent remainder or executory interest was created or, in the case of a devise, became effective. A possibility of reverter is the future interest that remains in a grantor after he has made a grant of a fee simple determinable. The American Red Cross held an executory interest because a remainder cannot follow a fee simple estate (and Alpha had been granted a fee simple determinable). Since there is a possibility that the land might be used for other than residential purposes more than 21 years after Alpha's demise, the executory interest held by the American Red Cross would be void under the Rule Against Perpetuities. Choice **A** is incorrect because a remainder interest cannot follow a fee simple interest (in this instance, a fee simple determinable). Choice **C** is incorrect because the interest held by the American Red Cross is invalid as a consequence of the Rule Against Perpetuities. Finally, choice **D** is incorrect for the same reason that choice **A** is incorrect.

60. A A possibility of reverter is the future interest that remains in the grantor after she has made a grant of a fee simple determinable. An executory interest is a future interest in land, held by one other than the grantor, that either (1) divests the grantor of a possessory interest at a subsequent date, (2) divests a prior grantee of a possessory interest prior to its natural termination, or (3) becomes effective upon the termination of a fee simple interest. Since the grant to the American Red Cross was void under the Rule Against Perpetuities and Alpha had received a fee simple determinable (i.e., the grant to Alpha was characterized by the words "so long as," which are ordinarily associated with a fee simple determinable), Owen, by law, had retained a possibility of reverter. This right was then transferred to Bill. Choices **B** and **C** are incorrect because an executory interest vests the land in someone other than the grantor when the event that terminates the preceding fee simple interest occurs. Finally, choice **D** is incorrect because Owen transferred his possibility of reverter to Bill.

61. A A possibility of reverter is the future interest that remains in the grantor after he has made a grant of a fee simple determinable. A fee simple determinable is an interest in land that is subject to a specified event or condition, upon the occurrence of which the land automatically reverts back to the grantor. Under the Rule Against Perpetuities, no contingent remainder or executory interest is valid unless it will vest, if at all, within 21 years after an ascertainable life that was in being at the time such contingent remainder or executory interest was created or, in the case of a devise, became effective. In this instance, the interest of the Salvation Army is **not** void under the Rule Against Perpetuities because the interest will vest, if at all, within 21 years after a life in being (i.e., Beta). By the terms of the conveyance, the interest must vest, if at all, within 20 years. However, if Beta were to use the land for other than residential purposes beyond the 20-year period, the land would revert to Owen by reason of his possibility of reverter. Thus, Beta and the Salvation Army could not convey a fee simple absolute (i.e., without qualification or condition) to Yates unless Owen relinquished his possibility of reverter. Choice **B** is incorrect because Beta and the Salvation Army did not own a fee simple absolute interest in Whiteacre. Choice **C** is incorrect because the Rule Against Perpetuities does not apply to a possibility of reverter. Finally, choice **D** is incorrect because there is ordinarily no strong public policy precluding a grantor from requiring land to be used for residential purposes.

62. **D** A fee simple determinable is an estate in land that is subject to a specified event or condition, the occurrence of which automatically causes the grantee's interest therein to terminate. An executory interest is a future interest in land (held other than by the grantor) that either (1) divests the grantor of a possessory interest at a subsequent date, (2) divests a prior grantee of a possessory interest prior to its natural termination, or (3) becomes effective upon the termination of any type of fee simple interest. Beta probably has a determinable fee since his use of Whiteacre for other than residential purposes will result in an automatic termination of his interest in the land. However, since the time frame is still within the 20-year period immediately following the conveyance, Beta's determinable fee is subject to an executory interest. The interest of the Salvation Army is an executory interest because it is held by someone other than the grantor and becomes effective upon the termination of a fee simple determinable. Thus, Beta's interest in Whiteacre can "best be described" as a determinable fee subject to an executory interest. Choice **A** is not the best choice because even though Beta has a determinable fee, it is subject to an executory interest. Choice **B** is incorrect because Beta's interest is a determinable fee rather than a fee simple subject to a condition subsequent. The latter type of interest is usually characterized by different language (i.e., "provided that," "on the condition that,"

"but if it should happen that," etc.). Finally, choice **C** is incorrect because Beta possesses a determinable fee rather than a fee simple absolute. A fee simple absolute is an interest that is not subject to any conditions or limitations.

63. **A** A reversion is the estate that remains in a grantor when he (1) has conveyed less than a fee simple estate; and (2) has not, in the same conveyance, created a vested remainder in fee simple. If Carla died without heirs prior to the death of Bea, Redacre would revert to Al. Choice **B** is incorrect because a possibility of reverter is the future interest that remains in the grantor after she has made a grant of a fee simple determinable. In this instance, Carla's interest is a vested remainder in fee simple subject to an executory interest. If the triggering event occurred (Carla enrolling in law school), the land would pass to the Legal Aid Society (rather than back to Al or his heirs). Choice **C** is incorrect because an executory interest is a future interest that is held by a party other than the grantor. Thus, Al could not retain an executory interest. Finally, choice **D** is incorrect because a right of reentry is the future interest that remains in the grantor after he has conveyed a fee simple subject to a condition subsequent. Again, Carla's interest is a vested remainder in fee simple subject to an executory interest (since the Legal Aid Society, rather than Al, would succeed to Redacre in the event that Carla enrolled in law school). Note that the Rule Against Perpetuities does not apply to vested remainders.

64. **B** A vested remainder is a future interest in land that is (1) created in an ascertainable person other than the grantor, (2) not subject to a condition precedent, (3) capable of becoming a possessory estate upon the natural expiration of the preceding possessory estate, and (4) created in the same conveyancing document as the preceding possessory interest. An executory interest is a future interest in land (held by other than the grantor) that either (1) divests the grantor of a possessory interest at a subsequent date, (2) divests a prior grantee of a possessory interest prior to its natural termination, or (3) becomes effective upon termination of a fee simple interest (there cannot be a remainder after any type of fee simple interest). Carla has a vested remainder because she is an identifiable person and her interest is not subject to a condition precedent (rather, her interest is subject to a condition subsequent — enrolling in law school). However, Carla's interest is subject to complete divestment if she were to enroll in law school. Choice **A** is incorrect because

Carla's interest is not absolutely vested (i.e., it is divested if she enrolls in law school). Choice **C** is incorrect because Bea is not divested of her possessory interest prior to its natural termination (i.e., Carla would not have a right to possession until Bea dies). Finally, choice **D** is incorrect because Carla is an identifiable person and her interest is not subject to a condition precedent.

65. **C** An executory interest is a future interest in land (held by other than the grantor) that either (1) divests the grantor of a possessory interest at a subsequent date, (2) divests a prior grantee of a possessory interest prior to its natural termination, or (3) becomes effective upon the termination of a fee simple estate (there cannot be a remainder after any type of fee simple interest). Assuming Carla's interest becomes possessory (i.e., she or any of her heirs survives Bea), she would then have a fee simple subject to an executory interest. The Legal Aid Society would have an executory interest because its right to possession would become effective upon termination of Carla's fee simple interest. Choices **A** and **D** are incorrect because a remainder cannot follow any type of fee simple interest. Finally, choice **B** is incorrect because the Legal Aid Society does not have a fee simple interest in Redacre. Rather, it has a future interest (not one that is present or possessory), which will become effective only if Carla undertakes specified conduct.

66. **D** One obtains title to land by adverse possession where she enters on and exclusively occupies another's land in an open, notorious, and hostile manner throughout the requisite statutory period. (Ordinarily, the statute of limitations period for real property actions is not more than 21 years.) The time during which the land must be occupied by the adverse possessor includes the period during which another occupies the land under or through the possessor's permission. Alex probably acquired title to Flatacre by adverse possession since the continuous occupation of Flatacre by Alex and/or Bill exceeded five years. Choice **A** is incorrect because even though Alex has not been in possession of Flatacre for five consecutive years, Bill's possession of Flatacre could be tacked onto her own. Choice **B** is incorrect because the rightful owner's actual knowledge that his land is being occupied is irrelevant for purposes of determining whether an adverse possession has occurred. Finally, choice **C** is incorrect because the adverse possession period must be continuous. While Alex has been in possession of the land for more than five years total, the two-and-a-half-year hiatus would prevent her

from claiming title to the land by adverse possession (unless she were to benefit, as she does here, from the tacking on of another's possession).

67. **A** One obtains title to land by adverse possession where she enters on and exclusively occupies another's land in an open, notorious, and hostile manner throughout the requisite statutory period. (Ordinarily, the statute of limitations period for real property actions is not more than 21 years.) Where real property is taken by eminent domain, the value of the land paid by the governmental entity is distributed amongst all of the parties with an interest (present or future) therein. If an appraisal of the land by the governmental entity exceeded the purchase price determined by the appraiser chosen mutually by Bill and Alex, Bill would be entitled to the excess. Since Bill has an option to purchase, he has an interest in Flatacre that could become possessory at a subsequent point in time (i.e., if Bill elects to purchase the land during Alex's life). Choice **B** is incorrect because Bill could not rightfully obtain possession to Flatacre without having previously paid the price set by the appraiser. Choice **C** is incorrect because Bill has an interest in Flatacre (i.e., a right to purchase) that could be exercised during Alex's life. Finally, choice **D** is incorrect because, as discussed in the preceding answer, Owen has no interest in Flatacre.

68. **C** One obtains title to land by adverse possession where he enters on and exclusively occupies another's land in an open, notorious, and hostile manner throughout the requisite statutory period. (Ordinarily, the statute of limitations period for real property actions is not more than 21 years.) Where an adverse possessor enters the land under color of title (i.e., pursuant to a defective conveyancing document), he acquires ownership to all of the real property described in the applicable documents. Since Alex entered upon Flatacre pursuant to a deed that she believed was valid, Alex would acquire all of Owen's land that was described in the deed. Choice **A** is incorrect because, under these circumstances, Alex acquired an ownership interest in all of Flatacre by adverse possession. Choices **B** and **D** are incorrect because, having entered Flatacre under color of title, Alex is entitled to the entire property.

69. **D** One obtains title to land by adverse possession where he enters on and exclusively occupies another's land in an open, notorious, and hostile manner throughout the requisite statutory period. (Ordinarily, the statute of limitations period for real property actions is

not more than 21 years.) One who occupies another's land without permission is liable to the latter for *mesne* profits (i.e., the reasonable rental value of the land). If Owen were successful in his ejectment action against Alex (i.e., Alex did not acquire title to the land under adverse possession), Bill's occupancy of Flatacre was wrongful. He therefore would be liable to Owen, the rightful owner, for the reasonable rental value of the land. Choice **A** is incorrect because Owen's lack of awareness of Bill's occupancy would not prevent Owen from successfully suing Bill for the reasonable rental value of the land. Choice **B** is incorrect because Steve never acquired any interest in Flatacre. Finally, choice **C** is incorrect because Alex, not having acquired title to Flatacre by adverse possession, would have had no legal right to rent the land to Bill.

70. **C** An express easement that has been properly recorded is binding upon the successors and transferees of the servient estate (here, Barrenacre). Since the Water District's easement has been recorded, it is binding upon Peterson (even though the deed from Owens to Peterson did not refer to the easement). A purchaser of an interest in land is charged with constructive notice of all documents within the grantor's chain of title. In addition, since the easement expressly included the right to "repair, maintain, and replace" the pipes, the proposed excavation is proper. Choice **A** is incorrect because Peterson is charged with constructive notice of any interest against the land within her chain of title. Choice **B** is incorrect because once an easement is acquired, it is not lost by nonuse alone. An easement may be lost by abandonment, but this does not occur unless the holder of the easement fails to use it *and* has the intention of abandoning it. Finally, choice **D** is incorrect because the fact that the Water District's plan may be "fair and equitable" is irrelevant. It is permissible for the Water District to make any use of Peterson's land that is within the scope of its express easement. There is no indication that the Water District ever intended to relinquish its easement.

71. **D** The holder of an easement is not liable for damages he causes to the servient estate owner as long as his use of the easement is reasonable. Since the Water District acted within the parameters of its express easement, it would have no liability to Peterson for disrupting her garden. Since Peterson is charged with constructive notice of the Water District's easement, she assumed the risk of interference with her garden if replacing the pipes became necessary.

Choice **A** is incorrect because one is charged with constructive notice of all interests within her chain of title. Choice **B** is incorrect because an easement holder is not required to maintain the servient estate in exactly the condition it was in prior to exercising the applicable use. The easement holder's obligation is only to refrain from using the easement in an excessive or an unreasonable manner. Finally, choice **C** is incorrect because the Water District would have to condemn the land and reimburse Peterson if the public had a strong interest in maintaining a continuous water supply.

72. **A** An easement is extinguished when a merger of the dominant and servient estates occurs. When Jane became the owner of Redacre through adverse possession, her easement across that parcel of land ceased to exist because a merger of Blackacre and Redacre had occurred. Choice **B** is incorrect because the mere nonuse of the easement does not extinguish it. An easement may be lost by nonuse if the holder concurrently intends to abandon it. However, there is no indication that Jane intended to abandon the express easement granted to her by Bill. Choice **C** is incorrect because the fact that Jane had no reason to use the easement would not, in itself, extinguish it. Choice **D** is incorrect because the easement was extinguished by reason of the merger of the dominant and servient estates.

73. **D** A tenancy by the entirety can exist only between a husband and wife. Where property is held concurrently and there is uncertainty as to how the estate should be characterized, there is a judicial preference for viewing concurrent ownership as a tenancy in common. Since common law marriage is not recognized in this jurisdiction, Wade and Mary probably would be deemed to be holding the land as tenants in common. Thus, Mary's prayer for partition probably would be granted because a co-tenant may successfully commence an action for partition at any time. Choice **A** is incorrect because, while legally true (i.e., a tenant by the entirety has no right of partition), Wade and Mary probably assumed title to the land as tenants in common; they had not wed, and common law marriages are not recognized in the state in question. Choice **B** is incorrect because the deed named both Wade and Mary as grantees. Choice **C** is incorrect because no tenancy by the entirety was ever created (despite the language in the deed given to Wade and Mary) because Wade and Mary were ***not*** married.

74. B Where one of two co-tenants transfers her interest in joint tenancy property, the transferee and the remaining joint tenant hold the land as tenants in common. A tenancy by the entirety is an estate in land held by a husband and wife, and neither spouse may validly convey his or her interest without the other's consent. A right of survivorship is characteristic of both a joint tenancy and a tenancy by the entirety. The facts are silent as to whether Celeste and Donald were married. Thus, the potential choices must be analyzed assuming both that Celeste and Donald were and were not husband and wife. If the co-tenancy were a tenancy by the entirety, Celeste's attempt to transfer her interest in the land would be invalid, and Donald (as the sole survivor) would be exclusively entitled to Lawnacre. If the co-tenancy were a joint tenancy, Celeste's transfer to Paula would be valid, and Donald would not prevail. Since we don't know what type of co-tenancy was created, choice **B** is the best choice. Choice **A** is not the best answer because Donald would be the sole owner of Lawnacre only if the land was initially conveyed as a tenancy by the entirety. Otherwise, Celeste's conveyance to Paula would, in most jurisdictions, have effectuated a severance of Lawnacre from joint tenancy to a tenancy in common. Choice **C** also is not the best answer because Donald's knowledge of Celeste's conveyance (or purported conveyance) has no effect upon the consequences of her actions. Finally, choice **D** is incorrect because Paula and Donald would not necessarily own Lawnacre as tenants in common as a result of Celeste's actions. If Lawnacre had been left to Celeste and Donald as tenants by the entirety, no severance would have occurred as a result of Celeste's purported transfer of her portion of the land to Paula.

75. C In the absence of an express agreement to the contrary, a co-tenant ordinarily may assign a fractional part of his leasehold interest. Since there was no express agreement to the contrary between Talbot and Rogers, Talbot cannot restrain Rogers from assigning a portion of her interest in the lease. The provision in question declaring any assignment to be null and void was intended to benefit Lane. Thus, Lane would be the only party capable of asserting it. Choice **A** is incorrect because a co-tenant ordinarily has the right to assign a part of his leasehold interest. Choice **B** is incorrect because the provision prohibiting assignment is assertable only by Lane. Finally, choice **D** is incorrect because even though clauses restricting the alienability of leasehold interests are strictly construed, they ordinarily have been sustained.

76. **A** When a tenant remains in possession of leased premises after termination of her tenancy, the landlord can elect to hold her to another term. Since Ted did not vacate the premises on or before December 31, 1997, Lin could elect to hold him liable for another term. With an original term of one year, Ted would be liable for the entire annual rental of $3,600. In some jurisdictions, the landlord cannot elect to hold a tenant liable for the full term when the tenant holds over due to circumstances beyond his control. However, the desire to avoid an unpleasant odor probably would ***not*** constitute a sufficient justification for failing to vacate the leased premises. Choice **B** is incorrect because even if Ted had informed Lin that he would be holding over for a few days, Lin would still have been legally entitled to elect to renew the initial term of the lease. Choices **C** and **D** are incorrect because a landlord may elect to hold a tenant to another full term if that person remains in possession of the premises after his tenancy has concluded.

77. **B** A landlord may be liable for breach of contract by failing to observe a provision within the lease. Since the lease contained a covenant to repair by Larry, his continuous failure to fix the faulty plumbing would constitute a breach of the agreement, entitling Tina to recovery. Choice **A** is incorrect because the constructive eviction doctrine ordinarily does not apply unless the tenant has vacated the premises within a reasonable time after the landlord breaches the implied covenant of quiet enjoyment of the premises. Because Tina has not vacated the premises, she could not successfully assert this theory. Choice **C** is incorrect because the implied warranty of habitability is ordinarily limited to situations involving uninhabitable premises. It is unlikely that the inability of a tenant to obtain hot water for two weeks would satisfy this standard. Finally, choice **D** is incorrect because the frustration of purpose doctrine (i.e., the special purpose of the tenant in leasing the premises, known by the landlord, has been frustrated by a post-contract event over which he had no control) is a defense to the nonpayment of rent rather than a theory for recovering damages.

78. **D** To the extent that an obligor performs his duties under an agreement (including a lease) prior to notification that the contract has been assigned to another, the obligor is relieved of obligations to the assignee. Since Tenant did not learn that the lease had been assigned to Owner until June 30, 2003, he would be relieved of his rental obligations to the extent that he paid rent to Landlord prior to that time. Owner could have avoided this situation by notifying

Tenant that, as of February 1, 2002, rent payments should be paid to her. Choice **A** is incorrect because, even though the conveyance by Landlord to Owner entitled Owner to receive Tenant's rent payments, Tenant was relieved of these obligations to the extent they were performed to Landlord before Tenant knew of Owner's interest. Choice **B** is incorrect because recording of the assignment by Landlord to Owner would not constitute notice of such transaction to Tenant. Tenant must have actually (rather than constructively) been aware of the transfer by Landlord to Owner, and here Tenant did not know of the assignment. Finally, choice **C** is incorrect because the fact that Tenant had assigned his interest in the lease to Assignee prior to the time Owner commenced the lawsuit is irrelevant. If Tenant had been aware of the assignment to Owner, Tenant would have been liable to Owner for the 17 months of rent that became due between February 1, 2002, and June 30, 2003.

79. **C** Where a landlord assigns her entire interest in a leasehold estate to another, her assignee is in privity of estate with the tenant. Where a tenant assigns his entire interest in a leasehold estate to another, his assignee is in privity of estate with the landlord, so long as that person occupies the premises. Since Tenant had assigned his entire interest in the lease to Assignee, Assignee stood in privity of estate with Owner. Choice **A** is incorrect because one can occupy land without paying the rightful owner, such as occurs when one acquires title to real property by adverse possession. Choice **B** is incorrect because Assignee owed rent pursuant to the lease to whoever occupied the position of lessor under the lease. Because Assignee did not make any rental payments, his lack of notice of the conveyance by Landlord to Owner is irrelevant. Finally, choice **D** is incorrect because even though transfers of interests in land must ordinarily be in writing, the Statute of Frauds can be asserted only by a party to the agreement (i.e., Assignee could assert the Statute of Frauds against Tenant, or Tenant could assert the Statute of Frauds against Assignee). Since Owner was not a party to the Tenant-Assignee agreement, she cannot successfully assert the Statute of Frauds.

80. **B** In the absence of a statutory or contractual restriction to the contrary, leasehold interests are alienable. To be enforceable, transfers of interests in land (including a leasehold estate for a term in excess of one year) ordinarily must be embodied in a writing that contains the essential terms and is signed by the party against whom enforcement is sought. Since the lease did not prohibit an assignment, Tenant's transfer of his leasehold interest to

Assignee would be effective, assuming the above elements were met. Choice **A** is incorrect because the assignment of a lease that still has a term in excess of one year must comply with the Statute of Frauds to be enforceable between the parties thereto. (Thus, without a writing, Tenant could **not** successfully sue Assignee for failing to meet his rental obligations to Owner.) Choice **C** is incorrect because leasehold interests are ordinarily assignable. Finally, choice **D** is incorrect because there is no legal requirement that the assignor of a lessee's interest give notice of the assignment to the landlord.

81. **C** A leasehold estate is ordinarily alienable, inheritable, and devisable. Since Assignee died testate, his interest in the lease would pass to whomever he had devised such property to. The devisee, however, would also be liable for any obligations of Assignee under the lease. Choice **A** is incorrect because a leasehold interest ordinarily survives the death of a lessee. Choice **B** is also incorrect because even if the distinction between freehold (fees, fee tails, and life estates) and nonfreehold estates was abolished, such action would have no effect upon Assignee's interest in the lease because leasehold interests are ordinarily devisable. Finally, choice **D** is incorrect because a leasehold interest does **not** automatically revert to an assignor upon the assignee's death.

82. **B** A leasehold estate is ordinarily alienable, inheritable, and devisable. Since the lease did not prohibit a transfer by Tenant, Tenant was free to sublease it. Choice **A** is incorrect because, absent a contractual or statutory provision to the contrary, a leasehold interest ordinarily may be subleased. Choice **C** is incorrect because a sublessee (as opposed to an assignee) does not stand in privity of estate with the landlord. In addition, for one to be an assignee, the assignor must have parted with his entire estate under the lease. Finally, choice **D** is incorrect because a sublessee does **not** stand in privity of estate with the landlord. (A sublessee, however, may be liable to the landlord if the landlord is deemed to be a third-party beneficiary of the sublease between the lessee and sublessee.)

83. **D** A trespass occurs when the defendant has intentionally intruded upon, beneath, or above the surface of the plaintiff's land. Restatement (Second) of Torts §159. If a trespass has occurred, the defendant is liable for at least nominal damages. The overhanging eaves would constitute a trespass. Restatement (Second) of Torts §159(f), illus. 1. Choice **A** is incorrect because a trespasser is liable to the plaintiff for at least nominal damages (whether or not the plaintiff

has suffered any actual harm). Restatement (Second) of Torts §158. Choice **B** is incorrect because Allen's intent to build the structure whose eaves now overhang Bates's land would constitute sufficient "intent" to intrude upon Bates's land. Choice **C** is incorrect because it is not necessary for Bates to prove that Allen's action actually interfered with her use of the land to recover in trespass.

84. C A landowner is strictly liable for the removal or alteration of his property in a manner that causes an adjacent owner's land in its natural state to subside. However, where an improvement is damaged because of a lack of lateral support, the defendant is strictly liable for damages only if the plaintiff can show that his land would have subsided even had the improvement not existed. Since Allen is unable to show that there would have been any settling or falling of his land if it had been in its natural condition, under the majority view, Bates would not be strictly liable to Allen as a result of the obligation to provide lateral support (although Allen could still bring a negligence action against Bates). Choice **A** is incorrect because Bates is only strictly liable to support Allen's land in its natural state. Choice **B** is incorrect because the mere fact that Bates failed to give Allen notice of the excavation is not a basis for recovery by Allen. Finally, choice **D** is incorrect because, in addition to the obligation to perform an excavation in a careful manner (i.e., in a nonnegligent manner), a landowner also has the obligation to provide lateral support so that a neighbor's adjoining land in its natural state will not subside.

85. A A landowner is strictly liable for the removal or alteration of his property in a manner which causes an adjacent owner's land in its natural state to subside. However, where an improvement is damaged because of a lack of lateral support, the defendant is strictly liable for damages only if the plaintiff can show that his land would have subsided even had the improvement not existed. Since Allen's land, even in its natural condition, would have subsided as a result of Bates' excavation, Bates is absolutely liable for the damages sustained by Allen. Choice **B** is incorrect because a landowner is ordinarily *not* entitled to support for her land in an improved condition (i.e., one is ordinarily entitled to support for her land only in its natural state). Choice **C** is incorrect because liability for failure to provide lateral support when required is absolute (i.e., foreseeability of harm to the adjoining landowner is irrelevant). Finally, Choice **D** is incorrect because liability for failure to provide lateral support is not predicated upon the malice or ill will of the party undertaking the excavation.

86. **B** A landowner ordinarily may modify or alter the flow of diffused surface waters without being held strictly liable for the consequences of his actions. Thus, Bates would not be strictly liable to Allen for her actions. Choice **A** is incorrect because there is no indication from the facts that Allen's building rested on an inadequate foundation. Choices **C** and **D** are incorrect because there is no rule imposing strict liability on a neighbor simply because improvement efforts resulted in harm to a neighbor's real property.

87. **B** A nuisance occurs when the defendant has, in a nontrespassory manner, caused an unreasonable and substantial interference with, or impairment of, the plaintiff's use of his land. In determining whether there has been an unreasonable interference with the plaintiff's use and enjoyment of his land, the court ordinarily will weigh (1) the social value or utility of the defendant's conduct or activity to the area, (2) the suitability of the defendant's activity to the character of the locality, and (3) the impracticability of precluding or avoiding the defendant's conduct. Polluting a stream used by an adjacent landowner and interfering with his ability to sleep together probably constitute an unreasonable interference, by West, with East's use of his property. Choice **A** is incorrect because the fact that one has interfered with another's commercial enterprise does not automatically require a finding that the former's activity is a nuisance (i.e., the interference must be unreasonable, and the utility to the community of both enterprises must be weighed). Choice **C** is incorrect because one may have liability for nuisance even though she did not intend to injure the plaintiff. It is only necessary that the defendant have intentionally or consciously engaged in the activity that unreasonably interfered with the plaintiff's use of his land. Finally, choice **D** is incorrect because the fact that West had been dumping waste into the slush pit prior to the time East commenced his chicken-raising business does not, *per se*, relieve West from liability under a nuisance theory.

88. **A** A nuisance occurs when the defendant has, in a nontrespassory manner, caused an unreasonable and substantial interference with, or impairment of, the plaintiff's use of his land. In determining whether there has been an unreasonable interference with the plaintiff's use and enjoyment of his land, the court will ordinarily weigh (1) the social value or utility of the defendant's conduct or

activity to the area, (2) the suitability of the defendant's activity to the character of the locality, and (3) the impracticability of precluding or avoiding the defendant's conduct. The relative wealth of West and East is irrelevant in determining whether West's activities have unreasonably interfered with East's use of his land. Choice **B** is pertinent in that it would show numerous persons were injured as a consequence of West's activities, which would weigh against permitting those activities to continue. Choice **C** would aid East because if West's oil well operation was only marginally profitable, then requiring its cessation would not impact severely upon her. Finally, choice **D** would aid East because a realization by West that she was polluting her neighbor's land would certainly weigh against West.

89. **A** To be enforceable, a contract for the transfer of an interest in real property must ordinarily be embodied in a writing that contains the essential terms and must be signed by the party against whom enforcement is sought or his duly authorized agent. Even though the contract was signed only by Arthur's agent, the Statute of Frauds is satisfied because Thomas was authorized to execute the agreement on Arthur's behalf. While a few states require that an agency agreement involving the transfer of real property be in writing, the majority rule is contrary to this position. Choice **B** is incorrect because the fact that Baker's agency agreement was in writing would **not** withstand a Statute of Frauds defense by Arthur if the contract was not signed by him (or his agent). Choice **C** is incorrect because it is not necessary that Baker (or her agent) have signed the contract. The agreement must merely be signed by the party (or his agent) against whom enforcement is sought (i.e., Arthur). Finally, choice **D** is incorrect because in most states it is not necessary that Arthur's agency agreement be in writing. It is necessary only for Arthur to authorize Thomas to sign the contract for him and for Thomas to sign the contract, which he did. (Conceivably, Arthur might deny that Thomas was authorized to sign the agreement on his behalf; if the jury believes otherwise, Baker's lawsuit would be successful.)

90. **A** Under the Statute of Frauds, for a contract for the purchase and sale of an interest in land to be enforceable, it must be embodied in a writing that contains the essential terms and is signed by the party against whom enforcement is sought. However, under the doctrine of part performance, where the party attempting to compel performance has done acts that are unequivocally referable to the

existence of a contract for the sale and purchase of land, many courts will permit evidence of the purported agreement to be admissible. Since Mrs. Williams moved into the dwelling and spent a substantial sum of money in renovating it, it is likely that a court would permit evidence of the oral agreement for the sale of Jones's summer home to be admissible. It would have been illogical for Mrs. Williams to have spent a significant amount of money to improve the summer home unless a contract for its sale to the Williamses existed. Choice **B** is incorrect because Mr. Williams was relieved of his obligation to tender the purchase price when Jones unequivocally advised Williams that he would not complete the transaction (i.e., when an anticipatory repudiation occurs, the aggrieved party is relieved of his prospective obligations under the agreement). Choice **C** is incorrect because the mere fact that Mrs. Williams was aware of the contract would not have any impact upon whether the oral agreement is admissible under the Statute of Frauds. Finally, choice **D** is incorrect because the fact that Mrs. Williams renovated the summer home without Jones's actual knowledge would not be dispositive. Since she was acting under the good faith belief that Jones would consummate the transaction with her husband, her possession of the dwelling prior to the time a contract had been prepared and signed would (at most) permit Jones to recover only the reasonable rental value of the summer home prior to the time the transaction would otherwise have been consummated.

91. B Under the merger doctrine, all promises and warranties (express or implied) contained in an agreement for the sale and purchase of real property are deemed to be merged into the deed. The terms of the deed that Peg accepted will control Sue's liability. Thus, if Peg accepted a quitclaim deed, no remedy against Sue may be available. On the other hand, if a full warranty deed was tendered to Peg, she might have a right of rescission or a right to recover damages. Choice **A** is incorrect because Sue's deed was not fraudulent. The facts indicate she believed that she had acquired title to the acre in question by adverse possession. This belief, albeit erroneous, precludes a finding of the intent to deceive that is necessary for one's actions to be deemed fraudulent. Choice **C** is incorrect because depending upon the type of deed Peg received, she might well have an action for rescission of the entire transaction. Finally, choice **D** is incorrect because, even though there is an implied covenant that title shall be marketable in all contracts for the sale and purchase of real property, an objection to the seller's title must be made ***prior*** to acceptance of the deed by the grantee. Once the deed is accepted, the implied covenant of marketable title is merged into the deed.

92. C Under the merger doctrine, all promises and warranties (express or implied) contained in an agreement for the sale and purchase of real property are deemed to be merged into the deed. Since Sue tendered, and Peg accepted, a quitclaim deed, Peg would have no action against Sue. Choice **A** is incorrect because Sue's deed was not fraudulent (i.e., there was no intent on her part to deceive Peg). Choice **B** is incorrect because the fact that the terms of the quitclaim deed control will cause Peg to lose her action against Sue. Finally, choice **D** is incorrect because a deed does ***not*** ordinarily incorporate the terms of a contract to purchase and sell real property.

93. B Under the applicable statute, a subsequent claimant who acquires land in good faith and for value has priority over earlier grantees. In most jurisdictions, receipt of a deed in exchange for a release of an outstanding obligation constitutes giving value by the grantee. In a few states, however, the grantee must part with contemporaneous consideration to have given value. Thus, whether Crider has priority will depend on this jurisdiction's view as to whether the release of a preexisting obligation constitutes giving value. Choice **A** is incorrect because receipt of a quitclaim deed does not automatically prevent one from having taken land in good faith. (In a few jurisdictions, receipt of a quitclaim deed is deemed to put the grantee upon inquiry notice with respect to the land being transferred.) Choice **C** is incorrect because, under the applicable statute, whether an earlier grantee paid value is irrelevant for purposes of determining whether a subsequent transferee will have priority. Finally, choice **D** is incorrect because Crider, not having parted with new consideration, probably could not contend that she relied on the apparent state of Owen's title in agreeing to accept Owen's deed.

94. A Under the applicable statute, a subsequent grantee who acquires land for value and without notice of a prior conveyance has priority over an earlier grantee who had not recorded. Since Allred recorded her deed after Niece recorded hers, Barrett's review of the grantor/grantee index would not have revealed the deed that Owen had given to Allred (Barrett would have checked for any transfers by Niece since her deed from Owen was recorded, as well as for any recorded deeds made by Owen prior to the time his deed to Niece was recorded). Choice **B** is incorrect because the fact that Niece recorded her deed before Allred's filing would not give Niece priority over Allred since Niece received her conveyance gratuitously (i.e., without parting with value). Choice **C** is incorrect because the applicable statute does not attach any importance to the type of deed received. Finally, choice **D** is incorrect because the fact that Niece had no notice of Allred's right would *not* give Niece priority over Allred since she had not given consideration for her deed.

95. D Under the applicable statute, a subsequent grantee who acquires land for value, and without notice of a prior conveyance, has priority over an earlier grantee who had not recorded. Since Allred had *not* recorded her deed, Leon's mortgage would have priority. Choice **A** is incorrect because Leon did give value to Owen (the loan was made to Owen at the time Leon received the mortgage). Choice **B** is incorrect because, while factually true, it offers no justification why a subsequent grantee who falls within the requisites of the priority statute should not have priority over Allred. Finally, choice **C** is incorrect because the fact that Leon recorded before Allred would not be the reason Leon obtains priority over Allred. The applicable statute assigns priority to a subsequent grantee if he or she has given value without notice of the prior grantee's interest, *not* on the basis of early recordation.

96. C Under the applicable statute, a subsequent grantee who acquires land for value, and without notice of a prior conveyance, has priority over an earlier grantee. Since Niece has not paid value (i.e., she received the deed to Farmdale gratuitously), she would not have priority to the land. Choice **A** is incorrect because, in addition to having no notice of Allred's rights when she accepted the deed from Owen, Niece would also have to have paid value to attain priority to Farmdale. Choice **B** is incorrect because recordation is not the focus of the applicable priority statute. Finally, choice **D** is incorrect because the fact that Allred paid value for Farmdale is irrelevant in this instance. Even if Allred had received the land as a gift, she would still have priority over Niece because Niece does not come within the statute that gives a subsequent grantee priority over an earlier one.

97. C Under the Statute of Frauds, for a contract for the sale of real property to be enforceable, it must be embodied in a writing that contains the essential terms and must be signed by the party against whom enforcement is sought. The price of a parcel of land, in virtually all instances, will constitute an essential term of the agreement. Therefore, Vetter cannot be forced to perform the contract. Choice **A** is incorrect because the circumstances underlying the doctrine of estoppel (i.e., the plaintiff has foreseeably relied on the contract to his substantial detriment) do not appear to be present. There is no indication from the facts that Prue will suffer in some significant way if the agreement is unenforceable. Choice **B** is incorrect because the law will *not* imply a reasonable price into a contract for the purpose of avoiding a problem with the Statute of Frauds. Finally, choice **D** is incorrect because there is no rule of law that a sale may be avoided simply because the seller agreed to accept a price that is less than the fair market value of the land.

98. A When an abstract of title is obtained by the owner of land for the purpose of delivering it to a prospective purchaser, the prospective purchaser probably will be deemed to be a third-party beneficiary of the agreement. An abstract company is ordinarily liable in both negligence and breach of contract for failure to include copies of all properly recorded instruments that affect title to the land under examination. Since Sloan contracted to have the abstract delivered directly to Jones, Abstract Company was on notice that Jones would be a beneficiary of its contract with Sloan. Since Abstract Company breached its contract by failing to include the deed to Power Company, Jones would have a cause of action against Abstract Company. Choice **B** is incorrect because an abstract does not guarantee title. An abstract only purports to include copies of all properly recorded instruments affecting title to the land. Guarantees are ordinarily purchased from a title insurance company. Choice **C** is incorrect because Abstract Company was obliged to include in its abstract all properly recorded documents affecting the land, not simply those of which it had actual knowledge. Finally, choice **D** is incorrect because Abstract Company was aware that its work product was to be delivered to Jones and that Jones would probably rely on it.

99. B A general warranty deed contains a covenant against encumbrances (i.e., that no other parties presently have an interest in the land that would impair the grantee's use of it). Since Sloan delivered a general warranty deed to Jones, Sloan warranted to Jones that Newacre would be free from any interests that could impair Jones's use of the land. Since Power Company has a right of way for the building and maintenance of a power line across Newacre, Sloan's warranty was breached. Choice **A** is incorrect because Sloan acted reasonably under the circumstances in retaining Abstract Company to prepare the abstract (presumably, Abstract Company was a reputable entity). Choice **C** is incorrect because Jones presumably relied on **both** the abstract and the general warranty deed he received from Sloan in taking title to Newacre. Finally, choice **D** is incorrect because the fact that Sloan did not have actual knowledge of Power Company's right of way would not preclude her liability to Jones as a result of the general warranty deed she delivered to Jones.

100. **A** Marketable title is that which is reasonably free from doubt (i.e., it would be acceptable to a reasonably prudent purchaser). If a seller of real property is willing and able to fully discharge a lien from the proceeds of the sale of land at the time of closing, an outstanding mortgage does not make the title unmarketable. A seller of land has the implied right to use proceeds to be derived from the purchaser to satisfy any outstanding monetary encumbrances. Since Venner is willing to apply the proceeds (placed in escrow) to satisfy the mortgage, Brier cannot legally withdraw from the contract. Choice **B** is legally incorrect, in that the mortgage would not shift to the contract proceeds. The mortgage would remain against the land until the obligation it secures is paid in full. Choice **C** is incorrect because, even though equitable title has passed to Brier, she would nevertheless be entitled to withdraw from the transaction if Venner could not furnish marketable title at the closing. Finally, choice **D** is incorrect because it is ordinarily implied into contracts for the sale of land that the seller will convey marketable title at the closing. Venner, however, is entitled to satisfy the mortgage with proceeds to be received from Brier upon the sale of Greenacre.

101. **B** Whether a chattel is deemed a fixture, and therefore the property of the owner of the land, depends upon the intention of the party who affixed the item to the real property, as determined from all of the circumstances. Since Barnes presumably desired to continue her hobby after the lease had expired and the chattels can (apparently) be removed without significant damage to the premises, a court probably would conclude that she did not intend the items to become fixtures. Choice **A** is incorrect because notice of a mortgage is irrelevant in determining whether a tenant intended her attached chattels to become fixtures. Choice **C** is incorrect because there is no rule of law that a residential tenant is automatically entitled to remove personalty that has been affixed to the premises. Finally, choice **D** is incorrect because even if Bank's

mortgage did not *expressly* extend to fixtures, a mortgagee of real property automatically has a claim to fixtures that exist on the land at the inception of the mortgage.

102. **A** Whether a chattel is deemed to be a fixture, and therefore the property of the owner of the land, depends upon the intention of the party who affixed the item to the real property, as determined from all of the surrounding circumstances. Because the items in question had been installed by Albert, Bank's chances of succeeding would improve. Albert (as the owner of the land) probably would have intended the chattels to become a permanent part of the real property. Choices **B** and **C** are incorrect because, as explained above, Bank's chances of succeeding would be improved if Albert were the party who affixed the chattels to the real property. Finally, choice **D** is incorrect because it is not necessary for a mortgage to explicitly refer to fixtures. Those fixtures that exist on the land at the inception of a mortgage are automatically covered by the mortgage.

103. **B** In order for a contract for the sale and purchase of land to be enforceable, all material terms must be sufficiently definite. In the absence of an explicit agreement designating the type of deed to be tendered at closing by the grantor, a court probably would imply delivery of whatever deed is customarily given in that type of transaction within the locale. Since a vendor of land is ordinarily required to convey marketable title, Chase will be obliged to do so in this instance. Choice **A** is incorrect because, as just stated, even though no reference was made to the type of deed to be conveyed, the court probably will imply whatever type (full warranty, special warrant, or quitclaim) is ordinarily given in this kind of transaction in this area. Choice **C** is incorrect because a vendor is required to convey marketable title at the closing, regardless of the status of his title on the date the contract was made. Similarly, choice **D** is incorrect because Chase is obliged to convey marketable title to Smith at the closing, regardless of whatever title he had when the contract was made or thereafter.

104. **C** Under the Statute of Frauds, for a contract for the sale of real property to be enforceable, it must be embodied in a writing that contains the essential terms and must be signed by the party against whom enforcement is sought. The material terms of the agreement must be sufficiently definite. Here, the amount of land adequate to "accommodate a garden and lawn" cannot be determined with reasonable certainty. Therefore, the agreement is

probably unenforceable. (It is also possible that the language "my dwelling" could be ambiguous if Arthur owns more than one piece of property with a dwelling on it, a fact not indicated by the fact pattern.) Choice **A** is incorrect because the Statute of Frauds is satisfied as long as the party against whom enforcement is sought (in this instance, Arthur) signed the agreement. Choice **B** is incorrect because the consideration in this instance is $20,000. The "$1" referred to in Arthur's writing alluded only to the deposit Arthur had received from Walter. Presumably, the balance would have been due at the closing. Finally, choice **D** is incorrect because, even though contracts for the sale of land are ordinarily enforceable by specific performance, this rule does not apply when an enforceable contract has ***not*** been formed.

Index

References are to the numbers of the questions raising the issue. "E" indicates an Essay Question; "M" indicates a Multiple-Choice Question.

Abandonment
Easements, M72
Nonconforming uses, E16

Abstracts of title, M98, M99

Acceptance
Gift, E21, M4
Sales and transfers of real property, E22, E23, E25

Accounting, joint tenancy, M17

Acknowledgment of deed, E21, M39, M47

Adverse possession
Generally, E12, E17, E19, E20, E21, M66, M67, M68, M69
Boundary disputes, M7
Claim of right, E12, E17, E19, E20, E21
Color of title, M68
Continuity of possession, M6
Eminent domain, M67
Holdover tenants, E12
Hostile possession, E12, E17, E19, E20, E21, M6, M7, M66, M67, M68, M69
Open and notorious possession, E12, E17, E19, E20, E21, M6, M7, M66, M67, M68, M69
Rental value of land, recovery of, M69
Tacking of possessions, M66
Taxes, payment of, E17, E20
Tenancy at sufferance, E12
Title insurance, M51

Aesthetics, zoning, E11

Animal *ferae naturae*, oil as, E17

Anticipatory repudiation of contract for sale of real property, E10

Anticompetition clause in lease, E9

Appurtenant easements, E5, E12, M29

Assignment
See also Assignment of lease
Licenses, E12
Profit in gross, E23

Assignment of lease
Generally, E8, M24, M25, M32, M75
Frauds, Statute of, M79, M80
Notice of assignment by landlord, M78
Privity, M79
Strict construction of prohibition, M25

Attorneys' fees, warranty deeds, E18

Bailment, duty of care under, M3

***Bona fide* purchasers**, E18, E25, M2, M41, M50

Boundary disputes, adverse possession, M7

Cases
In re Totten, M5

Claim of right, adverse possession, E12, E17, E19, E20, E21

Clean hands, enforcement of restrictive covenants, E11, E13

Color of title, adverse possession, M68

Commercial easements, E12

Condemnation
See Eminent domain

Consideration
Deeds, E18, E22, M93, M96
Sales and transfers of real property, E22, E25, M39

Constitutional law, nonconforming uses, M55

Constructive eviction
Destruction of property, E8
Negligence of lessor's employees or agents, E8
Noise, E7
Physical condition of property, E7, E9
Waiver by untimely vacation of premises, E9, M77

Constructive notice
Easements, E1, M70, M71
Restrictive covenants, E11, E15

Constructive trusts, sales and transfers of real property, E19

Contingent remainders, M10, M11, M13, M14

Continuity, adverse possession, M6

Contribution between joint tenants, M18

Crops, profits derived by joint tenants, E4

Cure, installment contracts, M54

Damages
Covenant against encumbrances, violation of, M44
Easements, damages caused to servient estate, M71
Sales and transfers of real property, E19
Trespass, M83

Death of tenant, M81

Deeds
Acknowledgments, E21, M39, M47
Bona fide purchasers, E18, E25, M41, M50
Consideration, E18, E22, M93, M96
Delivery, E21, E22, M39, M40, M43
Encumbrances, covenant against, M42, M43, M44, M49, M99
Equitable estoppel, E18, E23, E25
Estoppel by deed, E20
Identification of property and grantees, E21
Inquiry notice, M47
Legal interest, first to receive, E16
Merger of agreement into deed, M91, M92

Pure notice, E16, E18, E22, E24, M50
Pure race, E16, E21, E22, E24
Quiet enjoyment, covenant of, E18, M45, M46
Quitclaim deeds, E18, E19, E24, M91, M92, M93
Race-notice, E16, E18, E21, E22, E23, E24, M48, M49, M93, M94, M95, M96
Recording acts, E16, E18, E20
Recording of deed, generally, M47
Return of deed, M39
Revocation, E22
Seisin, covenant of, M42, M45, M46, M48, M49, M51
Shelter rule, E18, E23, M50
Warranty deeds, E18, M42, M43, M45, M91, M99
Wild deeds, E18
Witnesses, E21

Delivery
Deeds, E21, E22, M39, M40, M43
Gifts, M4
Leased property, E6, E7, M21
Sales and transfers of real property, E22, E23, E25

Destruction of easement, E1

Destruction of property, constructive eviction, E8

Devise of tenant's interest, M81

Downstream riparian owners, E17

Due process
See Eminent domain

Easements
Generally, E1, E5, E12, E13, M28
Abandonment of easement, M72
Appurtenant easements, E5, E12, M29
Burden on servient estate, increase of, M28, M29
Commercial easements, E12
Constructive notice of easement, E1, M70, M71
Damages caused to servient estate, M71
Destruction of easement, E1
Frauds, Statute of, M26
Gross, easements in, E12
Implication, easement by, E14
Merger of dominant and servient estates, M72

Necessity, easement by, E14, M26, M27
Notice of easement, E1, M70
Scope of easement, E15
Subdivision of dominant estate, M29
Termination of easement, E1
Tortious interference with easement, E5
Transfer of appurtenant easement, E5

Eminent domain
Adverse possession, M67
Inverse condemnation, E11
Nonconforming uses, E16, M55
Taking of property, E11

Equitable estoppel
Deeds, E18, E23, E25
Quiet title actions, E16
Sales and transfers of real property, E25

Equitable servitudes
See Restrictive covenants

Escrows and escrow agents, E25, M40, M41

Estoppel
See Waiver and estoppel

Eviction
See also Constructive eviction
Holdover tenants, E6, E7, M20, M21
Partition, E4

Executory interests
Generally, M57, M58, M59, M60, M62, M64, M65
Fee simple subject to executory interest, M9, M62, M65
Shifting executory interest in fee simple absolute, M10
Springing executory interest in fee simple absolute, M10

Extrinsic evidence, validity of deed, E22

Fee simple absolute, M8

Fee simple determinable, E1, E3, E12, M8, M9, M12, M61, M62

Fee simple subject to condition subsequent, E3, E12, M8, M9, M62

Fee simple subject to executory interest, M9, M62, M65

Fee tail, E12

Fixtures
Generally, E3, M101, M102
Insurance, requirement of, E8
Intent, E3
Mortgages, M101, M102

Foreclosure, installment contracts, M54

Frauds, Statute of
Agent, execution of writing by, M89
Assignment of lease, M79, M80
Collateral matters, E14
Easements, M26
Estoppel, E14, E19, M97
Lateral support, waiver of right to, E14
Leases, E7
Part performance of contract, E14, M33, M90
Price as essential term, M97
Promissory estoppel, E14
Sale or transfer of real property, E10, E19, E25, M33, M89, M90, M97, M104
Substantial improvements to land, E19, M90
Unequivocal reference of acts to oral contract, E10, E19, M33

Frustration of purpose of lease, E9, M77

Future assurances, warranty deeds, E18

Gas
See Oil, gas, and minerals

Gifts
Generally, M4
Acceptance, E21, M4
Delivery, M4
Intent, M4

Good faith, restitution for improvements, E21

Gross, easements in, E12

Holdover tenants
Generally, M20
Adverse possession, E12
Eviction, E6, E7, M20, M21
Notice of renewal, E8, E10
Reasonable rental value, recovery of, M20
Renewal of lease, E8, E10, M20, M76

Horizontal privity, restrictive covenants, M30, M31, M32

Hostility, adverse possession, E12, E17, E19, E20, E21, M6, M7, M66, M67, M68, M69

Implication, easement by, E14

Implied reciprocal covenants, E13, E15

Implied warranty of habitability of leased premises, E6, E7, E9, M22, M23, M77

Improvements
Joint tenancy, E4
Restitution for improvements made in good faith, E21

Inheritance of tenant's interest, M81

Injunctions
Life tenant, depletion of natural resources by, M56
Money damages, inadequacy of, E5
Multiple lawsuits, avoidance of, E5
Nuisance, E15, M52
Restrictive covenants, E11, E12, E15, M30, M32
Water rights, E17

Installment contracts for sale of real property, M54

Insurance
Fixtures, E8
Landlord and tenant, E8
Sales of real property, risk of loss, M37
Title insurance, M51

Intent
Fixtures, E3
Gifts, M4
Restrictive covenants, E11, E12, E13, E14, E15

Inter vivos **transfer of possibility of reverter**, E3

Inter vivos **transfer of right of reentry**, E3

Inverse condemnation, E11

Irrigation of land, E17

Joint tenancy
Generally, E2, E21, M15, M16
Accounting, right to, M17
Consanguinity of tenants, E21

Contribution, right to, M18
Crops, profits derived from, E4
Improvements, cost of, E4
Lease of property by joint tenant, E4
Mortgages, E2, M18
Ouster, E4
Partition, E4
Rent, sharing of, E4, M17
Taxes, M18
Tenancy in common, conversion to, E3, M74
Timber, sale of, E4
Waste, E4

Laches
Nonconforming uses, E16
Restrictive covenants, E15

Landlord and tenant
See also Assignment of lease; Constructive eviction; Eviction; Holdover tenants; Subleases
Anticompetition clause, E9
Death of tenant, M81
Delivery of possession, E6, E7, M21
Fixed term, E8, M19
Frauds, Statute of, E7
Frustration of purpose, E9, M77
Implied warranty of habitability, E6, E7, E9, M22, M23, M77
Inheritance or devise of tenant's interest, M81
Insurance, requirement of, E8
Joint tenant, lease of property by, E4
Mitigation of damages, E7
Mutual mistake, E9
Negligence of lessor's employees or agents, E8
Periodic tenancy, E8, E10, M19
Repairs, E6, E7, E9, E10, M23, M77
Surrender of premises, E7, E10
Termination of lease, E6, E10, M19, M23
Waiver of implied warranty of habitability, M22
Writing, requirement of, E4

Lateral support
Generally, E13, E14, M53, M84, M85
Frauds, Statute of, E14
Negligence, M53
Strict liability, M53, M84, M85
Waiver, E14

Leases
See Landlord and tenant

Licenses
Generally, E12, M26
Assignment, E12
Revocation, E12, M26

Liens and encumbrances
See also Mortgages
Deeds, covenant against
encumbrances, M42, M43, M44,
M49, M99

Life estates
Generally, M8, M11, M13, M14
Injunctions, depletion of natural
resources, M56
Waste, E4, M56

Limitations of actions
See Statutes of limitation

**Liquidated damages, sales of real
property**, M54

Lis pendens, M50

Lost property, M1, M2

Merger
Deeds, M91, M92
Easements, M72
Sales and transfers of real property,
M91, M92

Minerals
See Oil, gas, and minerals

Mislaid property, M1, M2

**Mitigation of damages for breach of
lease**, E7

Mortgages
Fixtures, M101, M102
Joint tenancy, E2, M18
Marketable title, M100
Restrictive covenants, enforcement
of, E2
Tenancy in common, E2

**Mutual mistake, landlord and
tenant**, E9

Natural flow doctrine, E17

Natural resources
See also Oil, gas, and minerals
Timber, sale by joint tenant, E4

Necessity, easement by,
E14, M26, M27

Negligence
Abstracts of title, M98
Constructive eviction, E8
Landlord and tenant, E8
Lateral support, M53
Sales and transfers of real property,
E18, E25

Noise
See also Nuisances
Constructive eviction, E7

Nonconforming uses
Eminent domain, E16, M55
Zoning, E16, M55

Notices
See also Constructive notice
Easements, E1, M70
Holdover tenants, renewal of term,
E8, E10
Restrictive covenants, E11, E15,
M30, M32

Notoriety, adverse possession, E12,
E17, E19, E20, E21, M6, M7, M66,
M67, M68, M69

Nuisances
Generally, E5, E13, E15, M52, M87,
M88
Injunctions, E15, M52
Zoning, E15, M52

Oil, gas, and minerals
Generally, E17
Life tenants, extraction by, M56
Tenancy in common, E23

Openness, adverse possession, E12,
E17, E19, E20, E21, M6, M7, M66,
M67, M68, M69

Options, rule against perpetuities, E1

Ouster, E4

Partition
Generally, E4
Death of joint tenant before
trial, E4
Joint tenancy, E4
Tenancy in common, M73

Police power, zoning, E11

Privity
Assignment of lease, M79
Subleases, M82

Profit in gross, E23

Promissory estoppel, Statute of Frauds, E14

Promissory notes, purchase money mortgages, M38

Public necessity, trespass, E5

Purchase money mortgages, M38

Quiet enjoyment, covenant of, E18, M45, M46

Quiet title actions
Generally, E2, E19, E25
Equitable estoppel, E16
Recording act, priority under, E16

Quitclaim deeds, E18, E19, E24, M91, M92, M93

Recording of deeds
See Deeds

Recording of restrictive covenants, M30

Reentry, right of, E3, M57, M63

Remainders
Generally, M9, M10
Contingent remainders, M10, M11, M13, M14
Vested remainders, M9, M63, M64

Rental value, recovery in action for ouster, E4

Repairs to leased property, E6, E7, E9, E10, M23, M77

Restitution, sales and transfers of real property, E24

Restrictive covenants
Generally, E13, M30
Balancing of hardships, E11, E13, E15
Constructive notice of covenant, E11, E15
Defects in title, status as, M34
Horizontal privity, M30, M31, M32
Implied reciprocal covenants, E13, E15
Injunctions, E11, E12, E15, M30, M32
Intent to run, E11, E12, E13, E14, E15
Laches, E15
Mortgagee, enforcement by, E2
Notice of covenant, E11, E15, M30, M32

Recording of covenant, M30
Running with land, E11, E12, E13, E14, E15
Touch and concern requirement, E11, E12, E13, E14, E15
Vertical privity, M30, M32

Reversions, M11, M57, M63

Reverter, possibility of, M12, M57, M58, M59, M60, M61, M63

Revocation
Deeds, E22
Licenses, E12, M26

Risk of loss under contract for sale of real property, E19, M36, M37

Rule Against Perpetuities, E1, E12, M13, M14, M57, M58, M59, M60, M61

Sales and transfers of real property
See also Deeds
Acceptance by transferee, E22, E23, E25
Anticipatory repudiation, E10
Appurtenant easements, E5
Consideration, E22, E25, M39
Constructive trusts, E19
Damages, E19
Definiteness of contract, M103, M104
Delivery, E22, E23, E25
Equitable conversion, E19, M36
Equitable estoppel, E25
Frauds, Statute of, E10, E19, E25, M33, M89, M90, M97, M104
Installment contracts, M54
Liquidated damages, M54
Marketable title, E19, M34, M35, M100, M103
Merger of agreement into deed, M91, M92
Negligence, E18, E25
Profit in gross, E23
Remedies, E19
Restitution, E24
Retraction of anticipatory repudiation, E10
Risk of loss, E19, M36, M37
Tenancy in common, M15
Unjust enrichment, E19, E24

Seisin, covenant of, M42, M45, M46, M48, M49, M51

Self-help abatement of trespass, E5

Shelter rule, E18, E23, M50

Shifting executory interest in fee simple absolute, M10

Slant-hole wells, extraction of oil, E17

Specific performance of sale of real property, M34, M35, M104

Spot zoning, E15

Statute of Frauds
See Frauds, Statute of

Statutes of limitation
See also Adverse possession
Reentry, right of, E3
Reverter, possibility of, E3

Strict liability, lateral support, M53, M84, M85

Subleases
Generally, E7, E8, M24, M25, M32, M82
Privity, M82
Strict construction of prohibition, M25

Surface waters, modification of flow of, M86

Surrender of leased premises, E7, E10

Tacking, adverse possession, M66

Taxes
Adverse possession, E17, E20
Joint tenancy, M18

Tenancy at sufferance
See also Holdover tenants
Adverse possession, E12

Tenancy by entirety, M73, M74

Tenancy for years, waste, E4

Tenancy in common
Generally, E2, E23, M15, M73
Joint tenancy, conversion of, E3, M16
Mineral resources, E23
Mortgages, E2
Partition, M73
Sale or transfer of interest, M15

Tenants
See Landlord and tenant

Termination
Easements, E1
Leases, E6, E10, M19, M23

Timber, sale by joint tenant, E4

Title insurance, M51

Tortious interference with easement, E5

Totten trusts, M5

Transfers of real property
See Sales and transfers of real property

Trespass
Generally, M83
Damages, M83
Public necessity, E5
Self-help abatement, E5

Unjust enrichment, sales and transfers of real property, E19, E24

Vertical privity, restrictive covenants, M30, M32

Vested remainders, M9, M63, M64

Voidable title to personal property, M2

Waiver and estoppel
See also Equitable estoppel
Bailment, liability under, M3
Constructive eviction, E9, M77
Deed, estoppel by, E20
Frauds, Statute of, E14, E19, M97
Implied warranty of habitability of leased property, M22
Lateral support, E14
Reentry, right of, E3
Reverter, possibility of, E3

Warranty deeds, E18, M42, M43, M45, M91, M99

Waste
Generally, E4
Joint tenancy, E4
Life estates, E4, M56

Water and water rights
Downstream riparian owners, E17
Injunctions, E17
Irrigation, E17
Natural flow doctrine, E17

Prior appropriation doctrine, E17
Reasonable use doctrine, E17
Surface waters, modification of flow
    of, M86
Water table, diminution of, E17

Wild deeds, E18

Witnesses to deed, E21

Writings
    See Frauds, Statute of

Zoning
Abandonment of nonconforming
    use, E16
Deprivation of property, E11
Nonconforming uses, E16, M55
Nuisance, E15, M52
Police power, E11
Spot zoning, E15
Violation of ordinance as rendering
    title unmarketable, M35